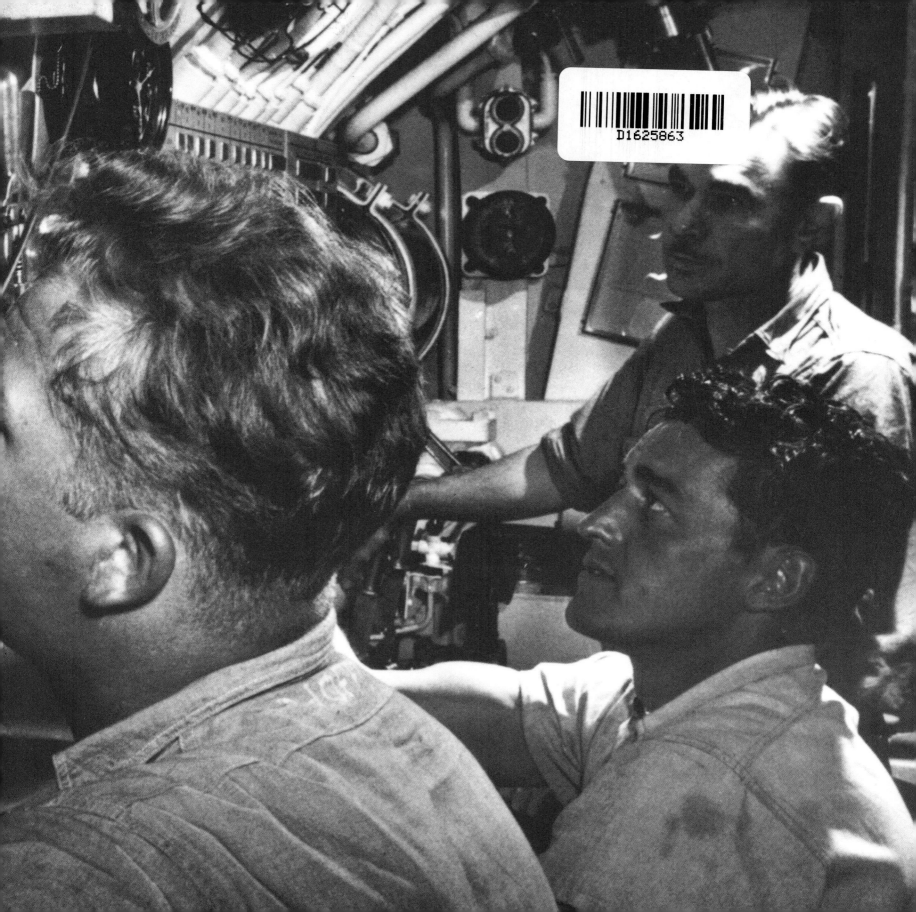

(2002)

£3

17114

RUN SILENT

RUN SILENT

PHILIP KAPLAN

AURUM PRESS

For Isabella, George, Charlie, Luis and Téa

First published in Great Britain 2002 by
Aurum Press
25 Bedford Avenue
London WC1B 3AT

Text copyright © 2002 by Philip Kaplan

Page 236 is an extension of this copyright page

A catalogue record for this book is available from the British Library.

ISBN 1 85410 815 8

1 3 5 7 8 6 4 2
2002 2003 2005 2004 2006
Printed and bound in Singapore by Imago

preceding spread: The USS *Nevada* (SSBN 733), a ballistic missile submarine based at the US Naval Submarine Base, Bangor, Washington, near Seattle. right: The launching of USS *Bluegill* (SS-242) at the Electric Boat Company, Groton, Connecticut in August 1943. Following page: The nuclear-powered USS *Georgia* (SSBN 729) at Bangor.

CONTENTS

SUBMARINE GLOSSARY

Abaft: towards the stern.

Acey-Deucey: Backgammon.

ADCAP: an advanced capability version of the US Navy's Mk 48 torpedo.

Akula SSN: large, ultra-quiet, third generation Russian sub; similar in many ways to the US Navy Los Angeles-class 688 SSN.

Aldis: A British signalling lamp.

AN/BSY-1: the integrated fire control and sonar system of the US Navy 688 I submarine.

Angles and Dangles: fast, steep climbing and diving turns.

Anechoic coating: a rubber decoupling coating on exterior hull surfaces of a submarine, intended to reduce noise emanating from the sub and to minimize detectability by active sonars.

Aphrodite: German device used to confuse enemy radar

ASDIC: Allied Submarine Detection Investigation Committee—established in WWI for research into submarine detection; a device in a dome under an anti-submarine vessel used to detect the presence of submerged submarines.

ASW: anti-submarine warfare.

Bauwerft: shipyard

B-Dienst: the German radio-monitoring and cryptographic intelligence service in WWII.

Belay: stop; disregard.

Biscay, Bay of: on the western coast of France; where the main German U-boat shelters were located in WWII.

Bletchley Park: location of the British Government Code and Cypher School in Buckinghamshire, England during WWII.

Blue/Gold crews: refers to the US Navy policy of manning its Trident missile submarines with two separate, alternating crews.

Bluewater: deep water.

Bow: forward end of a ship.

Bomber: Royal Navy nickname for a Trident sub.

Boomer: the US Navy sub force nickname for a Trident missile submarine.

Bridge: the observation area at the top of the sail of a sub.

Brow: gangway.

Bug juice: a KoolAid-like drink dispensed on US Navy ships.

Bunkers: exterior fuel tanks on a U-boat.

Cake hole: mouth.

Calibre: measurement of gun and shell size taken from the internal diameter, or bore, of the gun barrel.

Casing: a submarine's outer skin of light plating, which encloses the ballast tanks and pressure hull.

Cavitation: loud noise created by the accumulation of small air bubbles on a ship's propeller(s).

Cipher: a secret letter-substitution communication code system.

CO: Commanding Officer; captain, skipper.

COB: Chief of the Boat; senior enlisted man of a US submarine crew. The Coxswain is the Royal Navy equivalent.

Coffee pot: nuclear reactor.

Conn: steering responsibility for a boat; control room.

Conning tower: platform or observation tower of a sub.

Contact pistol: detonator on a torpedo that explodes on striking a solid object.

Control room: space on a sub where ship control, fire control and the periscopes are located. During internal communications the room is referred to as the Conn.

Convoy: a precise assembly of merchant ships organized in columns and escorted by warships.

Corvette: a small and highly manoeuvrable armed escort ship, smaller than a destroyer.

COW: Chief of the Watch, the supervising enlisted man of the watch. Responsible for the ballast control to dive and surface a submarine, under direction of the diving officer.

CVBG: an aircraft carrier battle group.

DD: US Navy reference to a destroyer-class warship.

DE: a destroyer escort-class warship.

Decrypt: a deciphered or decoded message.

Destroyer: a small, fast, highly-manoeuvrable warship, often armed with guns, torpedoes, guided missiles and depth charges.

Delta: series of Russian SSBN submarines classed I to IV.

Dolphins: identity symbol in use by the submarine forces of many nations to designate qualification as a submariner.

Duff: Royal Navy term for broken or useless.

EAB: a system providing low-pressure air to crewmen in an emergency situation on a sub.

Echo: an early nuclear-powered Soviet SSN submarine.

Eel: U-boat nickname for a torpedo.

Electric Boat Company: the submarine building firm that evolved from the union of the (John) Holland Torpedo Boat Company and a battery-making company in 1898.

Emergency blow: putting high-pressure air into the main ballast tanks of a sub to make it rise rapidly to the surface.

Enigma: the WWII cipher system of the Germans; the machine used in the encryption procedure.

Exocet: French anti-ship cruise missile.

Fairwater: US Navy reference to the sail of a submarine. The Royal Navy calls it the Fin.

Familygram: a brief (50-word) message from a loved one to a submariner in the US Navy.

Fathom: a depth measure; six feet or 1.829 metres.

Feindfahrt: an operational patrol by a U-boat.

First Lieutenant: Royal Navy title equivalent to the US Navy Executive Officer.

Fish: torpedo.

Flugboot: German for flying boat aircraft.

Freya: German radar detection apparatus.

Funker: German radioman.

Geedunk: candy or junk food.

George Washington, SSBN-598; the first US Navy SSBN missile submarine class.

Goat locker: the chief's quarters on a US Navy sub.

GPS: Global Positioning System; the Navstar satellite navigation system.

GRT: Gross Registered Tonnage; total displacement of a ship.

GQ: General Quarters—the call to man battle stations.

HE: high explosive.

Head: a toilet or bathroom in the US Navy.

Hedgehog: a type of bomb used by Allied vessels against U-boats in WWII.

HF: high frequency.

HF/DF: high frequency direction finder in WWII.

HMS Dolphin: the submarine school of the Royal Navy.

Hydrophone: underwater sound detection device.

Holland, SS-1: the first US Navy submarine. It was designed and built by the inventor, John Holland.

Hot-bunking: the alternating use of one bunk by two or more sailors as they come off watch at varying times.

Hotel SSBN: first-generation Soviet SSBN missile sub class.

Hot rack: see Hot-bunking.

Hunley: the Confederate Navy submersible; first sub to sink a surface warship.

Hydroplanes: the extended rudder fins on a submarine hull that allow the vessel to go up and down when submerged.

Jumping wire: a heavy cable with a cutting edge, stretched from the bow to the stern over the conning tower of a WWII U-boat, to cut or deflect underwater obstacles such as nets.

Jury rig: a temporary fix.

Kaleu; Kaleunt: diminutive form of KapitänLeutnant, the most common rank of a U-boat skipper in WWII.

Kilo SS: Russian diesel-electric coastal defence submarine class.

Knee-knocker: the coaming of a watertight door or bulkhead opening on a ship or submarine.

Knot: a ship's speed measured as one nautical mile per hour.

Kriegsmarine: the German Navy, 1939-45.

Kriegstagbuch: the German war diary kept by U-boats and ships at sea, and by shore-based headquarters staffs.

Lafayette, SSBN-616: the third generation US Navy SSBN submarine class.

LF: low frequency.

Los Angeles: SSN-688 and

688 I class fast attack sub based on the design specs of US Admiral Hyman Rickover.

Lose the bubble: to lose one's situational awareness.

Luftwaffe: German Air Force.

Maneuvering: reactor and propulsion control room in the engine area of US nuclear submarines.

Menopause manor: UK. See Goat Locker.

Messdecks: crew eating area.

MF: medium frequency.

MIDAS: mine detection and avoidance sonar system on the US 688 I Los Angeles-class subs.

Milch cow: nickname for the German WWII U-boats used for the resupply and refuelling of other U-boats at sea.

Midrats: meal served on sub at midnight.

Midwatch: a watch stood from midnight to 4 a.m.

Mixer: a torpedo mate on a German WWII U-boat.

Mk 8: a WWII-era non-homing torpedo of the Royal Navy; the type used against the 14,000-ton cruiser *General Belgrano* in the 1982 Falklands War.

Mk 48: the wire-guided active-homing torpedo currently used by submarines of the US Navy.

NATO: North Atlantic Treaty Organization.

Nautilus, SSN-571: the world's first nuclear-powered sub.

90-Day Wonder: derisive US Navy term for Officer Candidate School graduate.

November SSN: a first generation Soviet SSN class submarine.

OBA: oxygen breathing apparatus used in firefighting.

OCS: Officer Candidate School.

Ohio, SSBN-726: fourth generation US Navy SSBN class nuclear-powered missile submarine class.

OOD: US Navy officer of the deck. Responsible to the captain for the movement and safety of the submarine.

Oscar SSGN: third generation Soviet SSGN attack submarine.

Periscope: extendable, tube-like optical device containing prisms, mirrors, lenses and other equipment which allows submarine crewmen to view the sea surface while the sub is submerged at periscope depth.

Perisher: the Submarine Command Course of the Royal Navy.

Permit, SSN-594: the first US Navy production SSN anti-submarine warfare sub.

Plank owner: a member of the commissioning crew of a US Navy submarine or surface vessel.

Polaris: first generation US Navy submarine-launched ballistic missile.

Poopie suit: blue coveralls worn by submarine crewmen.

Poseidon: second generation US Navy submarine-launched ballistic missile.

Pressure hull: watertight structure containing the living and work areas of a submarine.

Pucker factor: the degree of stress in a given situation.

PWR: pressurized water reactor used on many nuclear-powered submarines.

Radar: radio detection and ranging system.

Rake: a patrol line of several WWII U-boats across the path of a convoy of merchant ships.

Resolution, S-22: the first Royal Navy SSBN missile sub.

Rig for Red: low-intensity red lighting condition in a sub.

Ring knocker: a US Naval Academy graduate.

Rocket: a written reprimand.

Rudeltaktik: the German technique of massing U-boats in a 'wolfpack' patrol line across a convoy's course and engaging ships of the convoy in a radio-coordinated attack.

SAM: surface-to-air missile.

Schlüssel M: the German Naval version of the Enigma cipher machine.

Schnorchel/schnorkel: a valved air pipe protruding above the surface of the sea, allowing a submerged U-boat to proceed on diesel power.

Screw the pooch: to make a serious mistake.

Scrubber: system for removing carbon dioxide from the air on a submarine.

Scuttlebutt: gossip or rumour.

Sea Lawyer: a know-it-all.

SEAL: US Navy special forces/commando Sea-Air-Land units.

Seawolf: the second US Navy SSN (SSN-575); also the name of a new class of SSN, SSN-21.

SHF: super high frequency.

Shutter door: outer door of a submarine torpedo tube.

Sierra, SSN: third generation Soviet SSN.

Signal ejector: small tube for launching noisemakers, flares and torpedo decoys from a submarine.

SINS: ship's inertial navigation system.

Skate, SSN-578: US Navy's first SSN class in production.

Skimmer: a surface ship or crewmember of same.

Skipjack, SSN-585: the first US Navy submarine to employ a teardrop hull shape.

SLBM: submarine-launched ballistic missile.

Snake-eater: a SEAL.

SNAPS: the Royal Navy's Smith Navigation and Plotting System.

Snapshot: an emergency launch of a torpedo by a submarine.

Snorker: sausage (Royal Navy).

Sonar: sound navigation and ranging.

Sparks/sparker: RN radioman.

Spearfish: the Royal Navy equivalent of the US Navy Mk 48 ADCAP torpedo.

SS: diesel-electric submarine.

SSBN: strategic ballistic missile submarine, nuclear-powered.

SSGN: nuclear-powered, guided (cruise) missile sub.

SSM: surface-to-surface missile.

SSN: attack submarine, nuclear-powered.

SSK: diesel-electric hunter-killer submarine.

START: Strategic Arms Reduction Treaty.

SUBGRU: Submarine Group.

SUBRON: US Navy Submarine Squadron.

SURTASS: surveillance towed array sonar system.

Swiftsure, S-104: third generation Royal Navy SSNs.

TASO: torpedo and anti-submarine officer—Royal Navy; junior officer responsible for torpedo launching system.

TB-16: "fat line" towed array system on US Navy SSN subs.

TB-23: "thin line" US Navy towed array system.

TDU: trash disposal unit on a submarine.

Tea kettle: nickname in the Royal Navy for the reactor on a submarine.

Tigerfish: the Mk 24 Royal Navy torpedo.

Tits up: broken, inoperative.

Tomahawk: cruise missile family used on SSN subs.

Torpedo: self-propelled weapon invented by Robert Whitehead in 1866.

Towed array: series of passive hydrophones towed behind a submarine.

Trafalgar, S-107: fourth generation Royal Navy SSN class submarine.

Trident I (C-4): third generation US Navy submarine-launched ballistic missile.

Trident II (D-5): fourth generation US Navy submarine-launched ballistic missile.

Trim: the balancing of a submarine's weight and equilibrium when it is being operated ßunderwater.

TSO: Royal Navy tactical systems officer; junior seaman responsible for a submarine's fire control system.

Turtle: the American Revolutionary War submersible designed and built by David Bushnell.

Type 2046: a towed array system used by the Royal Navy.

Typhoon, SSBN: Soviet; the largest submarine type ever built.

U-boat: *Unterseeboote*; the German term for submarine.

Ubootwaffe: the German submarine fleet.

UHF: ultra high frequency.

Victor, SSN: second generation Soviet SSN class of submarines.

VLF: very low frequency.

VLS: vertical launch system.

Vickers Shipbuilding Enterprises, Limited: British equivalent of Electric Boat Co.

WEO: Royal Navy equivalent of the US Navy weapons officer.

XO: US Navy term for Executive Officer, second in command of a submarine.

THE MISSION

Deep in the sea there is no motion, no sound, save that put there by the insane humors of man. The slow, smooth stirring of the deep ocean currents, the high-frequency snapping or popping of ocean life, even the occasional snort or burble of a porpoise are all in low key, subdued, responsive to the primordial quietness of the deep. Of life there is, of course, plenty, and of death too, for neither is strange to the ocean. But even life and death, though violent, make little or no noise in the deep sea.
— from *Run Silent, Run Deep*
by Commander Edward L. Beach

above: A torpedoman in the Los Angeles-class fast attack submarine USS *Jefferson City* (SSN 759). right: A torpedo tube in the *Jefferson City* which is based at Ballast Point, San Diego, California.

FOR THE FORTY-PLUS YEARS of the Cold War American and British attack submarines were tasked with the vital primary mission of intelligence gathering, in addition to their anti-submarine role. Being quick, stealthy and silent, these subs were tailor-made for the job of keeping an eye and an ear on Soviet submarine activity, missile test exercises, shipyards and harbour installations. They operated in nearly complete secrecy, utilizing some of the most sophisticated and advanced methods of information collection available. They kept tabs on and tracked the comings and goings of the enormous Soviet ballistic missile submarines in an effort to learn all they could about them, an effort so important to the security of the US and Britain that it was given highest priority by their navies.

Royal Navy Rear Admiral Mark Stanhope has commanded both conventional and nuclear-powered submarines as well as the aircraft carrier HMS *Illustrious* during his distinguished career.

"It was openly expressed, if not ever in any detail. The purpose of the attack submarine was to try and find the Soviet ballistic missile submarines. They were a key element in the nuclear balance. Additionally, its purpose was to sanitize the water that our own boats were in, making sure that we were keeping our ballistic missile-firing submarines clear of Soviet intruders. That area of engagement extended throughout the northern Atlantic a long, long way north. In the latter part of the 1980s, the Soviets were bastioning their submarines in the north. If they brought them south, into the Norwegian Sea, or further south, they knew that the chances of counter-detection were high, so they bastioned them further north, which caused us to go further north, looking for them.

"The purpose was to go and locate Soviet submarines. Therefore, the assumption is that we found them, and that's a good assumption. And once we found them, then the point was to remain in contact for as long as we could and, of course, in so doing we gained a lot of experience about how to do the job. We also gathered a lot of information about how they did their business. We could come home and tell people how they did the business so the next one to go out went with that information.

"There was also the developing role of defence of the fleet by means of anti-submarine warfare. Submarines are the best finders of other submarines. However, communications was a problem. If we found another submarine, was it enemy or one of ours? We had to find out. Eventually, communications got better. Satellite communications were a great breakthrough, so our engagement in fleet work was improving and increasing towards the end of the 1980s before the Berlin Wall came down.

"The intelligence gathering role has been fundamental in the mission of submarines ever since we managed to make them work. They can go places where they can't be detected, where they can raise masts above the water, where they can give early warning of activities that might only be available through other clandestine means.

"What's changed? The Russians still have nuclear submarines at sea, although it's fair to say, not very often. We still need to be able to counter these; we still need to be able to provide anti-submarine warfare defence to a fleet, but the concern now is less about nuclear submarine attack and more about conventional submarine attack. We are going through the mechanisms of learning about littoral or shallow water warfare, which is far more threatening to us now than the deep water challenges that we had before, when we had a horde of Soviet submarines coming down to meet us. If we put a fleet into shallow water, the potential presence of other conventional submarines is of increasing concern to us. It's much more difficult to find a submarine in 'brown water,' as we call it, where it's shallow and there is much more noise and where there

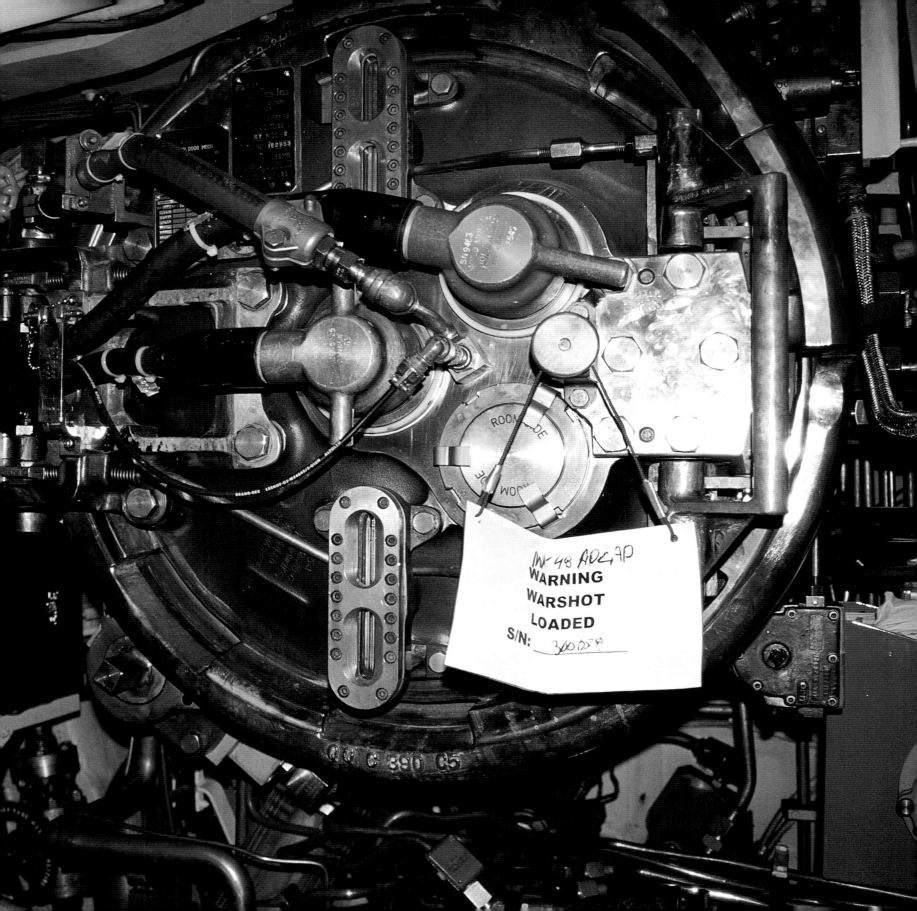

below: The firing of a vertically-launched BGM-109 Tomahawk land attack missile (TLAM) as seen through the periscope of the fast attack submarine USS *Pittsburgh*. The weapon was launched from the submarine during Operation Desert Storm on 19 January 1991.

Their feats, their fortunes and their fames are hidden from their nearest kin . . .
– Rudyard Kipling, 1916

If injury has to be done to a man it should be so severe that his vengeance need not be feared.
– Niccolo Machiavelli

are a lot more places for one to hide.

"We still are engaged in the principle of keeping our own submarines safe, so the ballistic missile threat is still important. It's important to provide the necessary protection to our ballistic missile capability, both in the US and the UK, and that's done by our SSNs. It's important that we don't lose the skills to be able to deal with the Russian nuclear submarines, both their ballistic missile-firing submarines and their SSNs. Some of their SSNs are extremely capable and still do venture wide and far, and we want to make sure we keep tabs on those if we can. And, of course, a submarine's ability to act in the provision of early warning is still a part of our business.

"In the future, I can't see us going back to the conventional submarine world. I think we will have to stick with the nuclear submarine or it's derivative. We are desperately keen to see something other than nuclear power being able to produce the same capability. Fuel cells, a new technology that's being developed, is heading that way but is not available yet, so we have decided to build the next generation of SSNs, the Astute class, to keep us in the business. There is another non-military but domestic pressure. If we stop building nuclear submarines, we lose the ability to do so. Without another order to follow on from the last of the T-boats [Trafalgar class], then Barrow-in-Furness, which is our only submarine builder, would have

had to pay off labour and lose all its design and development staff. Therefore, part of the decision taken to build the Astute class was in order to keep the building programme going, albeit at a low cost level, so as to maintain the structure we've got in Barrow. The balance is a fine one, but that's what we're doing at the moment. There are enormous financial pressures to restrict the programme, but the Government recognizes that if we want to stay a number one capable Navy, we've got to keep building these submarines. So, I think the near future is good, but the Americans and everybody are looking hard to find what's over the horizon. Nuclear submarines are a problem. What do you do when you get rid of them? Getting rid of them is, environmentally, a very hot potato and, as yet, unresolved. All of our paid-off nuclear submarines, *Dreadnought*, *Warspite*, *Valiant*, *Courageous*, *Conqueror*, *Churchill* and shortly the *Swiftsure*, are just sitting alongside in various harbours—most of them in Plymouth, some of them in Rosyth. The nuclear cores have been taken out and the really nasty bits are at Sellafield, but the reactor compartments themselves are radioactive and will be for many thousands of years. So, yes, I do think there is a future in the Royal Navy for submarines, but it's always going to be a challenge."

In the years since the collapse of the Soviet Union,

and the at-least-partial thawing of Cold War attitudes, these fast attack vessels have become multi-mission oriented. The intelligence gathering emphasis has shifted to tactical reconnaissance. Change has been the name of the game, the most fundamental being the adjustment from a strict posture of global deterrence to the support of US and British national interests in regional conflicts and crises. The anti-submarine warfare orientation against nuclear submarines has shifted to take full advantage of the current attack sub's multi-mission capability and her arsenal of Mk 48 torpedoes, Tomahawk land attack cruise missiles and other weapons.

The submarine forces have had to adapt from a bluewater emphasis to a littoral (shallow water) one and learn how to work even more effectively with other naval elements such as Amphibious Ready Groups, Special Warfare and Special Operating Forces like the US Navy SEALs (Sea-Air-Land teams) and, in the US Navy, in support of Aircraft Carrier Battle Groups.

The mission of the Royal Navy's fleet of attack submarines includes anti-ship and anti-submarine roles in addition to the support of land operations with Tomahawk (TLAM) missiles capable of striking targets up to 1000 miles from the launch point. Her four Vanguard-class submarines, with their Trident missiles, are the custodian of Britain's independent strategic nuclear deterrent.

Assigned to NATO, the Vanguards, like the US Ohio-class ballistic missile subs, are invulnerable while at sea.

The American submarine force includes attack, ballistic missile and auxiliary submarines, submarine tenders, floating submarine drydocks, deep-submergence vehicles and submarine rescue vessels.

For the US submarine force the primary roles are: Peacetime Engagement, Special Operations, Surveillance and Intelligence, Sea Denial, Precision Strike, Battle Group Operations and Deterrence.

Peacetime Engagement: While the United States and Britain are both at peace as the 21st century begins, the potential for regional crises erupting into wider armed conflict remains. US Navy submarines visibly represent American interests in specific regions, and are present, though invisible, in other areas where their detection must be avoided. With their great endurance and high transit speeds, these nuclear vessels are ideally suited for rapid deployment to trouble spots. They can operate with a high degree of visibility, as in their frequent port visits, or with no disclosure of their presence whatsoever. They can land small groups of special operations forces or do electronic surveillance for intelligence gathering. They can also operate in support of aircraft carrier battle groups and surface task forces, with other submarines or independently.

Underhand, unfair and damned un-English.
– Admiral Sir Arthur Wilson, Third Sea Lord, 1899, on submarine warfare

The essence of war is violence. Moderation in war is imbecility.
– attributed to Lord Fisher

Man is born unto trouble, and the sparks fly upward.
– Job. V. 7

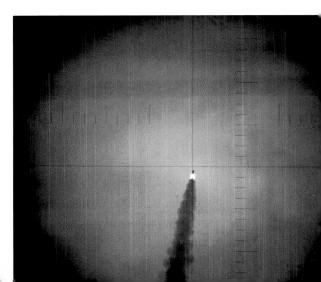

There's trouble in Russia, so they called us. We're going over there and bringing the most lethal killing machine ever devised. We're capable of launching more firepower than has ever been released in the history of war — for one purpose alone — to keep our country safe. We constitute the front line, an the last line of defense. I expect and demand your very best. Anything less, you should have joined the Air Force.
This might be our Commander-in-Chief's Navy, but this is my boat, and all I ask is that you keep up with me, and if you can't, that strange sensation you'll be feeling in the seat of your pants will be my boot in your ass.
— Captain Ramsey addressing the crew of the USS *Alabama* in the film *Crimson Tide*

Pay attention to your enemies, for they are the first to discover your mistakes.
— Antisthenes

Special Operations: The Sea-Air-Land teams of the US Navy (SEALs) can be transported to their missions, which are often behind enemy lines, by submarine in a covert way that is not possible by fixed-wing aircraft, helicopter, parachute or surface craft. The SEALs can then engage in reconnaissance, sabotage, search and rescue, diversionary attacks, communications and the monitoring of enemy movements, as well as other high-risk operations. The fast, stealthy attack submarine is effective in supporting Special Warfare Team operations including combat swimmer attacks, reconnaissance and surveillance, beach feasibility studies, hydrographic surveys and surf observation in support of amphibious landing operations.

Some US Navy submarines are specially designed to carry SWT swimmers and their equipment. They are fitted with Dry Deck Shelter (DDS) chambers which house Swimmer Delivery Vehicles (SDVs). The DDS is fitted aft of the submarine's sail structure and is connected to the deck over the after hatch, allowing free passage between the sub and the DDS while the sub is submerged and approaching the objective area. The sub is still submerged when it reaches the delivery point, and the SEALs can then emerge from the DDS and ascend to the surface with their rubber rafts and equipment. Alternatively, they can travel aboard SDVs entirely underwater to their objective landing area. Such SEAL teams are made up of two officers and fourteen enlisted men. Additional SEALs are carried in the submarine for assistance in mission planning and equipment handling.

Surveillance and Intelligence: The secret of the nuclear submarine's intelligence gathering and surveillance success is its ability to go into an area to watch, listen and collect information without being detected. While aircraft and satellites are also used for surveillance, their results can often be negated by cloud cover, weather conditions and target location. Their capability for observing

underwater activity is also limited. Submarines, however, are again ideally suited for such work and have been doing it very well throughout the Cold War years.

Sea Denial: Nuclear fast attack submarines can effectively deny enemy surface ships and submarines access to certain sea areas. In Sea Denial operations, fast attack submarines can conduct general warfare against a major maritime power, or blockade an enemy port. In a war of attrition situation, these subs can destroy much of the enemy's naval or merchant fleet, as US Navy submarines did to Imperial Japanese Navy and merchant ships in World War II. A more recent and very impressive example is the 1982 sinking of the Argentine cruiser *General Belgrano* by the British nuclear-powered submarine HMS *Conqueror*, S48, during the Falklands War. The threat demonstrated by this British submarine action served to deter the Argentinian surface fleet from further sorties in the conflict.

The key American weapon for attacking enemy surface ships and submarines is the Mk 48 torpedo, especially in the improved Advanced Capability (ADCAP) version. The Mk 48 is a long-range, heavyweight weapon with a large conventional high-explosive warhead and an advanced guidance system that lets it engage high-speed, manoeuvring target vessels effectively. The ADCAP version has a reduced vulnerability to enemy countermeasures, and a shorter warmup and reactivation time. The torpedo's engine runs on a liquid monopropellant fuel. As the weapon leaves the submarine launch tube, a thin wire spins out from it, linking the torpedo electronically with the sub, enabling a crewman to initially guide the torpedo towards the target. This helps the weapon avoid decoys and jamming devices deployed by the target vessel. In the final attack phase, the wire is severed and the passive/active sonar of the torpedo takes over to guide it to the target.

Able to engage enemy surface ships at ranges

beyond that of the Mk 48, the Tomahawk anti-ship missile can be launched while the submarine is completely submerged. Once launched, the guidance system of this "fire and forget" weapon takes over. Tomahawks can be carried instead of torpedoes and can be launched from the torpedo tubes, but about half of the US Navy Los Angeles-class submarines are fitted with twelve vertical tubes for launching the land-attack and anti-ship missiles. The fast attack subs also carry mines for use in denying sea areas, harbours and narrow sea passages to enemy ships and submarines.

Precision Strike: Tomahawk cruise missiles give British and American attack submarines the capability to make precision, long-range conventional warhead strikes against shore targets. The advantages they afford include flexibility, clandestine, non-provocative presence, no necessity for air superiority and no possibility of suffering lost aircraft or airmen. The missile is designed to fly at high subsonic speed and extremely low altitude over an evasive route to its target, directed by a mission-tailored guidance system. The Tomahawk Block III missiles incorporate a Global Positioning System (GPS) receiver for improved reliability and time-of-arrival control to allow the coordination of strikes with those by other missiles and aircraft.

The opening strikes of the Gulf War on the night of 16 January 1991 were delivered by US Navy Tomahawk cruise missiles which arrived over the heavily-defended Baghdad as US Air Force F-117 stealth attack aircraft bore in with their laser-guided smart bombs. In that conflict, US Navy surface warships and attack submarines fired a total of 288 Tomahawk land attack missiles.

Battle Group Operations: Attack submarines are fully integrated into US Navy carrier battle group operations, with two submarines normally assigned to each battle group. They participate with the battle group in all pre-deployment training and exercises. Where the battleship was once the

capital ship of the US fleet, signifying the nation's power wherever it went, that power projection is now the responsibility of the super aircraft carrier with her battle group. Her mere presence in a region can deter troublemakers from carrying out their aggressive plans, or deal with them forcefully if they choose hostility over prudence.

The carrier battle group exists to protect the carrier in hostile environments and to assist her in a variety of actions against enemy surface ships, submarines, coastal defences, aircraft and inland targets. The battle group is made up of cruisers, destroyers, frigates and submarines.

An enemy submarine armed with anti-ship cruise missiles poses the greatest threat to the US aircraft carrier and the US fast attack submarine provides the best defence against that other sub. The Russian ultra-quiet Oscar-class SSGN (anti-ship missile firer) submarine (see chapter seven The Downside) was designed specifically to be an aircraft carrier hunter-killer and is armed with 24 SS-N-19 Shipwreck heavy anti-ship missiles in addition to an array of torpedoes. The Oscar is seen by many western naval experts as the most powerful attack sub in the world, and a formidable challenge for the Los Angeles-class 688I attack sub.

The two SSN attack submarines assigned to a carrier battle group may range well out from the carrier and the surface ships of the group. Like a pair of German Shepherd dogs protecting their master as he walks along a forest trail, they move out and operate in anti-submarine warfare kill zones where they alone are permitted to roam and shoot, if necessary, thus avoiding possible friendly-fire encounters.

Deterrence: Former Chairman of the US Joint Chiefs of Staff, US Army General Colin Powell said in an address to submariners on the completion of the 3000th deterrent patrol by American submarines in April 1992, "No one, but no one, has done more to prevent conflict. No one has made a greater sacrifice for the cause of peace, than you. You stand

He who surpasses or subdues mankind must look down on the hate of those below.
– George Gordon, Lord Byron

There is a tide in the affairs of men / Which, taken at the flood, Leads on to fortune.
– from *Julius Caesar,* Act IV, Scene III by William Shakespeare

It cannot be denied that submariners of any nation are brave and skilful men; and that they are accustomed to continue to exercise their skill in conditions of acute danger, which is perhaps the bravest thing of all. But what they actually *do*, what constitutes their life work — killing by stealth, without warning and without quarter — is evil as well as skilful . . .
– Nicolas Monsarrat, from his foreword to *U-Boat 977* by Heinz Schaeffer

far right: The fast attack
submarine *Seawolf* (SSN
21) during her sea trials in
1997. bottom and right:
Postage stamps issued
to commemorate the
centennials of the
British and US submarine
forces which were
celebrated in 2001 and
2000 respectively.

tall among all our heroes of the Cold War."

At the end of the Cold War, in late 1991, the SSBN ballistic missile submarines of the US Navy carried 45 per cent of the nearly 12,000 nuclear warheads in America's strategic offensive forces; land-based intercontinental ballistic missiles carried 20 per cent and land-based bombers the remaining 35 per cent.

The Ohio-class missile submarines of the US Pacific Fleet, based at Bangor, Washington, near Seattle, carry the Trident I (C-4) Submarine Launched Ballistic Missile (SLBM) first deployed in 1979. It is a three-stage solid fuel missile that is powered only in the initial phases of flight. With the exhaustion of the third stage power, the missile follows a ballistic trajectory to its target. The Trident I technology and capability represents a quantum leap over the earlier Polaris and Poseidon ballistic missiles. Costing $13,000,000 each, the Trident I weighs 71,000 pounds and has a range of 4000 nautical miles. The latest version of the Trident is

the D-5, which has greatly increased accuracy and an improved payload. It became operational in 1990 and is deployed on the SSBNs based at the King's Bay, Georgia facility. The missile assembly buildings at the Strategic Weapons Facility Pacific (SWFPAC), US Pacific Fleet, Bangor, Washington base are to be reconfigured to handle the newer Trident II (D-5) missile.

When British or American Trident submarines go to sea they "find a hole to hide in" and the rest of the world understands that, with their deployment, annihilation awaits any state, rogue or otherwise, that is foolish enough to threaten the safety of the nations they represent.

Deterrence remains fundamental in US and British defence strategies and nuclear missile submarines continue to be the principal component of the defence mix. The Trident submarine forces will continue to carry the largest share of responsibility for the strategic nuclear deterrence strategies of the US and Britain well into the new century.

TRIAL AND ERROR

THE IDEA WAS SIMPLE. The realization was not.

In 1578 an English innkeeper named William Bourne proposed a type of military ship which could submerge to evade an enemy vessel. While adept at pulling a pint, Bourne was also a scientist, mathematician, inventor and naval theorist, and his daring concept was published in a series of articles called *Inventions or Devices. Very necessary for all Generalles and Captains, or Leaders of men, as wel by Sea as by Land*. "It is possible", he stated, "to make a Ship or Boate that may goe under the water unto the bottome, and so to come up again at your pleasure." Bourne believed intensely in the potential of his boat for the exploration of the sea bottom. His imagination and foresight enabled him to predict a system whereby such a craft would descend and rise by filling and emptying ballast tanks along its sides. It was the first recorded proposal for a submarine, but Bourne lacked the resources to develop his idea.

In Bourne's time scientists and inventors knew very little about the physical properties of the seas, the strange currents and variations in density between saltwater and fresh. But subsequent generations were to gradually solve the problem of developing such a submersible. It had to be able to submerge by counteracting its buoyancy. It had to be watertight and have some means of propulsion, and provision of fresh air had to be made for the crew.

Man has always been intrigued by the submarine world. According to legend, Alexander the Great's fascination with it led him in 332 B.C. to go under water in a sort of glass case or globe that was covered with asses' skins. He entered it through a door that could be shut tight with chains and a ring, and is said to have taken food with him and two friends for company. His pioneering undersea adventure has been portrayed in various works of art across the years.

In the fifteenth century Leonardo da Vinci, artist, inventor, musician, engineer, scientist and designer, talked about having devised a kind of military diving system, but he kept the details to himself "on account of the evil nature of men who practice assassination at the bottom of the sea."

One who did advance the practice of naval "assassination" was Frederico Gianibelli, an Italian military engineer. The Spanish siege of Antwerp, circa 1585, provided Gianibelli with an opportunity to test his belief in the potential of maritime explosives and break the siege. He set out to destroy a half-mile-long Spanish- built bridge which spanned the Scheldt River, by placing 7000 pounds of gunpowder in the hold of a small ship. He then covered the explosive with a six-foot-thick layer of flat stones and, on top of that, a thick layer of cannon balls and rubble. The detonation of Gianibelli's exploding ship beneath the bridge left a 200-foot gap in the structure and nearly 800 dead Spaniards. Gianibelli referred to his device as a "floating marine volcano". The Spanish called it "the hell-burner of Antwerp".

In Rostock, Germany, a teacher named Pegelius made drawings of futuristic mechanical inventions in 1604. One of them was a submarine, but nothing came of his design. It was the Dutch physicist/inventor Cornelius Van Drebbel who first made actual submersible boats using William Bourne's design (which had not provided for a means of propulsion). He built three vessels of different sizes in 1620. They were covered in leather to make them as watertight as possible and were propelled by oars fitted through holes cut along the sides. Though based on Bourne's idea, Drebbel's boats did not employ ballast tanks but relied on heavy weights to aid the efforts of the oarsmen in forcing the craft under the surface of the water. A friend of Drebbel, Constantyn Huygens, wrote in 1631: ". . . it is not hard to imagine what would be the usefulness of this bold invention in

. . . He went into the middle of the river Dart, entered his boat by himself, in sight of hundreds of spectators, sunk his boat himself, and tarry'd three quarters of an hour at the bottom; and then, by extending it with his screws, he rais'd it to the surface again without any assistance. He said, that tho', at last, the air began to be thick, he could bear it very well.
– Samuel Ley, 17 July 1749, describing a demonstration of the diving boat of carpenter Nathaniel Symons of Devon, England

time of war, if in this manner (a thing which I have repeatedly heard Drebbel assert) enemy ships lying safely at anchor could be secretly attacked and sunk unexpectedly by means of a battering ram—an instrument of which hideous use is made now-a-days in the capturing of gates and towns." Another prophetic view was offered with the publication in 1648 of an article by the Bishop of Chester, John Wilkins. Appearing in his treatise *Mathematical Magick: or the Wonders That May Be Performed by Mechanical Geometry*, the article was called "Concerning the Possibility of Framing an Ark for Submarine Navigation". He wrote: "Let there be several leather bags of several bigness . . . and strong to keep out the water . . . answerable to these, let there be divers windows, or open places in the frame of the ship, round the sides of which one end of these bags may be fixed, the other end coming within the ship being to open and shut like a purse." Wilkins continued: ". . . a man may thus go to any coast in the world without being discovered or prevented in his journey . . . It may be of very great advantage against a navy of enemies, who by this means may be undermined in the water and blown up."

Drebbel served as "inventor" in the court of England's James I and, in the pursuit of his interest in submersibles, is believed to have been the first to discover oxygen, which he referred to as "the quintessence in air that was necessary for life". His great achievement came in 1623 when he built what is generally acknowledged as history's first working submarine vessel. Reports of the time stated that his boat travelled down the Thames submerged at a depth of approximately fifteen feet, from Westminster Bridge to Greenwich. A later report appeared in 1645 in the *Chronicle of Alkmaar*, which was Drebbel's hometown in Holland: ". . . Drebbel built a ship which could be rowed and navigated under water from Westminster to Greenwich, the distance of two Dutch miles, even five or six miles, or as far as one

pleased. In this boat a person could see under the surface of the water and without candlelight, as much as he needed to read in the bible or any other book." As Drebbel's patron, James I may well have witnessed one of the inventor's submarine boat demonstrations, but whether or not he ever went along for an underwater ride has always been a matter of historical speculation.

Drebbel's submarine-related work took an especially interesting turn when he concentrated on the problem of "freshening the air" inside the boat. Chemist Robert Boyle had a serious interest in Drebbel's work and in 1662 wrote of it: "Drebbel conceived, that it is not the whole body of the air but a certain quintessence, or spiritous part of it that makes it fit for respiration; which being spent, the grosser body, or Carcasse of the Air, if I may so call it, is unable to cherish the vital flame residing in the heart. Besides the mechanical contrivance of his vessel, he had a chymical liquor, which he accounted the chief secret of his submarine navigation. For when from time to time he perceived that the finer and purer part of the air was consumed or over-clogged by the respiration and steames of those that went with his ship, he would, by unstopping a vessel full of this liquor, speedily restore to the troubled air such a proportion of the vital parts, as would make it again for a good while fit for respiration."

Cornelius Van Drebbel continued his work in the areas of submersible vehicles and maritime explosives after the death of James I in 1625 and in the following year was retained by the British to build a submarine and undersea weapons that they could use in their war of the time against the French. French Catholics had put the coastal town of La Rochelle (which was to become famous in World War II as one of the five principal submarine bases constructed and operated by the Germans in Brittany) under siege that the British were bent on breaking. Their Master of Ordnance directed Drebbel to produce "divers water mines, water-

Science is nothing but developed perception, Interpreted intent, common sense rounded out, and minutely articulated.
— from *The Life of Reason* by George Santayana

Amongst the manuscripts in the British Museum there is a quaint picture of a kind of a submarine barrel in which is sitting a crowned monarch. The barrel appears to have been transparent, and with the King, believed to be Alexander the Great, is shown a cockerel, and an animal which might conceivably be a cat; suspended from the roof of the submarine are three lamps with floating wicks. Above is a boat containing several people and the Queen, who appears to be holding a rope which is attached to the interior of the barrel.
— from *The Romance of The Submarine* by G. Gibbard Jackson

-Babcock-

JOIN ᵗʰᵉ NAVY
THE SERVICE FOR FIGHTING MEN

petards and two boates to conduct them under water". The order for boates was later amended to "water engines". Drebbel did as he was bid, but the British commander at La Rochelle was evidently unimpressed with the results, or at least failed to employ them against the French. Drebbel got the blame and was dismissed by the British government, his contract cancelled. He died in 1633, but members of his family persisted in efforts to promote his ideas. No less a figure than Samuel Pepys, in 1661 Secretary to the Admiralty, was persuaded by them to give due consideration to Drebbel's "engine to blow up ships". Oliver Cromwell had promised Drebbel's heirs a very substantial sum for "the invention to sink ships", but Cromwell died before making the formal agreement.

An Italian priest, Giovanni Alfonso Borelli, is credited with having first described, in 1680, the way in which fish controlled their depth through the use of a bladder. He then suggested a method by which a submarine's depth could be managed by employing goatskin bladders, a "ballast-bag system", which could be squeezed empty using levers. The method was subsequently tried in other submarines in the years after Drebbel and Borelli. Several inventors took up the challenge to work on various kinds of submarines and diving bells, none of them of any particular consequence, though their trial-and-error efforts undoubtedly contributed to the slow but steady progress in the field.

 In the late 1600s Denis Papin was working on his own submarine ideas as a laboratory assistant to Christian Huygens, the son of Cornelius Van Drebbel's old friend Constantyn. He later worked with Robert Boyle; both Huygens and Boyle being among Drebbel's greatest admirers. Papin was experimenting with a diving bell and wrote of it in a paper titled "How to Preserve a Flame Under Water", which attracted the interest of Prince Charles, Landgrave of Hesse, who assigned Papin the task of developing and perfecting one of Drebbel's submarine schemes as a workable war machine. He produced two boats, the first being a reinforced metal box accommodating one operator. It contained a pump to increase internal air pressure, a barometer to measure depth, and detachable ballast. When underwater the craft was propelled by oars and on the surface it would utilize a folding mast and sail. For military purposes the box contained holes through which the operator could "touch enemy vessels and ruin them in sundry ways". Papin's second effort was a bit larger and made of wood. It was operated by a two-man crew, one of whom was to lie in a six-foot-long copper cylinder that protruded from the front of the vessel. He could sight enemy ships through a viewing port and "touch" them after inserting his arms through the cylinder into water-tight sleeves. Papin believed he had solved the main problems associated with underwater submarine operation by 1696 and prepared to demonstrate his creations to the Landgrave. The Prince showed considerable enthusiasm when Papin told him about the progress he had made, but was preoccupied with other matters of the day. Denis Papin's craft were tested but never perfected.

The first recorded submarine disaster occurred in 1774. J. Day, a wagonmaker in Norfolk, England, had constructed a submersible boat on the Norfolk Broads and successfully tested it to a depth of 30 feet. He used a detachable ballast system of large stones suspended from the outer hull by ring bolts, and could release the stones from inside the craft. His accomplishment caught the attention of a gambler who persuaded Day that they could make money taking bets on how long Day could remain underwater in his craft. Investors enabled the pair to purchase a sloop to serve as a tender for the submersible, and in the summer they went to Plymouth Sound where a further shallow descent was made. Encouraged by this latest success, the pair accepted a bet that Day could not achieve a

successful dive in deeper water. What Day evidently did not understand or allow for were the changes in buoyancy, density and pressure that his craft would encounter at the 132-foot depth it was to reach. The submersible undoubtedly collapsed or imploded in the pressure, killing Day. Witnesses attempted to raise the boat in the belief that Day might have survived by finding trapped air in the vessel, but the attempt failed.

In the time of the American Revolution, Yale graduate and native of Westbrook, Connecticut, David Bushnell designed and built the first submarine to be used in an actual attack on an enemy naval vessel. His boat, the *Turtle*, was similar to a Papin design in that it carried a pump to bring air in and out, a barometer, valves to admit water and pumps to control buoyancy. But his real interest was underwater munitions and his work on *Turtle* was an effort to develop a means of delivering such explosives to a target vessel.

The *Turtle* was egg-shaped with the pointed end down and was made of thick wood. It remained upright with the aid of 700 pounds of lead ballast at its bottom. At its top was a crown-like rim containing four portholes, an access hatch, and sleeved armholes. Propulsion up and down, forward and reverse, was achieved through the turning of two hand-operated screws. Foot-operated controls for a valve and pump allowed water to come in during descent and be expelled for ascent. Other fittings included a ballast gauge, a fresh air vent for use when on the surface (the air supply lasted just 30 minutes), an air pressure gauge and a compass.

In actual naval operation *Turtle* was intended to arrive at a target partially submerged whereupon the operator would take it down beneath the hull of the enemy vessel in order to afix a magazine containing a 150-pound explosive charge near the vessel's rudder. In the crown-rim of *Turtle* the operator would use a vertically-mounted augur to

. . . be so kind as to communicate to me what you can recollect of Bushnell's experiments in submarine navigation during the late war, and whether you think his method capable of being used successfully for the destruction of vessels of war.
— from a letter by Thomas Jefferson, then American Ambassador to France, to George Washington in 1785

I then thought, and still think, that it was an effort of genius; but that a combination of too many things were requisite, to expect much success from the enterprise against an enemy, who are always on guard. — That he had a machine which was so contrived as to carry a man under water at any depth he chose, and for a considerable time & distance, with an apparatus charged with Powder which he could fasten to a ship's bottom or side & give fire to in any given time (sufft. for him to retire) by means whereof a ship could be blown up, or sunk, are facts which I believe admit of little doubt—but then, where it was to operate against an enemy, it is no easy matter to get a person hardy enough to encounter the variety of dangers to which he must be exposed. 1 from the novelty 2 from the difficulty of conducting the machine, and governing it under water on acct. of the Currents and 3 the consequent uncertainty of *continued on page 24*

hitting the object of destination, without rising frequently above water for fresh observation, wch., when near the Vessel, would expose the adventure to discovery, & almost certain death. To these causes I have always ascribed the non-performance of his plan, as he wanted nothing that I could furnish to secure the success of it — This to the best of my recollection is a true state of the case.
– from George Washington's 26 September 1785 reply to Thomas Jefferson

bore a hole in the enemy hull, into this hole a hook was screwed to hold the explosive charge. The operator would then put his arms through the armhole sleeves and attach the charge. The charge was to be subsequently detonated by a clockwork mechanism attached to a gun lock. The timer would be started when the operator released the drill bit, leaving it in the enemy hull and pulled on a lanyard. He would then crank to drive the craft away and raise it to an awash attitude before making his escape. He would have thirty minutes to make his withdrawal before the charge blew up.

In trials on Long Island Sound, *Turtle* made successful descents and ascents and Bushnell also established the effect of large gunpowder charges when detonated underwater. *Turtle* was deemed ready for action in August 1776. She was later brought to the Hudson River to launch an attack on HMS *Eagle*, flagship of Admiral Earl Howe, which was spearheading the British blockade of New York. Bushnell's brother was set to operate the submersible in this action but became ill and the job went to Sergeant Ezra Lee of the American Patriot Army. The *Eagle* lay off Governor's Island in Upper New York Bay [some accounts place it off Bedloe's Island, rather than Governor's Island, on 7 September, the date of the attack by *Turtle*]. After experiencing mechanical problems with the submersible, Lee was spotted by the British who quickly launched boats to intercept him. Lee responded by jettisoning his magazine charge which blew up as the British sailors approached. In the ensuing confusion, Lee was able to get away. There followed two further failed attempts by *Turtle* to attack enemy ships. Then, in September, the British captured New York. They soon found and destroyed the *Turtle*. Thanks in part, though, to the efforts of the French Navy, which was causing Britain considerable difficulty on the trans-Atlantic supply route, the balance of power shifted and American independence was secured.

In the Anglo-American War of 1812, David

Bushnell was back with a new, improved *Turtle* and in July 1813 the little craft saw action in an attack on the 74-gun ship of the line, HMS *Ramillies* off New London, Connecticut, where the United States Navy Submarine Service would later be headquartered. Again the little craft was sighted by the British crewmen and the *Ramillies* weighed anchor to depart the area, but the *Turtle* operator somehow managed to reach the enemy vessel and began drilling into the keel. The drill broke, however, and the operator was forced to withdraw without having attached his explosive charge. While Bushnell's creation had not achieved its mission goals, it sparked keen interest among several nations in the military possibilities of undetected attack from beneath the seas.

Robert Fulton was born in Little Britain Township, (now Fulton), Pennsylvania in 1765. He was a portrait painter, gunsmith and inventor, and had also studied civil engineering. Among his many achievements were the first commercially successful steamboat and the first steam-powered warship.

In 1797 Fulton went to France where he was befriended by a fellow expatriate, Joel Barlow, a writer and poet. Barlow and his wife invited Fulton to share their home, which he did for seven years. They had a common interest in the subject of underwater warfare and he and Barlow began a collaboration on the design of a self-propelled torpedo device. Fulton was well aware of the work of David Bushnell and had a profound, if critical interest in it. He and Barlow were intrigued by the possibility of a weapon which could be launched in a particular direction and would travel for a predetermined distance to its target whereupon it would explode. Their work proved both dangerous and unsuccessful. Certainly, they were motivated by the war that was going on between France and England, and, despite their torpedo failure, Fulton wrote, unsolicited, to the French government on 13 December 1797: "Considering the great importance of diminishing the power of the British Fleets, I have contemplated the Construction of a Mechanical Nautilus. A Machine which flatters me with much hope of being Able to Annihilate their Navy . . . ." His proposition to the French was that he would form a company that would, at his own expense, build and operate a device [submarine] to be deployed against the blockading British fleet. He asked that he be compensated for each British ship destroyed, on a sliding scale based upon the size of each target ship, an example being 400,000 French francs for a 30-gun frigate. Further, he was to be given possession of any captured British ships and cargoes, and, should the war end before his craft could be deployed, he was to be reimbursed for his out-of-pocket expenses. He asked too, that he and his crew be given naval commissions. The French denied this last request and countered with a schedule of fees at roughly half the rate proposed by Fulton. Furthermore, they would only compensate him in the event of an early conclusion to the war if it could be established that Fulton's terror weapon had actually frightened the British into surrendering before any of their vessels had been sunk. In February 1798 a contract was drawn up incorporating the French changes to Fulton's proposal, but it was never signed. Instead, Fulton looked to private sources for sponsorship and proceeded with some of his other developing interests, including steam engines and propellers.

Fulton chose the name *Nautilus* for his undersea creation, ancient Greek, via Latin, for the underwater mollusc. It was destined to become the most famous name in submarine fact and fiction.

In July 1798 the French Marine Minister had been replaced, and Fulton decided to re-submit his *Nautilus* proposal. With it he wrote: "The destruction of the English Navy will ensure the independence of the seas and France, the nation which has most natural resources and population, will alone and without a rival hold the balance of

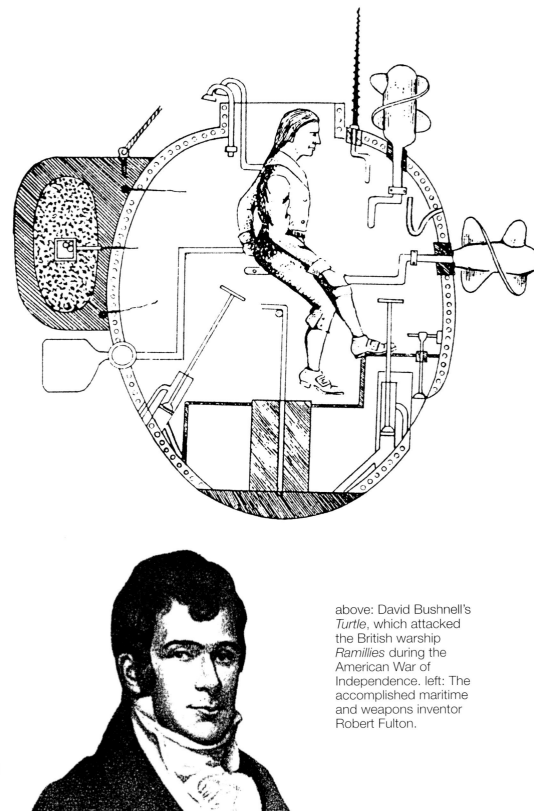

above: David Bushnell's *Turtle*, which attacked the British warship *Ramillies* during the American War of Independence. left: The accomplished maritime and weapons inventor Robert Fulton.

power in Europe." His dealings with the French government seem to have produced continuing interest but little else. Still, Fulton went on with *Nautilus* and, on his own initiative, started construction of the submarine, completing it in Rouen in July 1800. He conducted trials in the River Seine and on 30 July reported to the Marine Minister: "Citizen Minister, Yesterday I tryed my experiments with the *Nautilus* in water 25 feet deep and have succeeded to Render the sinking and Rising easy and fameliar . . . [and now] having succeeded to sail like a common boat and plunge under water when I think proper to avoid an enemy—it may be sufficient at present to render an operation against the enemy successful . . . ." Fulton took *Nautilus* to the French coast where he completed the essential sea trials including one dive which lasted an hour and two minutes and a shallow descent lasting more than six hours in which he utilized a tube to the surface for ventilation. The submarine itself was very like Bushnell's *Turtle* in concept, though larger and more evolved and sophisticated in design. The explosive weapon and the method of attaching it to an enemy hull were also similar to that of *Turtle*, but seemingly improved.

Believing *Nautilus* to be ready for operation against the British ships, Fulton again requested French naval commissions for himself and his crew. Again, the answer was no. He then wrote to his friend Barlow asking him to appeal to the Marine Minister and, though Barlow could not say why, *his* request was agreed. Fulton was made a rear admiral and his two crewmen were also commissioned. Off to war they went.

Twice that September *Nautilus* set out to attack ships of the British fleet and each time the sub was sighted and evaded by its quarry. Though unsuccessful, Fulton made a new proposal to the government of Napoleon. In it he asked for funds to build a new, larger and better *Nautilus* that would carry twenty bombs (the term torpedo had

above: German poster requesting contributions to finance submarine construction in 1917.

not yet come into use). He also requested two small support ships and additional funds to cover sea trials. A French commission studied Fulton's proposal and recommended to Napoleon that he authorize a test in which the inventor would be required to use *Nautilus* to destroy one of France's obsolete ships in return for the financing. But Fulton was having second thoughts and new ideas, including some new methods of delivering his weapons. The French had doubts too, but in February 1801 provided Fulton with 10,000 francs and agreed to his sliding schedule, from 400,000 francs for a ship of 30 guns or more, down to 60,000 for a small sloop. He now had his deal, but his submarine needed considerable refitting at this point to make it combat-ready and, as the work proceeded through July, he inexplicably seems to have either lost interest in the sub or became distracted by his interest in other new projects, one of which he called the "bomb submarine". This was a copper container filled with gunpowder. It had a gun lock and was to be carried to its point of use by the submarine which he referred to as the "plunging boat". It was to be the first primitive wire-guided torpedo.

Fulton's continuing attempts to attack British ships met with failure. The British were aware of his efforts and were very much on their guard. He seems to have elected to end his experimental submarine work in the summer of 1801, for he then disassembled *Nautilus*, selling the parts for scrap. He had most likely become convinced that the reliance upon hand-power in such a craft was just too limiting to merit further effort and expense. By October the French had signed a preliminary peace treaty with Britain and, with peace breaking out, albeit a brief one, Fulton was seemingly done with both France and underwater warfare.

In mid-May 1804, with Britain and France again at war, Robert Fulton quit France and, using the assumed name Francis, supposedly as protection against French reprisals, went to England where he proposed to help the British attack and defeat the French invasion fleet that was being assembled at Boulogne. The proposal was based around a new and larger submarine than the earlier *Nautilus*, 35 feet long, manned by a crew of six and carrying 30 bombs with 100 pounds of gunpowder in each. In a change of tactics from those used by *Nautilus*, the new boat would lie in ambush until nightfall before surfacing to attack. Waiting in close proximity to the enemy hull for an opportune moment to leave her bombs, she was now, in effect, a minelayer that could do her work and then withdraw in relative safety. But the British were really only interested in Fulton's bombs, not his submarine.

In 1806 Robert Fulton returned to the United States, where in 1810 he convinced the Congress to spend $5,000. on his new steam-powered submarine project, an 80-foot vessel with a 21-foot beam. It would be, claimed the inventor, so quiet that it was to be named *Mute*. Work progressed on *Mute* and the boat seemed quite promising, but then in 1815 Fulton died and with him the interest in his final project. He did, however, leave a legacy to future submariners, in the shape of solutions to some of the more challenging technical problems. His final maritime achievement was not a submarine, but a 38-ton steam-powered paddle-wheel surface warship, the USS *Fulton*.

As a young corporal in the Prussian artillery in 1849, Bavarian Wilhelm Bauer, was stationed for a time in Schleswig-Holstein where he observed blockading Danish naval ships during a coastal dispute. There it occurred to him that the blockaders could be attacked from underwater using a craft called a *Brandtaucher* (incendiary diver). It was the first *unterseeboot* or U-boat. Bauer somehow persuaded a Kiel shipyard, Howaldt-Werke, to build the 27-foot-long boat for him in 1850 and by the end of that year he

At the end of the year 2000 a controversy surrounded the British submarine *Resurgam*. Built in 1880 to an 1879 design by George Garrett, *Resurgam* was a 45-foot, coal-fired vessel which carried a three-man crew. She sank in shallow water off the North Wales coast on 25 Feburary 1880 while being towed to Portsmouth where she was to undergo sea trials with the Royal Navy.

Sheltered for more than a century in a sandy crater, the submarine was found again in 1995 when apparently uncovered accidentally during trans-Atlantic cable laying.

According to Miss Alex Hildred, an archeologist working with the Mary Rose Trust in Portsmouth, the protective pine cladding around the *Resurgam* has virtually disintegrated and the vessel has been damaged by collisions and vandalism. "She's like a Coca-Cola can lying on a motorway, waiting to be hit. At any moment we could lose her. She just needs to be hit once more by an anchor and that's it. It really is a race against time. As every day passes we are lucky she is still there."

But there is disagreement about the notion of raising and relocating *Resurgam*. Dr Sian Rees, an inspector of ancient wrecks for the Welsh Heritage organization also has concerns about the sub. Having dived on the vessel, Dr Rees believes that it may be settling back into the relatively *continued on page 28* protective environment that had previously held it, and that it may be better to leave the submarine intact where she lies until a future home for her is secure, rather than move her now, risking further damage in the process.

The situation with *Resurgam* is further complicated by the view of other experts that a Spanish submarine, the *Ictineo II*, which was built a few years before *Resurgam*, was actually the first mechanically-powered submarine and was thus a more direct link to the design of modern submarines. This view has kept prospective institutions from offering a new home to *Resurgam*. For now, the vessel waits where she has rested since 1880.

commenced trials in the Kiel Fjord. This caught the attention of the Danes who were sufficiently intimidated by the imagined threat of *Brandtaucher* to abandon their blockade. In later sea trials, however, the sub sank on two occasions, the second costing three crew members their lives.

Bauer lost favour in Germany and later in Austria-Hungary, but re-surfaced in England where his ideas for underwater craft soon earned him a £7000 grant to build another submarine for use against the Russians in the Crimean War. Once again misfortune plagued Bauer when several crewmen died in his experiments with the craft.

The inventor's next port of call was St Petersburg in 1855, where he switched sides and built a 52-foot version of the *Brandtaucher* for the Russian Navy. He called it *Diable Marin* or Sea Devil and it began sea trials in 1856. It, too, had problems and Bauer soon moved on, first to France, and then in 1857, back to Bavaria where in 1864 he started work on the design of yet another submersible, the *Küstenbrander* (coastal incendiary), for Prussia. It was revolutionary in that its power was to come from some form of internal combustion engine which was to produce its own oxygen. It didn't happen. Bauer and the Prussians didn't get along and he moved on to concentrate on what apparently was a genuinely promising paraffin engine project. He died in 1875, largely unheralded and underappreciated for the worth of his contribution to submarine development.

The outbreak of the American Civil War led to keen interest in the potential of the submarine on the other side of the Atlantic. In 1862, with the war in its second year, Horace Hunley, a well-to-do Alabama engineer with a consuming interest in submarine boats and their potential military application, financed construction of the *Pioneer*, an ironclad 34-foot, three-man submarine for his beloved South. The Navy of the Confederacy of

southern states was in need of a way to break the siege of their key port of Charleston, South Carolina by the United States Navy. The *Pioneer* was either lost in action or scuttled at the war's end to prevent its capture by Union forces. Hunley soon built a successor to *Pioneer*, cleverly designed to be propelled by a battery-powered electric motor. However, no such satisfactory motor was available and the new boat had to be hand-cranked. She was lost off Mobile in an attempted attack on a US ship.

The first combat fatality in submarine warfare history occurred on 5 October 1863 when a small "David" Confederate States Navy semi-submersible manned by Lieutenant W.T. Glassell and three volunteers rammed the USS *New Ironsides*, the flagship of Rear Admiral John Dahlgren, USN. When approaching *New Ironsides*, the little sub was spotted by Acting Ensign C.W. Howard, USN, who was killed by a shotgun blast fired from the hatch by one of Glassell's crew. Glassell's spar-torpedo did significant damage to *New Ironsides* but did not sink her. Two of his crew were captured.

Submarine warfare finally began to develop on 17 February 1864 when a larger, more capable submersible, the CSS *Hunley*, with a crew of nine (eight of whom cranked the propeller shaft) attacked the 1400-ton Yankee sloop USS *Housatonic* near the mouth of Charleston harbour. In her trials the *Hunley* sank five times, taking 41 lives including that of Horace Hunley. Re-floated and manned by a sixth volunteer crew, *Hunley*'s weapon was a towed mine, which was referred to then as a "torpedo", (the name of a type of electric eel). It was a beer barrel full of gunpowder equipped with contact fuses. The plan called for *Hunley* to make a surface approach to the enemy ship, then pass beneath it, trailing the mine which was intended to detonate when it contacted the *Housatonic*'s hull. But the commander of *Hunley*, Lieutenant G.E. Dixon,

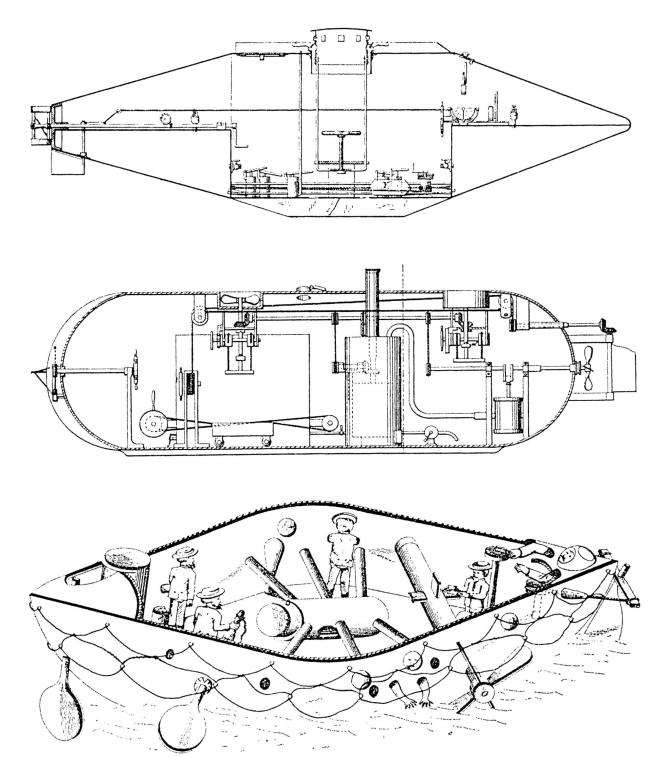

left: A submarine boat design of 1883. centre: A submarine designed for use in the American Civil War, but not built. bottom: A submarine design patented in 1889.

Always design a thing by considering it in its next larger context—a chair in a room, a room in a house, a house in an environment, an environment in a city plan.
— Eliel Saarinen

God will not look you over for medals, degrees or diplomas, but for scars.
— from *Epigrams*
by Elbert Hubbard

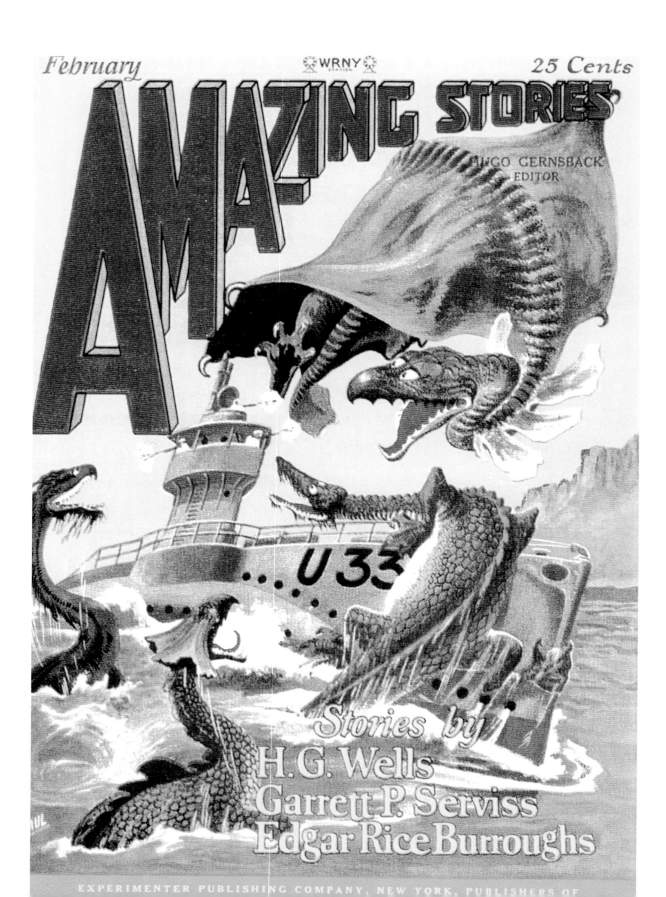

CSN, preferred the proven spar-torpedo to the towed mine, and an awash approach to the enemy ship, rather than a submerged one. He headed in towards *Housatonic* and was sighted at a distance of 100 yards, but *Housatonic*'s crew was unable to depress her guns low enough to shoot at *Hunley*. *Hunley*'s torpedo blew a hole below the target's waterline, killing five of *Housatonic*'s crew and settling her in the shallow water in less than five minutes. While *Hunley* is credited with being the first submersible to sink an enemy ship, she was also a casualty of the action. It is believed that she was swamped by turbulence from the explosion of her torpedo and sank. All nine of her crew were lost. The long-term effect of *Hunley* and this action was to spur considerable interest in submarine warfare as well as important new thinking about underwater military operations that was to alter the course of naval warfare and strategy. Serious attention would soon be given to the main problems still facing the would-be submariners:
a sensible and practical means of surface and underwater propulsion, endurance when submerged, and a truly effective weapon system.

Together with Captain Giovanni Luppis, Robert Whitehead, an engineer from Lancaster, England, created the first viable, self-propelled and self-contained torpedo in 1868 for the Austrian government. It was powered by compressed air and could deliver an eighteen-pound dynamite charge to a distance of 200 yards; an improved model extended that to 300 yards. Whitehead then solved the problem of maintaining a constant depth and in the same year designed and built the first torpedo-launching tube, also powered by compressed air. The first production model of the Luppis-Whitehead torpedo came on stream in 1870. It was sixteen feet long and carried a 76-pound charge of guncotton over a 400-yard range at a speed of eight knots.

The Austrians invited foreign naval officials to see their marvellous new weapon and representatives of the Royal Navy were impressed. They in turn invited Whitehead back to Britain where his launching tube was fitted to the deck of a warship and firing trials were conducted off Sheerness. The British government, acting with unusual speed, purchased the manufacturing rights, including future improvements, from Whitehead for £15,000. It seems that the Austrians had not bothered to protect the new weapon with patents.

The type of torpedo developed by Whitehead was soon in favour with the Imperial Japanese Navy which used it very effectively against the Russians in the Russo-Japanese War. And before that, in 1878, the Russian Navy had made the first real torpedo attack when they sank a Turkish ship in the Black Sea utilizing two of the weapons. And in 1895 the Japanese used torpedo boats quite effectively against Chinese warships. These activities all involved tubes mounted on surface ships firing at surface ships and ultimately led, in the 1920s, to the development of the high-speed motor torpedo boat. Thus, torpedo development was making great strides as the century ended, but submarine technology lagged well behind. By 1907 Whitehead was building a torpedo of amazing capability; a 4000-yard range at a 36-knot speed with a warhead containing 300 pounds of guncotton. Leading up to this significantly advanced weapon was the creation by a Trieste inventor named L. Obry of the gyroscope, which made it possible to automatically maintain both the course and depth of the torpedo. Whitehead installed the device in his torpedoes beginning in 1898. In the same period a Berlin firm called Schwarzkopf was engaged in the design and construction of some excellent torpedoes which were notable for their resistance to corrosion, a hugely important factor at sea.

Submarine development got a boost in 1879 when

far left: In 1927 this cover of the popular pulp magazine *Amazing Stories* featured a submarine in the image illustrating the Edgar Rice Burroughs story *The Land That Time Forgot*. below: An early Jolly Roger. Such pirate flags were often flown by Royal Navy subs in World War II to display symbols of their combat achievements.

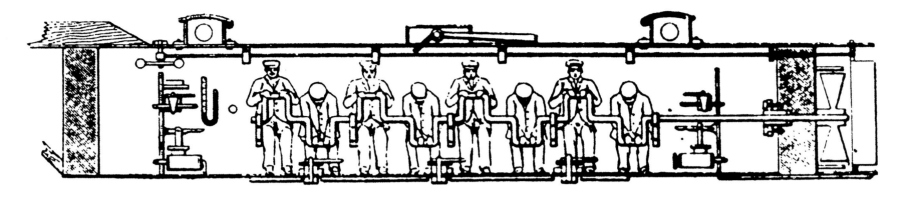

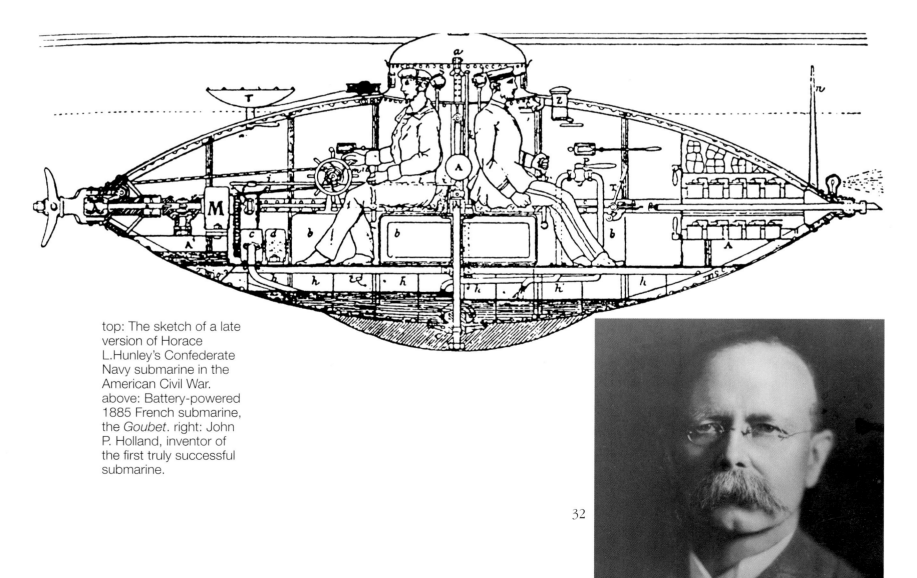

top: The sketch of a late version of Horace L.Hunley's Confederate Navy submarine in the American Civil War. above: Battery-powered 1885 French submarine, the *Goubet*. right: John P. Holland, inventor of the first truly successful submarine.

32

the Reverend George Garrett built a submersible similar to the Confederate Navy's *David*. He called it *Resurgam* (I shall rise again). It featured a method of underwater propulsion based on steam stored in pressure cylinders and was capable of a ten-mile range, submerged, at up to three knots. Test results of *Resurgam* were mixed, but Garrett soon joined forces with a Swedish gunmaker, Thorsten Nordenfelt, and the pair built a submarine in 1882 at Stockholm, the first to incorporate a gun in addition to a deck-mounted torpedo tube. Garrett's original hull design was now streamlined and expanded to a length of 64 feet with a nine-foot diameter and a 60-ton displacement. It, too, was steam-powered using stored steam for underwater operation. The specs called for a 150-mile range on the surface and fifteen miles submerged at four knots. It was most impressive, despite having a number of early developmental problems, not least being the accumulation of smoke, carbon monoxide, and carbon dioxide (a problem of all submarines until the advent of the nuclear boats). Like most early submarines, the Garrett-Nordenfelt boat was really a semi-submersible, but it made a powerful impression and gave new impetus to the development of submarine technology.

Thorsten Nordenfelt went on to associate with Britain's Barrow Shipyard (where the Royal Navy's ballistic missile submarines have been built). There he and Garrett built the Mark III; a submarine 125 feet long, able to dive to a depth of 100 feet and powered by two steam engines. Her range was 1000 miles. She displaced 230 tons submerged and was the first sub with internally-mounted torpedo tubes. She promised a lot but suffered unstable depth-keeping, was never accepted and was eventually scrapped.

With the work of other British inventors of the time, Ash, Campbell and Waddington, the solution to the problem of underwater propulsion was finally achieved. Their efforts resulted in electric motors that ran on banks or "batteries" of accumulators. Such electric motors required no air and this proved to be one of the greatest accomplishments in submarine evolution.

There followed a series of submersible creations in France, most of them fascinating, but utterly unstable and invariably unsuccessful, until the early 1900s when all of their experience and experimentation began to pay off. As early as 1906 the French proved that they could build 800-ton genuine ocean-going submarines capable of ten knots submerged and with a range of 2500 miles. France was now leading the world in the design and construction of the most advanced and sophisticated submarines and was able to deploy them in considerable numbers.

In the United States the Navy had allocated $200,000 of its 1893-94 budget for the design, construction and testing of an experimental submarine and bids were invited, with just three bidders submitting proposals. Of the three, only John Philip Holland, an Irish immigrant living in New Jersey, whose earlier submersibles had earned him some acclaim, was offering something no one else could—a submarine that could actually descend by tilting large hydroplanes, remain level at the desired depth, and ascend by using forward motion with its hydroplanes tilted in the other direction. One of his earlier boats, the USS *Plunger* which resulted from a US Navy contract of 1895, performed on a par with the much later subs of World War I; fourteen knots on the surface and eight knots submerged. *Plunger* failed though, due to heat that accumulated within the hull. Still, Holland was on the right track.

The Electric Storage Battery Company entered into an agreement with John Holland by which it provided financing for his next submarine in return for the patents to it. It was to become the Electric Boat Company and the primary contractor to the US Navy for its future submarines. This new

"Soggy she grew, 'n' she didn't lift, 'n' she listed more 'n' more, / Till her bell struck 'n' her boiler pipes began to wheeze 'n' snore; / She settled, settled, listed, heeled, 'n' then may I be cust, / If her sneezin', wheezin' boiler-pipes did not begin to bust!
– from *One of the Bosun's Yarns*
by John Masefield

boat was to be called the *Holland*. She was 54 feet long with a surface displacement of 75 tons. Power came from a petrol engine which drove her at seven knots on the surface, and an electric motor taking her to five knots submerged. She could recharge her own batteries at sea, the first submarine with that capability. *Holland* was fitted with a bow torpedo tube and carried three torpedoes as well as a gun for surface use. She successfully completed sea trials in 1899 and was purchased by the US Navy in 1900 for $150,000.

On the strength of *Holland*'s performance, the first production model drew interest, and orders, from many of the world's navies. This production version was 63 feet long with an eleven- foot diameter. She had a 160 hp engine with a dynamo to charge the batteries. The boat carried air flasks with sufficient capacity to provide air for a nine-man crew for up to nine weeks. It could also be used to blow the ballast tanks for rapid surfacing and to fire the torpedoes. The new *Holland* had a main ballast tank as well as an auxiliary one, and additional tanks for fore and aft trim. *Holland* was the first wholly successful submarine in history. Her performance and reliability were good and despite occasional mishaps due with her petrol engine, she showed the world that the submarine had come to stay.

In addition to the US Navy and others, the Royal Navy adapted the Holland and was licensed to build five of the boats at Vickers' Barrow-in-Furness yard. The Royal Navy operated them for twelve years. The first of these boats, called *Holland 1*, was being towed to the breaker's yard in November 1913 when she foundered off Plymouth. On 14 April 1981, a Royal Navy mine-hunter, HMS *Bossington*, made a contact which proved to be the wreck of *Holland 1* at a depth of 190 feet. *Bossington* was searching an area of sea off the Eddystone Light on behalf of the Royal Navy Submarine Museum, Gosport. By midnight

I think the Holland submarine boat should be purchased. Evidently she has in her great possibilities for harbor defense. Sometimes she doesn't work perfectly, but often she does, and I don't think that in the present emergency [the Spanish-American War] we can afford to let her slip. —Teddy Roosevelt, then Assistant Secretary of the Navy in a letter to Navy Secretary John D. Long, 1898.

left: American painter Thomas Hart Benton worked aboard the USS *Dorado* in 1943 on a series of paintings and drawings called *The Year of Peril*, powerful images of submarine action in World War II. The project was financed by Abbott Laboratories and Benton collaborated on it with the painter Georges Schreiber. This example from is called *Score Another for the Subs*. Following its commissioning in the fall of 1943, *Dorado* sailed for the Canal Zone, but never arrived. Air searches discovered oil slicks and widely scattered debris, but no identification was made. A German submarine was known to be operating in the area, but the actual fate of *Dorado* is unknown.

There be of them, that have left a name behind them, that their praises might be reported. And some there be which have no memorial.
—Ecclesiasticus IV. 9

Long ago it was and yet, who amongst us dare forget.
—John Bell

the diving vessel *Seaforth Clansman* had lowered a diving bell and an underwater television camera. At noon the next day the Museum received a signal from the ship: "Submarine in reasonably good condition. Hull is heavily encrusted but easily identifiable and sits with keel approximately two feet into the seabed with slight list . . . ." *Holland 1*, the only surviving example of the inventor's first

really successful submarine, had been found. Subsequent salvage was relatively simple in the skilled hands of naval experts at Devonport. The conservation and restoration were started immediately. There was very little corrosion; internal wooden decking had not softened, and one of the battery cells, returned to Chloride Ltd where it was made, delivered 35 ampere-hours.

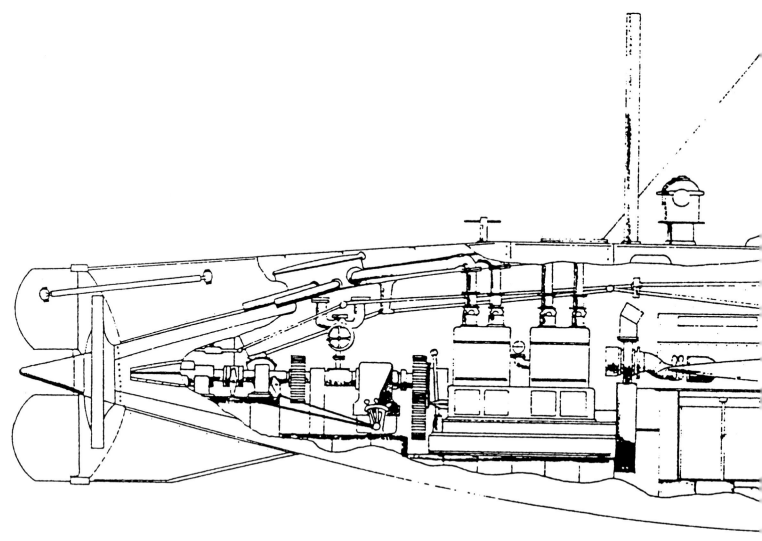

Today the Royal Navy's first submarine looks much as she did when in service.

In the period leading up to World War I, the submariners were experiencing a rough and ready existence. Conditions in the submarines of the day were crude, insanitary and dangerous. Among the hazards they faced were the possibility of collision, flooding and explosion when their petrol engines malfunctioned. This last threat was finally eliminated when the engines were replaced by the safer, more powerful and efficient diesel engines that were to become the standard surface power-plant of submarines until the introduction of nuclear-powered subs in the 1950s, the first being the USS *Nautilus*.

below: A cutaway view of the Royal Navy's first Holland submarine of five ordered. The first Holland was launched on 2 October 1901. It was powered by a four-cycle Otto petrol engine and a 60-cell battery unit.

The widespread interest [in the submarine] is out of all proportion to the actual fighting value of this type of vessel.
— *Scientific American*, April 1899

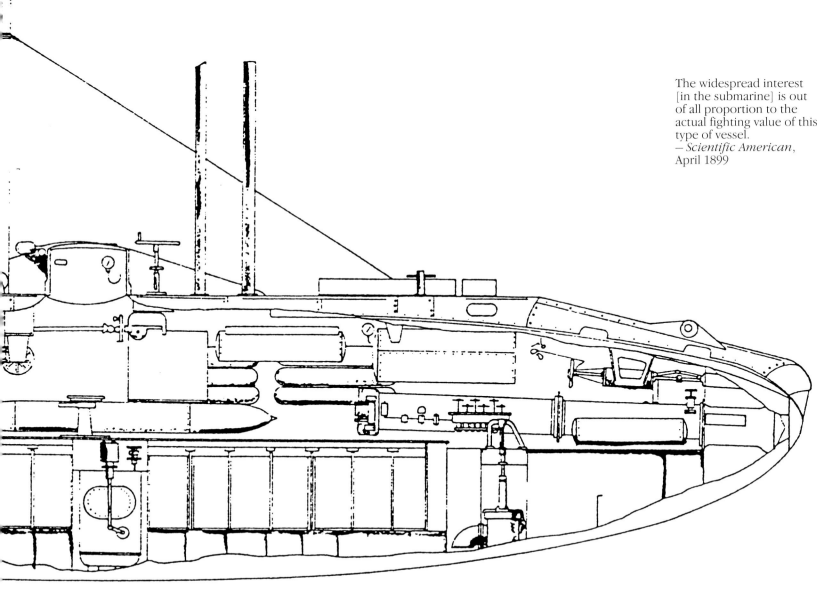

DIESEL BOATS

above: Aboard the USS *Seadog* (SS 401) in search of enemy shipping in the western Pacific, May 1945. right: The conning tower of the USS *Pampanito* (SS 383), a Balao class submarine currently serving as a fully-restored floating museum in San Francisco bay. Built in 1943 at the Portsmouth (New Hampshire) Naval Shipyard, *Pampanito* made six patrols during World War II, sinking six Japanese ships which totalled 27,000 tons.

IN THE RUN-UP to World War II, American military planners saw the submarine as essential in helping to protect the country from the fleets of hostile foreign governments, and the submarines of the US Navy were given the dual role of patrol and attack.

At the 1921 Washington Naval Conference (which specified the number of ships in each class that each power should be permitted) the British had wanted to abolish the military use of submarines by international treaty, but they were opposed by the other powers, including France and the United States, who wanted as much allocated submarine tonnage as possible. The meeting also focused on an attempt to devise a humanitarian code for the use of submarines, but the input was so contradictory that the effort ultimately collapsed.

As war began for the US in December 1941, the United States Naval Staff realized that their previous ideas about using submarines to target hostile battleships and aircraft carriers would have to widen, and the policy soon became: 'Against Japan, unrestricted submarine warfare.' With the prospect of a demanding and protracted war in the Pacific, and with few support bases there, the US Navy went to work on the design of new, long-range subs, bluewater boats able to venture far from their bases. These subs had to be large, with substantial range, reasonably good habitability and good speed on the surface. They would have an 11,000-mile range at an economical 10-knot speed. They would carry ample food and consumable supplies for up to 75 days at sea. They would be able to stay submerged for up to 48 hours at a speed of 2.5 knots. They would have a sustained submerged speed of 9 knots. On the surface they would cruise at up to 20 knots and they would operate to a depth of 300 feet.

The armament of the Gato/Balao-class boats, the best of the American World War II submarines, consisted of six forward torpedo tubes and sixteen Mk 14 torpedoes, four aft torpedo tubes and four spare torpedoes, and either a three-inch or four-

In both world wars, the depth charge was the weapon of choice used against enemy submarines. Loaded with high explosive, depth charges were weighted steel cylinders (sometimes referred to in the US Navy as "ash cans"). Prior to releasing these weapons, a detonation depth was set on the hydrostatic pistol. The charges were either dropped or launched from various types of surface ships, often from destroyers on convoy escort duty. When the charges hit the water they sank quickly and exploded on reaching the pre-set depth. The explosion caused an expanding spherical pressure wave intended to cause significant damage to the target sub. For the depth charges to be effective, the crew of the surface ship delivering them needed very accurate information about the target sub's position, course, speed and depth, all factors that would be changed immediately when the sub skipper learned that his boat was about to receive the attentions of an enemy surface vessel. For the attacker, targetting a submarine with depth charges was often a lengthy and difficult and frustrating task. For the men on the receiving end in the submarine, the sometimes protracted depth charging experience ranged from annoying to terrifying; a testing time for both men and boat. Later World War II developments included *continued on page 43*

continued on page 43

inch deck gun. In lieu of the spare torpedoes, the boat could carry 40 mines.

The Gato-class sub was 312 feet long, with a 27-foot beam and normally displaced 2420 tons submerged. Its diesel power was supplied by four General Motors or Fairbanks Morse units; with electric power came from four Elliot or General Electric units. The surfaced power was 5400 hp, and the submerged power was 2740 hp.

The Gato-class submarine is divided into nine watertight compartments or sections. The first, in the bow, the forward torpedo room, contained six torpedo tubes with war shots loaded, up to ten spare torpedoes and bunks accommodating 25 per cent of the crew. Just aft of the forward torpedo room is the wardroom and officers' quarters, which are located above the forward battery space. Through the next watertight bulkhead is the control room and the radio room. There is a hatch in the control room leading up to the conning tower and the combat centre with the periscopes, radar, torpedo data computer and the navigational plot.

Beyond the control room is the galley and the crew mess, followed by the crew sleeping area with bunks for another 36 men. The galley staff was responsible for three meals a day, snacks and coffee round the clock. The enlisted mess seated 24 men at the four tables. It also served as the crew area for recreation, study and relaxation. Beneath this area is the after battery space. Beyond the crew berthing area are the forward and after engine rooms, each of them housing two 1600 hp diesels, and under these rooms lay the four 1100 kw generators. The boat's four electric motors turn the twin propellers from the next compartment aft. Above the motor room is the maneuvring compartment. The last area of the sub is the after torpedo room with four stern torpedo tubes and bunks for an additional fifteen crewmen. There is also an escape and rescue hatch.

When riding on the surface the Gato class fleet submarine normally kept a low profile and low

centre of gravity for stability. On the surface she was about two-thirds submerged.

The captain had a very small stateroom containing a bunk, with a depth gauge and a compass mounted in the wall behind it, a small fold-down desk, a chair, a telephone and a lockable cabinet above the desk.

The Gato-class boat was manned by 70 enlisted men and five or more officers. Then, as now, the senior chief petty officer was called the chief of the boat. Routine required the crew to be divided into three work sections or groups, with each group standing a four-hour duty watch followed by eight hours off duty. On watch, a working section performed routine maintenance, operated the machinery and stood lookout. In their off-duty hours, they slept, had meals, played poker and other games such as acey ducey and cribbage, wrote letters and studied for their submariner qualifying examinations. Typically, the commanding officer was a lieutenant commander, a Naval Academy graduate, about 30 to 35 years old. His number two, as today, was the ship's executive officer who was charged with much of the administrative detail. He assisted the skipper in combat situations. The remaining officers headed the departments, including communications, torpedo/gunnery and engineering. The crew was composed of electricians, torpedomen, gunner's mates, machinists, quartermasters, cooks, radio-men, firemen, a pharmacist's mate, a yeoman and several ordinary seamen, all under supervision by the petty officers and department heads. Submariners enjoyed perks such as higher pay and better food than surface sailors, as they do today, in partial compensation for the added dangers that come with the submarining business.

With the fall of France in May 1940, a concerned United States Congress authorized funding for 67 new submarines in addition to the six already funded for the fiscal year 1941. At that time there were only three American shipyards in the

42

business of building submarines and together they had just a dozen construction ways. They quickly went on an emergency basis, working to add more building ways, and the US Navy Bureau of Ships drafted the services of two other yards that had no experience building subs. One of them was Manitowoc Shipbuilding whose yard was located in Wisconsin, a very long way from the nearest ocean. For the Navy to take delivery, the Manitowoc-built subs had to be towed more than 1000 miles down the Illinois and Mississippi Rivers to the Gulf of Mexico. Submarine production at the Manitowoc yard was managed by Electric Boat of Groton, Connecticut, a company with a long and proud history of building submarines. Both the Wisconsin yard and the Cramp Company shipyard of Philadelphia adapted readily to submarine construction techniques, producing some of the tightest and best-built boats of the war. The first subs of this particular congressional buy became operational at the Navy's Pearl Harbor base early in 1942. Training the crews to man them required significant changes in normal procedure at the Navy Submarine School, New London, Connecticut. It was then that the "ninety-day wonder" was created. With the exigencies of war, the peacetime six-month officer course had to be condensed to just three months. For the students it meant many eighteen-and twenty-hour-days of study and work. The output of officer graduates quickly accelerated from a prewar 50 a year to 1000, and the number of enlisted men completing the course grew from a monthly 336 in 1940 to a wartime high of more than 4700 in March 1944.

Even with the staggering nationwide demand for skilled industrial workers, machinists, electricians, pipe fitters, welders and metal workers for all the various war-related industries, the American shipyards engaged in submarine construction somehow found and hired the people they needed. The Portsmouth Navy Yard in New Hampshire worked extremely efficiently and reached a productivity rate of one new sub each month by mid-1943, the high point of submarine construction during the war. The Portsmouth yard increased its workforce from 4200 in 1940 to about 20,000 in 1943. The expression "swing shift" entered the vernacular in the early war years as factories and shipyards strove to build their efficiency by operating with three working shifts on an around-the-clock basis. Efficiency resulted, too, from the adoption of auto- industry assembly line production methods and the prefabrication of submarine sections. Such sections could be made and stored independently of the schedule for a given boat and retrieved as needed for assembly into a new hull.

Electric Boat built 74 submarines at the Groton yard during World War II. Its productivity went from one boat a month in 1941 to 16 a year in 1942; 25 in 1943 and 23 in 1944. The motto at their shipyard was KEEP 'EM SLIDING. Electric Boat also managed the submarine construction at its Manitowoc River yard where 28 World War II subs were built.

The namesake of the Gato-class of submarines happened to be the boat whose design and assembly had reached an acceptable standard, in the judgement of Navy authorities, at a point when high-efficiency mass production was of paramount importance to the US war effort. At that point these experts declared the *Gato* to be the standard to which all subsequent submarines would be built. No further alterations to the design or construction method would be allowed. With the design plans frozen, construction times fell and the man-hours needed to build the subs dropped dramatically.

In all of World War II, the submarines of the Imperial Japanese Navy managed to sink only 184 Allied merchant ships, totalling 907,000 gross registered tons. They accounted for many warships, among them two aircraft carriers, two cruisers, ten

the Hedgehog, a mortar firing an array of 24 small impact-fused bombs, each having 32 pounds of Torpex explosive, supposedly ample to pierce the hull of any submarine of the time. Squid followed in 1943, a three-barrelled mortar firing full- sized depth charges, each containing 300 pounds of explosive, could be used with devastating effect in a near miss as well as a hit.

preceding page: John Mills and Richard Attenborough in a scene from the movie *Morning Departure*. above: A construction worker on the hull of a new vessel at Electric Boat's Groton yard in August 1943.

Good taste demands I keep my jacket on

The largest submarines in the world during the Second World War were the Japanese Type STo class ocean-going boats. Only three such boats were operational. Each carried three high-performance float planes. The STo displaced 5223 tons surfaced and 6560 tons submerged. They were 400 feet long and had two diesel engines producing 7700 hp and two electric motors of 2400 hp. The surfaced speed was 19 knots and submerged they could do 6.5 knots. Cruising surfaced at 16 knots, they had a range of 30,000 miles. The armament included eight torpedo tubes and twenty torpedoes, as well as one 140mm deck gun and ten 25mm anti-aircraft guns. The complement was 144.

right: The commander of a US Navy submarine scans the sea surface for enemy vessels near the end of World War II in the Pacific.

destroyers and other escort ships, as well as several submarines. Japanese losses included 129 submarines of which 70 were sunk by Allied surface ships, 19 by submarines, 18 by aircraft, and 22 due to accidents and other causes.

Of the many submarine types and classes built by Japan before and during the war, the best may have been the Kaidai-class, Variant KD.7, which had evolved from the earlier Kaidai variants. The KD.7 was a large, ocean-going boat with good speed and range, good seakeeping characteristics and an effective armament. Constructed by the Kure Dockyard, the KD.7 displaced 1833 tons on the surface and 2602 tons submerged. The length was 346 feet, the beam 27 feet and the draught 15 feet. Power was supplied by two diesel units and two electric units, producing 8000 hp surfaced and 1800 hp submerged, respectively. The maximum speeds were 23 knots surfaced and 8 knots submerged. The range was 8000 miles at 16 knots surfaced. Armament included six forward-fitted torpedo tubes and a load of twelve torpedoes, as well as one 120mm gun and two 25mm guns. The complement was 88.

For the Japanese there were few big moments in their entire World War II submarine effort. One came with the assembly of their carrier strike force in preparation for the multiple surprise attack on the American capital ships and facilities at Pearl Harbor, Hawaii in December 1941. The Imperial Japanese Navy sent 24 of its submarines to sea ahead and in support of its carrier force. While losing one of their number to attacking US aircraft that were returning to their carrier, the USS *Enterprise*, the Japanese subs had their greatest successes in that first month of the war with America. They sank eight Allied merchant vessels (six of them American) with a combined tonnage of 40,700 and damaged seven more with tonnage totalling 47,500.

Their most impressive attack was that made by Lieutenant-Commander Takaichi Kinashi of the

submarine *I19* on 15 September 1942. Kinashi was in command of the large sub with a 101-man crew and was patrolling in the Coral Sea when he encountered a US Navy convoy of transports and troopships which was being escorted by the battleship USS *North Carolina*, several destroyers and the aircraft carriers USS *Wasp* and USS *Hornet*. The prize the Americans were fighting for was the strategic island of Guadalcanal in the Solomons and its urgently-needed airfield. Kinashi found *Wasp* and attacked her with a four-torpedo salvo, hitting the 21,000-ton carrier twice below the waterline. The ensuing explosions in her fuel and ammunition stores resulted in the sinking of the carrier. In one of the strangest events of the war, the other two torpedoes from the Japanese sub carried on past the *Wasp* for nearly six miles, one of them striking and seriously damaging the *North Carolina*, while the other hit and blew the bow off the destroyer USS *O'Brien*. The battleship struggled back to base at Pearl Harbor for repairs, but the *O'Brien* broke in half and sank while under tow to New Caledonia. This attack by the Japanese sub had a devastating effect on the US Pacific Fleet, which was then left with only one serviceable aircraft carrier and one relatively modern battleship. Still, the convoy got through and delivered its 4000 US Marines to Guadalcanal, leading to American success in the campaign there. Lieutenant-Commander Kinashi's fortunes turned in July 1944 when he and the crew of the submarine *I29* were lost while returning from Germany, the victims of torpedoes from the submarine USS *Sawfish* off Singapore.

The submarine *I58* of the Imperial Japanese Navy was responsible for the greatest sea disaster in the history of the US Navy. By 1945 the Americans had concluded that the Japanese submarine force had never really developed into the threat that it might have become, and, in essence, dropped their guard. The heavy cruiser *Indianapolis*, flagship of Admiral Raymond Spruance's Fifth Fleet, had been

right: The vital moment for which a submarine was built, as depicted in *Stand By To Fire*, by Georges Schreiber.
below: A British poster of World War II, by Norman Wilkinson.

There is no margin for mistakes in submarines. You are either alive or dead.
— Admiral Sir Max Horton, Royal Navy, Flag Officer, Submarines, 1940-1942

A FEW CARELESS WORDS MAY END IN THIS—

Many lives were lost in the last war through careless talk
Be on your guard! Don't discuss movements of ships or troops

chosen to deliver the first atomic bombs to the US Army Air Force at Tinian in the Marianas Islands. The cruiser had completed her assignment and was heading for Leyte in the Philippines, unescorted. She was not bothering to zigzag or take any anti-submarine precautions and passed right through the patrol line of the *I58* on 29 July 1945. The skipper of the Japanese sub, Lieutenant-Commander Mochitsura Hashimoto, could not believe his luck. It was just before midnight and Hashimoto struck at the *Indianapolis* with six Long Lance torpedoes, hitting the cruiser with at least two of the weapons. In just twelve minutes the American ship sank. Of the 1199 crew members 850 survived the sinking, but they waited for 84 hours before being spotted by a Catalina flying boat on 2 August. After their ordeal by exposure, wounds and repeated shark attacks, only 316 men were still alive when rescue finally came. The *Indianapolis* was the last American warship to be lost in the war, the final success of the Japanese submarine force. It would be 37 years before another vessel would be the victim of a submarine.

In World War II it was the lot of the Royal Navy submarine branch to go on long patrols and attack heavily-defended trade routes near enemy-occupied shores. They had the largely unrewarding task of operating against merchant shipping to North Africa in the difficult and dangerous conditions of the Mediterranean. There, in relatively shallow and clear water, British subs were very effective in support of the North African desert campaign; in all they sank nearly two million tons of enemy shipping in the Med and North Sea. Casualties suffered by the Royal Navy sub crews, however, were quite high, with 70 submarines lost.

The British submarines had considerable success in sea denial missions against German and Italian warships and submarines and, in February 1945, HMS *Venturer* attacked and sank the *U864*, and so became the first submarine ever to sink another

sub while both were submerged.

Unlike the larger American submarines of the time, British subs had little impact on the war in the Far East, largely because they lacked the range to cover the vast ocean distances in that part of the world. Of the many submarine types employed by the British in the war, the S- and T-classes were probably the best and most effective in their roles. The smaller S-boats were designed as medium-range vessels of 990 tons submerged displacement (Group 3 units), with an operational depth of 300 feet. This sub was intended for operation in the North Sea, the Mediterranean and other restricted waters. It was designed to have very good handling characteristics, dive-time, surface and dived speeds. Up to the 1930s, the S-class boats were the largest class ever built for the Royal Navy, with a 217-foot hull. With greater fuel capacity than in previous RN subs, the S-boats were capable of a 6000 mile range at 10 knots surfaced. Storage capacity for food and ammunition made it possible to undertake patrols of up to 48 days. They were among the most successful submarines of the war.

The British T-class submarines, the first of which was HMS *Triton*, launched on 5 October 1937, were built to be true ocean-going subs and were among the most successful of the British World War II subs. The second and more refined group of T-boats had a submerged displacement of 1575 tons, an 8-11,000 mile range, a surface speed of 15 knots and a submerged speed of 9 knots. These subs had a crew complement of 65. They had six internal and two external bow torpedo tubes, and three external stern tubes, as well as one four-inch deck gun and one 20mm anti-aircraft gun. Their power came from two 2500 hp diesels and two 1450 hp electric motors. The T- boats were simple and reasonably low-maintenance craft with better safety and underwater handling qualities than their predecessors. They performed well wherever they were sent, but they also suffered the highest loss rate of any Royal Navy submarine class in

In peace there's nothing so becomes a man / As modest stillness and humility; / But when the blast of war blows in our ears, / Then imitate the action of the tiger. . .
— *Henry V,* Act III, Scene I by William Shakespeare

below: Harry Farmer, a diesel-era US Navy submariner who now serves as a guide aboard the USS *Pampanito* in San Francisco bay.

Undoubtedly the greatest strains of the war at sea fell on the shoulders of the masters and deck officers of the tramp ships. Their charges were slow and manoeuvred like the lumbering barges they were. Station-keeping in convoy was for these men an unending ordeal. On a dark, moonless night it required nerves of steel and the eyes of a cat; in poor visibility or stormy weather it was an impossibility. They straggled, they romped and they veered, becoming the easiest of targets for the stalking U-boats. The men in the engine room suffered the tortures of the damned, never knowing when a torpedo might tear through the thin plates of the hull, sending their ship plunging to the bottom before they had a chance to reach the first rung of the ladder to the deck. Burdened, as they so often were, with heavy bulk cargoes, the tramps sank like punctured tin cans filled with lead shot. For those who took to the lifeboats or rafts, the process of dying was more prolonged. Lacking protection from the sun and storms, and striving to exist on rations measured in ounces per day, many eventually succumbed to exposure, starvation, thirst or sheer mental exhaustion.
— from *The Merchant Navy Goes To War*
by Bernard Edwards

World War II.

In his fine book, *War Beneath The Sea*, British naval historian Peter Padfield provided a superb description of the World War II diesel submarine and its operation and use in war:
"A submarine was a thick-skinned steel cylinder tapering at both ends, designed to withstand enormous pressure at depth. Buoyancy chambers termed main ballast tanks, fitted in most cases as lozenge-shaped bulges outside this pressure hull on either side, kept the cylinder afloat. An outer steel 'casing' liberally pierced with openings to let the sea flood in and out provided a sharp bow, a faired stern and a narrow deck atop the cylinder; only a few feet above the sea, this was washed in any weather like a half-tide rock. About midway along its length rose a low structure enclosing another small pressure chamber called the conning tower, accessible from the pressure hull via a circular hatch and allowing access to the bridge above it by another small, pressure-tight hatch.

"To submerge, the diesel engines which drove the craft on the surface, sucking air in through ducts from the tower structure, were shut down, and electric motors which took their power from massed batteries and consequently used no air were coupled to the propeller shafts. Buoyancy was destroyed by opening valves in the main ballast tanks, allowing the trapped air to be forced out by sea water rushing in; and horizontal fins, termed hydroplanes or just planes, projecting either side at bow and stern were angled against the water flow caused by the boat's progress to impel the bows down. Approaching the required depth as shown on a gauge in the control room below the conning tower, the diving officer attempted to balance the boat in a state of neutral buoyancy, 'catching a trim' in which they neither descended further nor rose. He did this by adjusting the volume of water in auxiliary tanks at bow and stern, and either side at mid-length,

flooding or pumping out, aiming to poise the submarine so perfectly that she swam on an even keel weighing precisely the same as the space of sea she occupied, completely at one with her element and floating firm and free as an airship in the air. It was an art attained by minute attention to the detail of prior consumption of stores and fuel, and by much experience. Sea water is seldom homogenous; a boat passing into a layer of different temperature or salinity, and hence density, becomes suddenly less or more buoyant, dropping fast or refusing to descend through the layer until more tank spaces have been flooded; when going deep the pressure hull would be so squeezed between the ribs by the weight above that it occupied less space and the boat had to be lightened by pumping out tanks to compensate. Most vigilance was required at the extremes: going very deep the boat might plunge below the point at which the hull could withstand the pressure; near the surface at periscope depth she might porpoise up to break surface in sight of the enemy.

"Submerged, a submarine stole along at walking pace or less, either to conserve her batteries which could not be recharged by diesels until she surfaced again or, when hunted, to make as little engine and propeller noise as possible. With both sets of batteries 'grouped up' in parallel she might make twice a fast walking speed, 8 or 9 knots, but only for some two hours at most before the batteries ran dangerously low. This was her shortcoming: while she had great range and speed on the surface, once submerged she lost mobility by comparison even with the slowest tramp steamer. Against a battle squadron she could not hope to get within range for attack unless already lying in ambush very close to its track. For this reason the submarine was held to be 'a weapon of position and surprise'.

"Once her presence was detected and she became the hunted her submerged endurance was limited by the amount of air within the pressure

...the periods at sea—cramped in mold-ridden, diesel-hammering, oxygen-lacking, urine-reeking, excrement-laden, food-rotting, salt-encrusted steel cockleshells, firing torpedoes in exultation, searching for convoys in frustration or receiving depth charges, our side or theirs.
— from the forward by Edward L. Beach to *Iron Coffins* by Herbert A. Werner

A man has his distinctive personal scent which his wife, his children and his dog can recognize. A crowd has a generalized stink.
— W. H. Auden

above left: Crewmen of HMS *Unseen* displaying their Jolly Roger flag at the end of a World War II patrol. left: Shipmates and their mascot share tea aboard *Unseen*.

hull, which of course was all the crew had to breathe; as they exhaled it became progressively degraded with carbon dioxide, after twenty-four hours or so reaching dangerous and finally fatal levels. Headaches and dizzyness were common in operational submarines, but they were accepted among the other discomforts of an exacting life; remarkably little was known of the speed of deterioration of air. It was, for example, not appreciated that when the carbon dioxide content reaches 4 per cent thinking becomes difficult and decisions increasingly irrational; by 10 per cent extreme distress is felt, followed soon after by unconsciousness; at over 20 per cent the mixture is lethal. No doubt this was not realized, and air purifiers were not installed—although in the German service individual carbon dioxide filter masks with neck-straps were provided—since before the advent of radar a submarine could usually surface at night to renew her air while remaining invisible. That indeed was the usual operational routine: to lurk submerged on the lookout for targets by day, coming up after nightfall to recharge the batteries, refresh the air and perhaps cruise to another position.

"The submarine's main armament was provided by torpedoes, each a miniature submarine in itself with a fuel tank and motor driving contra-rotating propellers, a depth mechanism actuating hydroplanes to maintain a set depth, and a gyro compass linked to a rudder to maintain a set course. At the forward end a warhead of high explosive was detonated by a mechanism firing on contact or when disturbed by the magnetic field of the target ship. These auto-piloted cylinders, known as fish or in the German service as eels, were housed in tubes projecting forward from the fore end of the pressure hull and often aft from the after end as well. In some classes two or more tubes were housed externally beneath the casing, but unlike the internal tubes from the pressure hull whose reloads were stowed in the fore and after compartments, external tubes could not be reloaded until return to base.

"While devastating when they hit the soft underpart of a ship or exploded beneath her, torpedoes were neither as accurate as shells from guns, nor for several reasons could they be 'spotted' on to the target. They were launched from their tubes—after these had been opened to the sea—set to steer a collision course to a point ahead of the target ship, ideally at or near a right angle to her track. Whether they hit depended largely on whether the relative motion problem had been solved correctly, which before radar meant how accurately the target's course and speed had been estimated. The most certain data available was the target's bearing read from a graduated ring around the periscope. Range was obtained by reading the angle between the waterline and the masthead or bridge of the target, either from simple graduations of minutes of arc or by a split-image rangefinder built into the periscope optics. Using the height of the mast or whatever feature had been taken, the angle was converted into range by a sliding scale. Since in most cases the masthead heights had to be estimated from the assumed size or class of the target ship, usually a difficult judgement to make from quick periscope observations, and since there was a tendency to overestimate size, ranges were often exaggerated. In addition the observer made an estimate of the angle between the ship's heading and his own line of sight, known as 'the angle on the bow'; this too was often overestimated. Speed was deduced from a count of the propeller revolutions audible through the submarine's listening apparatus, the distance of the second bow wave from the stem, or simply from the type of vessel and experience. With this data a plot was started incorporating both the target's and the submarine's own movements; updated by subsequent observations as the attack developed, the plot provided increasingly refined estimates which were fed into computing devices of greater or less mechanical ingenuity according to the nationality of the submarine. In British and Japanese navies the firing solution was expressed as an aim-off or director angle (DA) ahead of the target, in the US and German navies as a torpedo-course setting. Finally, a salvo of two or usually more torpedoes was fired with an interval of several seconds between each; this was to avoid upsetting the trim with such a sudden release of weight as would result from the simultaneous discharge of all tubes, and to allow for errors in the estimated data or the steering of the torpedoes themselves. In the British service, where it was assumed that at least three hits would be required to sink a modern capital ship, COs were trained to fire a 'massed salvo' of all torpedoes—usually six—at 5-second intervals, so spreading the salvo along the target and its track. In the American and German services particularly, where the torpedoes themselves could be set to run the desired course, 'spread' was often achieved by firing a 'fan' with a small angle between each torpedo.

"Few attacks were as straightforward as this description might imply: the target was generally steering a zigzag pattern; surface and air escorts were often present to force the submarine into evasive alterations during the approach. The periscope could be used only sparingly, the more so the calmer the sea, lest the feather of its wake were spotted by lookouts; and between observations the submarine CO had to retain a mental picture of the developing situation, continuously updating calculations of time, speed and distance in his head as he attempted to manoeuvre into position to catch the DA at the optimum time when the torpedoes would run in on a broad angle to the enemy's track. There were other situations when snap judgements had to be made on a single observation or while the submarine was turning with nothing but the CO's experience and eye to guide him."

left: Another Thomas Hart Benton painting, *Up Periscope*, from the USS *Dorado* in World War II. above: A sailor sleeps above spare torpedoes in the torpedo room of a US Navy submarine near New London, Conn. in August 1943.

right: A member of the USS *Batfish* (SS 310) crew reading his mail during a May 1945 war patrol in the Pacific.
below: A *Batfish* sailor fastens battle flags to a line. They would be flown when the sub entered harbour at the end of her war patrol.
far right: Officers of the USS *Bonefish* (SS 223) playing cribbage in their wardroom, August 1943.

UNTERSEEBOOTE

THROUGHOUT THE CENTURIES Britain has looked to the sea lanes for transport of her essential supplies, a fact which prompted Germany's attempt to deny the safe use of the trade routes to British merchant ships in World War I. The Germans wanted to cut Britain's vital supply lines and force her to throw in the towel. To do this they employed a powerful force of *unterseebootes*, U-boats, beginning in 1914. These boats generally had their way with the British merchantmen until 1917, when the Allies adopted a policy of assembling and sailing their merchant ships in convoys that had the protection of escorting warships. Prior to that year the U-boats had accounted for the loss of several hundred vessels, their crews and their vitally needed cargoes of food, fuel and war materiel. The famous ASDIC sound-detection system had not yet been invented, and the German submarines had the great advantage of being virtually undetectable by Allied vessels, except when the subs were on the surface.

Both British and German naval commanders were feeling their way in an effort to define a realistic, viable warfare policy. By November 1914 a British naval blockade of Germany and her allies had been established, including the stopping and searching of neutral vessels, and in response Admiral Friederich von Ingenohl, Commander in Chief of the Imperial German Navy pressed his Chief of Naval Staff to advocate a counter-blockade which would utilize their submarines: "As England is trying to destroy our trade it is only fair if we retaliate by carrying on the campaign against her trade by all possible means. Further, as England completely disregards international law in her actions, there is not the least reason why we should exercise any restraint in our conduct of the war. We can wound England most seriously by injuring her trade. By means of the U-boat we should be able to inflict

the greatest injury. We must therefore make use of this weapon, and do so, moreover, in the way most suited to its peculiarities. . . . Consequently a U-boat cannot spare the crews of steamers, but must send them to the bottom with their ships. The shipping world can be warned of these consequences, and it can be pointed out that ships which attempt to make British ports run the risk of being destroyed with their crews. This warning that the lives of steamers' crews will be endangered will be one good reason why all shipping trade with England will cease within a short space of time. . . . The gravity of the situation demands that we should free ourselves from all scruples which certainly no longer have any justification."

In a fervour born of the conviction that, with their U-boat weapon, they were invincible, the Germans declared in February 1915 "all the waters around Great Britain and Ireland, including the whole of the English Channel, a war zone" and warned that "from February 18th, all British merchant shipping in those waters will be destroyed." The proclamation went on to explain that "it would not always be possible, in view of the misuse of neutral flags ordained by the British Government . . . and owing to the hazards of naval warfare . . . to prevent the attacks meant for hostile ships from being directed against neutral ships." An example of alleged "misuse of neutral flags" was the Cunard liner *Lusitania* which was then sailing under an American flag, arguably because she carried some American passengers. There was, in fact, a "neutral corridor" north of Scotland through which innocent neutral ships were supposedly guaranteed safe passage. But, by the end of February, unrestricted U-boat warfare had begun.

Before the *Lusitania* sailed from New York on 1 May 1915 bound for Liverpool, the German Embassy to the United States placed an ad in New York newspapers near the Cunard Line notices.

H R ERDT

U BOOTE HERAUS!

. . . a U-boat cannot spare the crews of steamers, but must send them to the bottom with their ships. The shipping world can be warned of these consequences, and it can be pointed out that the ships which attempt to make British ports run the risk of being destroyed with their crews. This warning that the lives of steamers' crews will be endangered will be one good reason why all shipping trade with England will cease within a short space of time.
— Admiral Friederich von Ingenohl, Commander in Chief, Imperial German Navy, November 1914

left: German World War I poster — The U-boats Are Out! far left: A 1917 British war poster. far left above: German *Lusitania* medal.

right: U-boat lookouts dressed in foul-weather oilskins. The sailor in the foreground has just completed his watch and is going below to rest and warm up.

"Notice! Travellers intending to embark on the Atlantic voyage are reminded that a state of war exists between Germany and her allies and Great Britain and her allies; that the zone of war includes the waters adjacent to the British Isles; that, in accordance with formal notice given by the Imperial German Government, vessels flying the flag of Great Britain, or of any of her allies, are liable to destruction in those waters and that travellers sailing in the war zone on ships of Great Britain or her allies do so at their own risk." On 7 May at 9.15 p.m. one torpedo struck the liner as she cruised off the south coast of Ireland. She was six days out of New York when sighted by Walter Schweiger, commanding officer of the German submarine, *U-20*. *Lusitania* appeared in Schwieger's copies of *Jane's Fighting Ships* and *The Naval Annual*, listed as an Armed Merchant Cruiser and a naval auxiliary. She sank in just eighteen minutes carrying 1198 passengers to their deaths, 128 of them Americans. Was this great ocean liner a legitimate military target? The evidence suggests she was. Many years after the war the identified wreck was searched by divers who discovered large quantities of military stores in the cargo hold, confirming a statement by the Collector of the Port of New York shortly after the sinking, that the *Lusitania's* manifest listed 173 tons of ammunition.

President Woodrow Wilson's initial response to the sinking of *Lusitania,* and to the increasing public pressure on him to enter the war against Germany was, in part, that: "The objection to the present method of attack against trade lies in the practical impossibility of employing U-boats in the destruction of commerce without disregarding those rules of fairness, reason, justice and humanity, which all modern opinion regards as imperative."

The people of the United States were deeply divided over whether the country should become embroiled in the great war with Germany. Not since their own War Between The States had there been such a division and diversity of opinion. Some worked to whip up the populace in favour of war with the Germans, the sooner the better. Others, unsympathetic to Britain and her plight, nursing anti-British and/or pro-German feelings, favoured Germany's cause in the conflict. There were also many who simply took the position that America must avoid all foreign wars no matter what. This domestic tug-of-war persisted through early 1917 when the German government resumed wholly unrestricted U-boat operations and so informed the government of the United States.

By March, American merchant ships were regularly slipping beneath the waves, victims of a vigorous new campaign by the submarines of the German Navy. The US President called a special session of the Congress and there the various factions met in ferocious verbal combat on the question of what America should do in this situation. Wilson got his declaration of war against Germany on 6 April and, at last, the American nation was committed to the fray. It was the last thing the Germans wanted.

At the beginning of the Second World War the German Navy (*Kriegsmarine*) submarine force found their torpedoes to be unreliable. They had some success in the offensive they had launched in 1939 against Allied shipping, but it was not until the summer of 1940 that they resolved this problem and began to achieve truly punishing results.

The failure of the German Air Force (*Luftwaffe*) to subdue the British Royal Air Force and gain air supremacy over the English Channel and southern England by the end of that summer led the Germans to renew their effort to starve the British into submission. Now, the German Navy engaged in an all-out savage campaign of U-boat attacks on Allied merchant ship convoys. With the fall of France the Germans had gained the use of the main Brittany ports and put the organization

Shipboard routine had replaced the excitement of the chase and the battle. And it was a maddening routine. The small ship rolled and slapped, listed and shuddered endlessly. Utensils, spare parts, tools, and conserves showered down on us continually; porcelain cups and dishes shattered on the deckplates and in the bilges as we ate our meals directly out of cans. The men, penned up together in the rocking, sweating drum, took the motion and the monotony with stoicism. Occasionally, someone's temper flared, but spirits remained high. We were all patient veterans. Everyone aboard looked alike, smelled alike, had adopted the same phrases and curses. We had learned to live together in a narrow tube no longer than two railroad cars. We tolerated each other's faults and became experts on each other's habits—how everyone laughed and snarled, talked and snored, sipped his coffee and caressed his beard. The pressure mounted with the passage of each uneventful day, but it could be relieved in an instant by the sight of a fat convoy.
— from *Iron Coffins* by Herbert A. Werner

True bravery is shown by performing without witness what one might be capable of doing before all the world.
— La Rochefoucauld

of Doctor Fritz Todt, and many thousands of slave labourers, to work building immense and impenetrable concrete structures, or "pens," to shelter, repair, re-arm, refuel and re-supply their submarines. It was from these formidable bases at Brest, Lorient, Saint Nazaire, La Pallice and Bordeaux that the flotillas of U-boats were then launched across the Bay of Biscay to seek and destroy their targets. The French bases on the Atlantic coast saved the Germans many hundreds of miles and sailing days *en route* to their hunting grounds, enabling them to remain on station at sea for up to ten days longer than was possible when operating from ports in Germany.

The campaign gained strength and momentum as the U-boat force increased in size until, in early 1943, with more than 100 U-boats operating against the convoys, it seemed near to achieving its objective. At that point the submariners were sinking twelve merchant ships for every U-boat lost in action. The situation changed, however, with the introduction of long-range Allied air patrols able to locate the U-boats through the use of radar, with strengthened surface escort groups and with improved training in the art of U-boat hunting. By May, the balance of terror had firmly shifted in favour of the Allies who, in that month alone, sank 41 German submarines. In real terms, the month the German submariners called "Black May" spelled victory for the Allied cause in the ferocious Battle of the Atlantic.

The U-boat force consisted predominantly of Type VII vessels, favoured by the Commander of Submarines, the then Captain Karl Dönitz because of his belief in the need for a very large fleet of medium-sized ocean-going subs. He rejected the view of the German Naval Staff that Germany should be building larger submarines. In the late 1930s, as he planned for the coming war, Dönitz argued that Germany required a large number of the ocean-going boats which would be tasked with sinking the greatest possible number of hostile merchant ships in order to starve the enemy into submission. He intended to deploy his U-boats against the escorted convoys. In groups, they would attack mainly at night and on the surface, operating submerged only when under threat of air attack or in situations where a submerged attack on enemy ships made sense. His method would involve several U-boats launching a coordinated attack from different sides of a convoy to confuse and scatter the enemy escort ships. These tactics would lead to the development of the "wolfpack" which involved the deployment of as many as twenty U-boats patrolling a line across the convoy's anticipated course. Any of the U-boats spotting the convoy would signal its composition, speed and course to the U-boat headquarters in France. The spotting U-boat would then stalk the convoy, noting and reporting any changes in its behaviour and U-boat HQ would order the pack of submarines to close on the spotting/stalking U-boat. By night the pack of subs would assemble, infiltrate the convoy and launch a surface attack at speed from within its ranks. Before daylight the U-boats would submerge and spend the day shadowing the convoy in order to repeat the procdedure that evening, and so on until the convoy had finally been destroyed.

The Type VII submarine was well-suited to the wolfpack assignment, being highly manoeuvrable and fast with good range, ample torpedo reserves and a fairly small tower structure making the boat rather hard to spot.

The design and performance of the Type VII developed significantly between the initial variant and the final version, the F. The Type VIIC was the version produced in the greatest quantity. It normally displaced 769 tons surfaced and 871 tons when submerged. It was 218 feet long with a 20-foot beam and a 15-foot draught. Power was provided by two diesel units and two electric motors, all from various manufacturers. The C

generated 3200 hp surfaced and 750 hp submerged. On the surface the boat was capable of 17.5 knots; it could do 7.5 knots submerged. It had an 8500 mile range at 10 knots surfaced and 130 miles at 2 knots submerged. The armament was five 21-inch torpedo tubes and fourteen torpedoes. It had one 37mm gun and two 20mm guns. The boat was operated by a crew of at least 46 men. Including all variants, A through F, more than 700 Type VII U-boats were built by German shipyards between 1935 and 1945.

In total, 1162 U-boats of all the operational types served in the German submarine fleet between mid-1935 and the end of the European war in May 1945. The submarine force numbered 55,000 men sailing on the 3000 patrols made by 920 subs during the war. Their torpedoes and guns sank 2840 merchant ships for a total of 14,333,082 gross registered tons, and 150 warships of various types. Of the 1162 operational German submarines, 1060 were lost, either in action or through scuttling at the war's end. The submarine force lost 27,491 men dead or missing, and approximately 5000 as prisoners of war. Roughly three-quarters of the submarines lost were lost in action; more than 40 per cent were lost in attacks by aircraft.

Until his death in May 1941, Günther Prien was the leading U-boat commander of World War II and a recipient of Germany's highest military decoration. Prien was skipper of *U-47* and on the night of 14 October 1939, under the intense green and orange glow of the northern lights, he attacked and sank the British battleship *Royal Oak* as she lay at anchor in Scapa Flow. His two torpedoes cost the Royal Navy 833 officers and men. In Hitler's Third Reich, Prien was a popular hero. Here he recounts an experience from his first patrol.

"At last, early in the morning of the fifth September, we sighted another plume of smoke. I happened to be on the bridge. A light mist lay over the waves and beyond, the sun rose, blood

Enemy submarines are to be called U-boats. The term 'submarine' is to be reserved for Allied underwater vessels. U-boats are those dastardly villains who sink our ships, while submarines are those gallant and noble craft which sink theirs.
– Prime Minister Winston S. Churchill

ZEICHNET
KRIEGS-ANLEIH
FÜR U-BOOTE GEG
ENGLAND

left: An Atlantic convoy bringing vital supplies to Britain during World War II. U-boats hunted individually and in "wolfpacks", successfully preying on ships in the convoys during the early years of the war.

red. It was difficult to see clearly in the half-light. By the time we had sighted the smoke, the ship had already come over the horizon. She was steering a curious zig-zag course like a dragonfly flitting over a stream. Endrass remarked, 'She seems to have a bad conscience.'

"We dived. I stood at the periscope and watched the ship approach. She was a short and dumpy freighter painted in weird colours. The stack was flaming red, the superstructure black and the bottom grass green. On the bows *Bosnia* was painted in large letters.

"The English merchantman had obviously been warned and was prepared for the worst. It would have been a mistake to surface in front of her as she was possibly armed or might be tempted to ram us. So I let the ship go past and we surfaced a short distance astern and fired a shot over her. The ship altered course and turned stern to us and I noticed the foam of the propeller swirling up. She was trying to escape. We fired a second round, this time so close that the column of water splashed on deck. But she refused to stop. At the same time my signaller sang out; 'Signal to Commander: Enemy sending radio messages.'

"A runner came hurrying up the ladder. 'Here is the intercepted message, sir.' He gave me the slip of paper: *Under attack and fire from German U-boat. Urgently require assistance.* Here followed his position and the message ended with *SOS, SOS*.

"That settled it. I gave Endrass a sign. Swiftly and with precision the crew loaded the gun. Then Endrass barked 'Fire.' A sharp report and the *Bosnia* was hit amidships. A cloud of smoke rose up, but still the *Bosnia* continued her flight.

" 'Five rounds rapid fire,' I ordered.

"Again we could clearly see the second shell hit its target, then the third.

"At last the ship hove to and lay there like a wounded animal. From the hold heavy blue and yellow smoke belched up and formed a column over the ship like a pine tree swaying in the wind.

The cargo must have included a large quantity of sulphur. We closed in on the *Bosnia*, as the crew rustled to the boats and launched them.

"Hansel sang out behind me, 'Column of smoke in sight.' I turned about. On the north-west horizon appeared a thick streak of smoke, heavy and black, like a mourning flag. Swiftly I considered my situation. It could be a destroyer coming to the aid of the freighter.

" 'Keep that ship well in sight,' I told Hansel, 'and report at once if you can see what her nationality is.'

"The crew of the *Bosnia* had been over hasty in their efforts to escape. One boat had filled with water and was foundering. It was pathetic to see the men drift helplessly away. Some of them shouted for help while others beckoned to us. We steered towards the sinking boat. Samann and Dittmer reached down to help the floating men aboard, leaning far overboard so that their hands nearly touched the water.

"By now the lifeboat of the *Bosnia* had filled with water and the sea swept over it. A few heads were floating close together, then a wave separated them. In the space of a few seconds only a handful were left.

"A few non-swimmers thrashed about with their arms. Others were swimming with long strokes towards a sea-worthy lifeboat of the *Bosnia*, which had turned towards the men in the water.

"Reaching out, Dittmer and Samann grabbed one of the men and heaved him on board. He was a small red-headed boy, probably the mess-boy. He sat up gasping, while water was running down his face and dripping from his clothes.

"Behind me Hansel reported, 'It is a Norwegian freighter, sir.' I turned round and took up the glasses. The ship that was coming up from the sou'west lay high; apparently she had no cargo on board.

" 'OK Hansel,' I said, and heaved a sigh of relief. I would not have welcomed an encounter with a destroyer before I had sunk the *Bosnia*.

"In the meantime the boy recovered his breath,

left: A U-boat victim, the SS *Tiger*. below: An ace World War II U-boat commander, Erich Topp.

The only thing that ever really frightened me during the war was the U-boat peril. Invasion, I thought, even before the air battle, would fail. After the air victory it was a good battle for us. We could down and kill this horrible foe in circumstances favourable to us, and, as he evidently realised, bad for him. It was the kind of battle which, in the cruel conditions of war, one ought to be content to fight. But now our life-line, even across the broad oceans and especially in the entrances to the island, was endangered. I was even more anxious about this battle than I had been about the glorious air fight called the Battle of Britain.
— from *The Second World War: Their Finest Hour* by Winston S. Churchill

got up and stepped to the rail beside Dittmer.

"He was shivering with fright. I beckoned him to the bridge..

" 'Are you the mess-boy?' I asked.

" 'Yes, sir.'

" 'What was your cargo?'

" 'Sulphur, sir.'

" 'Where were you bound for?'

"He spoke in a cockney accent but his answers were completely unselfconscious. He was a boy from the London slums, a type of person who is impressed by no one and nothing.

" 'You are trembling. Are you afraid?'

"He shook his head. 'No. I'm only cold, sir.'

" 'You will have a spot of brandy later on,' I said. He nodded his head and added, perhaps to show his gratitude, 'Of course, we got a fright, sir. You can't imagine what it's like; you looks over the water and sees nothing, on'y sky and water and then suddenly a bloomin' big thing pops up beside yer, blowing like a walrus. I thought I was seein' the Loch Ness monster.'

"We approached the second boat of the *Bosnia*.

" 'Where is your Captain?' I called over the water.

"An officer stood up and pointed to the *Bosnia*.

" 'He is on board,' he said.

"I gazed at the ship which was wreathed in clouds of smoke and flaming like a volcano.

" 'What is he doing there?'

" 'He is burning his documents.'

"I understood. There was a man alone on the burning ship, hundreds of miles from land and without a lifeboat, destroying his ship's papers lest they fall into the hands of the enemy. I had to admire his courage.

" 'And who are you?', I asked the officer.

"He raised his hand to his cap, 'I am the First Officer of the *Bosnia*.'

" 'Come aboard.'

"Dittmer helped him to climb on board. On the whole he did not look very much like a seaman; pale, fat and tired. When he stood on the deck he

saluted again.

"In the meantime the little mess-boy had been taken on board the other lifeboat of the *Bosnia* and we steered towards the new arrival, the large Norwegian vessel which floated almost completely out of the water.

"On our way we came across one of the shipwrecked men and while we stopped Samann and Dittmer hauled him on board.

"I came down from the tower to have a look at the man they had brought up. He lay there lifeless, a small skinny man still fairly young in years, but worn out like an old horse. There were traces of coal dust on his clothes. He had probably been a stoker on board the *Bosnia*.

"Samann had removed his jacket and shirt; the fellow was painfully thin and his ribs showed up clearly like the bars of a cage. Dittmer grasped him by the arms and began artificial respiration.

"The First Officer of the *Bosnia* was standing beside me. Looking down at the man he said abruptly, 'You Germans are good-hearted people, sir.' I looked at him standing there, fat, well-fed and probably mighty satisfied with himself. I could not contain myself and said gruffly, 'It would have been better if you people had given that poor fellow something to eat in your ship.' Leaving him standing there I returned to the tower.

"The Norwegian vessel had now approached so close by that her large national flag flying from the fore-mast was clearly visible. I flagged her to a stop and she hove to, so close to our boat that the sides towered over us like a cliff.

"We signalled, 'Please take crew of English ship on board.'

"The Norwegian ship replied, 'Ready.' A boat was lowered and when it came alongside, the little stoker, still unconscious, was put aboard first, followed by the First Officer who saluted once more before he left.

"I talked with the officer in charge of the Norwegian lifeboat, and explained the situation to

HOLDING THE LINE !

far left: A German torpedo calculator from World War II, a primary aid to a U-boat skipper in the complex business of attacking enemy shipping. above: The badge of the German submarine crewman.

top right and centre: World War II U-boat crewmen on deck and at rest. below: U-boat planesmen. below right: Torpedo mates, known as "mixers" in the German Navy.

DO NOT REPORT TOO MUCH BAD NEWS, SO AS NOT TO DEPRESS THE OTHER BOATS.
— signal from Admiral Dönitz to all U-boats, 5 August 1943

far left: WWII U-boat commander Reinhard Hardegen. left: A U-boat gun crew struggling with their weapon, the deck awash. below: The strain of war patrol is apparent in the faces of these U-boat lookouts.

him. I pointed to the *Bosnia*'s lifeboat, with the *Bosnia* burning close beside. Just then a man on board the *Bosnia* jumped into the water, probably the Captain who had managed to destroy his papers.

"I pointed towards him and said, 'You must save that man also.' The Norwegian officer nodded and cast off.

"We waited until they had finished the rescue work. It took quite a time, while our lookouts nervously scanned the horizon; the *Bosnia* had wirelessed for help and her cloud of smoke stood like a huge pillar over the burning ship, which must have been visible for hundreds of miles.

"At last the Norwegian vessel dipped her flag and steamed off.

"We were obliged to sacrifice a torpedo to finish off the *Bosnia*.

"It was our first torpedo release and everyone wanted to observe its effect. So, nearly the whole crew came on deck. We had, of course, seen from photographs from the First World War how the stricken steamer appears to rear up in the water and then swiftly slide to the bottom. But this was quite different, much less showy and all the more impressive because of that. There was a dull explosion and huge columns of water rose up high on the mast. And then the stricken ship simply broke in two pieces which, in a space of seconds, disappeared into the sea. A few bits of driftwood and the empty boats were all that was left."

Again, Günther Prien: "As we were doing our trim dive on the twelfth day, I was standing at the periscope and called over to Bohm, 'Gustav, your bloody periscope is covered in muck again.'

" 'But I've cleaned it, sir.'

"At the same instant I caught sight of a steamer. It was like an electric shock.

" 'Action stations,' I shouted.

"We rapidly approached the solitary tanker of about six thousand tons that was trying to evade us by zigzagging wildly. We dived underneath him and came

all: Views of *U-995*, a World War II Type VIIC U-boat that is displayed on a beach at Laboé, near Kiel on the Baltic coast of Germany. right: The high and low pressure distributor panel. far right: Public access is permitted to the meticulously restored submarine.

Dawn was approaching and with it the danger of aircraft patrols. From 500 yards he fired another torpedo at the *Invershannon*, which suddenly broke in half, and for a few minutes the crew of *U-99* were the sole witnesses of a sight reserved only for sailors in wartime. The two separate parts of the oil tanker sank gently inwards and the two masts locked together at their tops, forming a great Gothic archway, under which black smoke and flames were thrust upwards from the bowels of a ship in its death throes—a magnificent and terrifying scene bathed in pale moonlight. Around them the flurrying sea heaved and subsided, while over in the west a huge bank of black cloud gathered to emphasise the loneliness and vastness of the watery desert around them. *Invershannon* gave its last, almost human, gasp of pain and was swallowed up by the waves.
– from *The Golden Horseshoe* by Terence Robertson

up close astern. 'Prepare guns for firing,' I called.

"I happened to turn around and the blood froze in my veins. Over on the west horizon a forest of masts had appeared. It was a large convoy. We dived immediately.

"We had very nearly been caught in a U-boat trap, for the single vessel had been sent on alone as a decoy, but I decided to go for the convoy.

"For three hours we followed the convoy with the intention of cutting it off and coming to meet it. But it was hopeless, for underwater we were far too slow. When we surfaced again the forest of masts was floating far away on the horizon. Only a trawler was coming towards us with a foaming bow wave. We dived again and surfaced once more. This time a Sunderland came out of the clouds down at us so that we had to submerge quickly to take cover beneath the water.

"By this time the convoy had disappeared. I cursed our luck as I looked through the periscope, but suddenly I noticed a steamer leisurely approaching us. It had apparently dropped out of the convoy. I estimated it at about six thousand tons.

"The deck was laden with huge crates and on the fo'c'sle I counted eight guns. We dived and sent him a torpedo which hit him amidships. Through the periscope I watched the crew take to the boats. Then the steamer slowly vanished in a foam. As we turned away we could still see the crates bobbing about in the water.

"I saw through the slats in the crates that they contained aeroplane parts, wings, propellers and so on. We watched them sink one by one.

" 'There goes a flock of birds that will never fly,' said Meyer with satisfaction.

"Now I thought that the spell had been broken, but ill-luck stayed with us for the next seven days and we saw nothing but sky and water. The polar sickness on board assumed epidemic proportions. We couldn't stand the sight of each other any more and to see anyone eat or clean his teeth was enough to make one vomit.

"On the seventh day the watch on the tower sang out, 'Steamer in sight.' It was a convoy again. There were about thirty ships which appeared in a long line over the horizon.

"As we were lying in an unfavourable position I let the convoy pass, came up astern of it and circled it in a wide sweep. It was evening before we made contact again, but this time we were well placed.

"They made a lovely silhouette against the evening sky. I chose the three biggest ones, a tanker of twelve thousand tons, another of seven thousand tons and a third, a freighter, of seven thousand tons. We approached them underwater. I glued myself to the periscope and watched while the First Officer relayed my commands. Tube one was discharged, followed by tube two and a few seconds later tube three should have fired also. But tube three did not fire. From forrard came the sound of argument but just then I could not bother about it. I observed the effect of the explosion. The first hit the *Cadillac*, the twelve thousand tonner. There came the dull thud of the detonation, the up-spout of the water and behind it appeared the ship enveloped in yellow-brown smoke.

"The second hit. I could hardly believe my eyes. It was a steamer we had not aimed at. The *Gracia* of five thousand, six hundred tons.

"All three ships had been well and truly hit and not one of them could be saved.

"We pushed off as fast as we could, while behind us depth charges stirred up the sea in our wake.

"I sent for the torpedo man. 'What the hell happened just now?' He looked sheepish and said, 'I am sorry, sir. I slipped and fell on the hand-trigger and the torpedo went off too soon.'

"I had to laugh. 'Well, anyhow, at least you hit something with it, but still you did us out of fourteen hundred tons.' He was silent for a moment. Then he asked, 'How much was it all together, sir?'

" 'Twenty-four thousand tons,' I said.

"The news swept through the boat and faces

below: A German submariner observing the results of the attack by his U-boat on an enemy merchant ship during the Battle of the Atlantic. far right: A recruiting poster of the German Navy in World War II.

shone like the sky after a long spell of rain. At last our luck had changed. Two nights later we spotted a blacked-out steamer loaded with wheat; about two thousand, eight hundred tons. In order to conserve torpedoes I made the crew take to their boats and sank the vessel with shells. We were fairly far from land and I followed the lifeboats and gave them bread, sausages and rum.

"The following day brought us two ships. At the crack of dawn we got a four thousand tonner with a cargo of timber which we dispatched with a few shells below the waterline. In the late afternoon we met a Dutch tanker loaded with diesel oil. On his bridge he carried a huge barrier of sandbags.

"Finally, we aimed our gun at his engine room and at last the ship began to sink. The lifeboats and the crew were already some distance away when we spotted three men floating in the water. They were the Third and Fourth Engineer and the Stoker. Their Captain had not bothered about them but had left them to drown in the engine room. I picked them up and followed the lifeboats and handed them over. Then I addressed a short speech to this Christian Captain beginning: 'You bloody bastard,' and ending in a similar strain.

"By now we had accounted for nearly forty thousand tons on this war patrol. Thirty-nine thousand and eighty-five tons to be precise. We were beginning to be pleased with ourselves. But then we received a radio message, 'German U-boat just returned from war patrol has sunk fifty-four thousand tons.' Her commander had been trained by us.

"My men made long faces and Steinhagen, our sparks, gave expression to the general opinion, 'It is annoying to see these young upstarts leave us standing.' His chagrin struck me as rather childish but all the same I was glad to see the spirit of the crew under this provocation.

"I called for the First and Second Officers. The result of our discussion was devastating. We had only six rounds of high explosive and a few torpedoes left. The following night we shot one of the torpedoes into the blue. A steamer went past us in the distance at considerable speed and we had to shoot quickly if we were to get her at all. When the torpedo had left the tube we began to count. First to fifty seconds . . . every second made a hit all the more improbable. One minute . . . one minute twenty. . . . 'My beautiful torpedo,' moaned Barendorff between set lips. We took up the chase but the steamer eluded us and darkness swallowed it up.

"I was awakened with the news that the First Officer had spotted the *Empire Tucan*, a liner of seven thousand tons.

"Our boat was rolling heavily in the swell. 'We shall have to attack her with shells,' I said. 'I don't know whether we can hit her in this sea,' remarked the First Officer. I shrugged my shoulders. 'In any case we shall have to be even more sparing with our torpedoes.'

"The bo'sun Meyer was called to lay the gun. He refused to come. 'To shoot in this weather is mad,' he told the man who woke him. 'There is far too much swell to take proper aim.'

"We sent the runner a second time with a formal order from the bridge. Finally, he turned up, sleepy and annoyed. I gave him my instructions. 'Your first shot will be on the guns which you can see clearly on the quarterdeck and your second will hit the bridge so he can't radio.

" 'Very good, sir,' he said, clicking his heels. But to judge by his expression he thought that we should economise with our shells as well. We stood on the bridge and observed the fire, for it was the last of our ammunition. The first shell hit the ship exactly between the guns and the second went into the fo'c'sle and the third into the stern.The fourth missed the target, the fifth was a dud and the sixth and last hit the bridge and was caught in the windsail. It was a weird sight. The pressure of the detonation within the sail pushed up what looked like a huge white ghost in the dawn and threw it right over the mast. In spite of the last hit, the radio was operating furiously and sent out its SOS. The crew manned the boats and drew away from the ship. Only the wireless operator remained behind and continued sending messages.

"There was nothing else we could do! We had to sacrifice a torpedo if we did not want to have the whole mob at our heels. The *Empire Tucan* was hit exactly amidships. The ship broke, dipped deep into the sea and then reared up again against the skyline. The operator was still at his station.

"Suddenly we saw a man run across the sloping deck. He grasped a red lamp in his hand and, holding it high above his head, he leaped from the sinking ship. As he struck to water the red light went out. We stopped at the place where he had disappeared but we could not find him. Then shadows appeared in the north, dark shapes in the dusk, probably destroyers. As we had only one useable torpedo left we decided to push off. Three minutes later Steinhagen brought me a radio message. It was the last message of the *Empire Tucan. Torpedoed by U-boat. Sinking fast – SOS,*

The men are the heroes; the heroines are the ships, the only villain is the sea, the cruel sea, that man has made more cruel.

For us the Battle of the Atlantic was becoming a private war. If you were in it you knew all about it. You knew how to keep watch on filthy nights, how to bury the dead, and how to die without wasting anyone's time.
— from *The Cruel Sea* by Nicholas Monsarrat

Vernon Howe Ba

and then a long dash. It was the operator's last signal.

"The next ship we encountered [was] two days later. It was a Greek freighter which we finished off with our last torpedo. It was only four thousand tons. Steinhagen put his head through the door. 'Have we got enough, sir? he asked breathlessly. I had been counting already.

" 'No,' I said. 'We have fifty-one-thousand tons and the other U-boat has got three-thousand tons more.'

"A wave of disappointment swept through the boat. We began our return journey with one defective torpedo left on board. I called the torpedoman. 'Have one more shot at getting the torpedo in order.'

"It was a clear and calm summer morning. We were steaming along in the vicinity of the coast in a calm sea. The lookout reported, 'A steamer on our starboard bow.' A huge vessel with two funnels approached us out of the sun in wild zig-zags. Against the light it was impossible to determine her colour, but by her silhouette I recognised that it was a ship of the *Ormonde* class; that meant over fifteen thousand tons. 'Fellows,' I said, and I felt their excitement, 'cross your fingers and let's try and get it.' Then the command, 'Fire'.

"Then we waited, counting. Painfully slowly the seconds slipped by. The ship was a great distance away, too great a distance I feared. Then suddenly, right amidship a column of water rose up far beyond the mast and immediately after, we heard the crash of the detonation.

"The liner heeled to starboard. In great haste lifeboats were launched, many of them. In between them hundreds of heads were bobbing in the water. It was not possible to help them because the coast was too close and the ship still afloat. On her fo'c'sle a number of guns were clearly visible. We retreated underwater. When a few minutes later we surfaced only the lifeboats were visible on calm sea.

"I descended to my hole to make up the war diary. As I passed the control room I caught sight of a board which hung on the door. On it was written: 66,587 TONS. LEARN BY HEART."

There was a submarine. I'm sure of it. It's where a submarine making an attack would have been. And if it was a submarine, how many more men in ships would it have killed? I had to do it. Anyway, it's all in the report. Nobody murdered those men. It's the war, the whole bloody war. We've just got to do those things and say our prayers at the end.

We didn't get any medals, Number One. And we only sank two U-boats. Two in five years. It seemed a lot at the time.
— from *The Cruel Sea* by Nicholas Monsarrat

Dönitz was a sour looking character, resembling Calvin Coolidge, but, like Coolidge, he had a sly sense of humor. They say he had an oil seascape hanging in his headquarters with nothing but whitecaps visible in it. When visitors asked him what the picture represented, he replied, 'The fleet passing in review in 1955.' When they said, 'But I don't see any ships,' his answer was, 'There are hundreds of them—submarines cruising in submerged formation.'
— from *Twenty Million Tons Under The Sea* by Rear Admiral Daniel V. Gallery, US Navy

left: The USS *Barracuda* in Drydock at Portsmouth Navy Yard, New Hampshire, by Vernon Howe Bailey, 1941.

"SUBMARINERS have extraordinarily thick skins. One of the sayings we have on the ships is: 'You always find the weak chick and peck it to death.' If you have a foible, or something that you are sensitive about as an individual, as soon as your shipmates detect that sensitivity, they will bore in on it and attack it until you have become completely thick-skinned on that issue and it no longer bothers you. One of the things that amazes me most about submarines is that we can take a bunch of 18—23-year-olds, lock 'em up inside a ship with no girls, no distractions, no sports, no real means of blowing off steam; you can trap them on the ship for months and not have fights or arguments be a daily occurrence. I can count on one hand the number of fights I have seen on a submarine in my career, and every one of those was ten seconds or less. One or two swings and that was it. You learn very quickly how to concede space to your fellow shipmate. You stay out of his way. He stays out of your way. When he needs slack, you give him slack. When a guy is feeling tense, you cut him some slack. When he is feeling tense about something he shouldn't, you 'poke him in the eye' and give him some heat about it until he learns how to be less agitated about that minor detail.

"You end up with a bunch of guys who are very cool-headed, they're very calm, they're relaxed, and as a result, really exciting things can happen to them and they don't get all wound up. They know how to go coasting right through it as if it's just a little bump in the road, not too much of a problem."
– Commander William Hoeft, skipper of the USS *Salt Lake City*, SSN 716

"Most of the time you are six hours on [watch] and twelve off. In the last few days of sea trials, I've had three hours' sleep in a day and a half. That's because stuff breaks and you have to try and fix it. When I first came in [14 years ago] if there was an underway limiting item, you were up until it was

ROUTINE

top: The captain's cap from the USS *Michigan* (SSBN 727) above: The gold and silver dolphins of the US Navy submarine officer and enlisted man, respectively. far left: Electronics Technician 3rd Class Christopher Bruce "drives" the fast attack submarine USS *Tucson* (SSN 770).

On a submarine, more than on any other type of ship, each of the men who will live together for a year or so has a very high stake in the welfare and efficiency of this boat—his own life. Every man in a submarine knows that whatever future he has in life is bound to the fate of that submarine. If the boat dies, the odds are three to one he dies with her. He therefore not only does his own job to the very best of his ability, he checks to see that every other man does likewise. There is no such thing as an unimportant job and everybody knows that a single mistake by any one of them can be the end for the whole lot of them. Everybody resents any carelessness or inefficiency because the guilty party gambles with all their lives when he does anything that risks his own. A crew can be reconciled to a daring skipper who takes long chances and wins great glory for them to share, but they can't tolerate a stupid shipmate who doesn't pull his weight in the boat. After a submarine crew have made a couple of war cruises together, there is a bond between them that lasts for life. It bridges whatever gaps there may be in their background, education, and station in life, and makes them permanent members of an exclusive club who have shared certain experiences together that no other group in the world have shared. They may not all like each other, but for a certain period they pooled

fixed. A lot of that has changed now. They will rotate people in. They try to be a little easier on people now, which is better.

"I think the military is good for everybody, for at least a couple of years. It gets you out of the nest, away from mom and dad. It teaches you to be a man. A lot of kids nowadays need it. It's a structured life style. It teaches you to deal with people from different ethnic backgrounds, people from different parts of the world. I've been on submarines with guys from the Philippines, Jamaica, Puerto Rico. You see a lot of the world if you get on a good boat. This is a good boat, and the crew is excellent, a very good crew. How do people get along on an extended cruise? You just do. You're stuck here with 130 people. The ones you've had your differences with, you just kind of steer clear of, and they steer clear of you. That's the way I do it. I just walk around in my own little world and minimize the interference with other people's troubles. It just works out. You're busy and you don't think about it."
—Douglas Cushman, sonarman, USS *Jefferson City*, SSN 759.

Mike Sizeland served as a navigator in submarines of the British Royal Navy in the 1950s and 1960s. "HMS *Truncheon* broke down in Halifax, Nova Scotia, and it was decided to let her limp slowly home for a major engine overhaul in Portsmouth, rather than undergo an expensive repair in Canada. Royal Navy submarine authorities became a bit concerned when they had heard nothing from her for a week, and signalled, 'REPORT ETA' [estimated time of arrival]. Back came the cautious reply, 'Easter.' 'BE MORE PRECISE' was the curt response. After some deliberation came the more accurate assessment, 'Easter 1961'.

"After acting as the loyal opposition during exercises in the English Channel, it was common practice, particularly on Friday afternoons, for the Surface Forces to wind on maximum revs and head

for home and weekend jollifications without the courtesy of letting the submarine know of her position before surfacing. After one such occasion our submersible heroes were somewhere south of the Isle of Wight on an easterly course heading (they presumed) for Portsmouth, when they sighted another submarine on a directly opposite course. The standard exchange of signals between warships was flashed by Aldis lamp in the gathering misty gloom as they rushed past each other, 'WHAT SHIP? WHERE BOUND?', to which the reply came, 'HMS ARTEMIS BOUND FOR PORTSMOUTH.' 'SO AM I.' was the perplexing response just before visual contact was lost between the two.

"The control room is the nerve centre where all the sensors deliver information, and from where the attack is conducted. It is kept scrupulously clean and in spotless condition. A particularly fastidious and irascible commanding officer was obsessed with the immaculate condition of his control room, and much spit and polish was devoted to this area of his sub. Any shortfall from his impossibly high standards rebounded on his First Lieutenant in scathing, histrionic reproval. As cleanliness involved much soap, water and scrubbing, inevitably a single drop of water was left on the deck unnoticed by all except the eagle-eyed captain. His customary precise attack and salvo of torpedoes missed the target and, searching for someone to blame for his own failings, he summoned the hapless First Lieutenant to the control room. 'Number One, how on earth do you expect me to conduct a sensible attack when I am up to my arse in water!'

"Of all the aspects of submarine warfare, perhaps the least accurate was gunnery. All World War II boats, and many in later years, were equipped with a four-inch gun which, exposed to full diving depth, was not the most precise of weapons. Its most effective role lay in the element of surprise. The tactic employed was to approach the enemy while submerged, to the closest possible range (half a mile or so), surface quickly and open fire before the opposition had time to react. To achieve the maximum effect, the drill was to put a pressure in the boat by bleeding in air from the bottle banks, blow the main ballast tanks and keep the boat down by increasing speed and putting both hydroplanes hard a'dive until positive buoyancy prevailed, when the planes were reversed and the boat bobbed up to the surface like a cork. Just before exposing the upperworks, the gun hatch was opened and the first member of the gun crew leapt out with a shell under his arm, usually in a bubble of air, followed by the remainder of the crew. The object was to get the first round off in less than half a minute, roughly in the direction of the opposition, and continue firing until retaliation became too hot for comfort, when we would dive to safety again. To practice this art, a tug was employed to tow a battle target some hundreds of yards astern which would record the fall of shot and report back results. HMS *Tally Ho!* was engaged in a gunnery exercise of this nature, and such was the gun crew's enthusiasm that the first shot went seriously awry and dangerously close to the towing tug. 'HOW AM I DOING?' signalled the *Tally Ho!* 'RATHER POORLY. I AM PULLING THIS TARGET, NOT PUSHING IT' came back the reply.

"The coxswain, whose many responsibilities included victualling, made a real effort for Christmas Dinner and actually provided some freeze-dried reconstituted turkey with a limited supply of festive garnishing The captain initiated proceedings by wishing the crew a Happy Christmas over the intercom, which was followed smartly by the coxswain's stricture: 'ANYONE WHO WANTS STUFFING REPORT TO THE COXSWAIN IN THE GALLEY.'

"Submarine design left little space for freshwater tanks and the rather inadequate evaporators could never quite keep up with demand, causing strict water rationing on lengthy patrols. Washing was discouraged and many submariners sported

beards. The general rule was that the more hygenically inclined should wash in their allotted ration, shave in it and then drink it afterwards. It is little wonder that few of us were big water drinkers.

"In HMS *Andrew* we had a most attentive if somewhat wayward wardroom steward called Buckweed Harris. When he wasn't AWOL (absent without leave), which was quite often, he supplied our every need with a commendable sense of duty. In harbour the wardroom seldom needed to buy such luxuries as fresh milk because Buckweed on his way in usually managed to liberate the odd bottle from the doorsteps of those unfortunate enough to live along his route to work. If upbraided his revenge was often pretty effective and we took good care not to displease him. On one occasion when we did he nailed an elderly kipper to the underneath of a wardroom bunk and there, concealed, its malodorous presence soon became evident and, ultimately, intolerable. 'Buckweed, we know what it is, but where is it?' we complained. The offending corpse was not revealed until a full, unreserved apology was offered. But his *pièce de resistance* was the delivery of a cup of hot cocoa to the Officer of the Watch on the bridge on surfaced passage. This was virtually impossible since, with the diesel engines running, the supply of air came rushing down the conning tower with hurricane force and most of the contents of the cup were invariably blown away in the gale. What little survived was stone-cold. When asked how he achieved this miracle of deliverance, Buckweed explained that, at the bottom of the ladder in the control room, he sucked in and pouched the contents into his capacious mouth, then rushed up the ladder to the bridge where he disgorged it back into the cup on arrival before presenting it. Cocoa never tasted quite the same after this revelation."

In order to become a submarine officer in the US Navy, the successful candidate must first survive a

their lives together in a dangerous business and brought each other through it safely. They can therefore make allowances (ashore) for the failings of these shipmates which they wouldn't make for anyone else. – from *Twenty Million Tons Under The Sea* by Rear Admiral Daniel V. Gallery, US Navy

According to Salvador Dali, a sardine on the seabed who, seeing a submarine pass overhead, said to his children: 'There goes our revenge; a great tin made of sheet-iron in which men, covered in oil, are held inside, pressed against one another.'

A submarine in harbour is a lifeless, dead thing. It lies quiet, waiting, but with the hidden menace of a sheathed sword. – from *Down The Hatch* by John Winton

None will improve your lot if you yourselves do not. – Bertolt Brecht

above: Officers on the nuclear-powered Trident submarine USS *Michigan* (SSBN 727) at the navigation table in the control room. right: At the main console aboard the USS *Michigan*. above right and centre: Meal preparation and consumption on HMS *Turbulent*, a Trafalgar class nuclear-powered attack submarine in February 2001.

above: Mess Specialist 2nd Class Wilbur Fifield prepares desert while standing night watch on the USS *Seawolf* (SSN 21). left: Machinist Mate 2nd Class Chris Fitchet enjoying a novel in his rack aboard the USS *Pasadena* (SSN 752).

Stuffed Cabbage Rolls

Yield: 100 portions
24 lbs cabbage, fresh, trimmed and cored
3 gals water, boiling
2 1/4 tsp salt
Add cabbage to boiling salted water in steam-jacketed kettle or stock pot; cover; cook 10 minutes or until leaves are pliable. Drain well; separate 200 leaves; remove larger ribs; set aside for use later. Shred remaining cabbage coarsely. Set aside for use later.
24 lbs beef pattie mix, bulk or beef, ground, thawed
3 qts rice, long grain, cooked
2 1/2 qts onions, dry, chopped
2 cups catsup, tomato
1 cup Worcestershire sauce
3 tbsp salt
3 tbsp pepper, black
1 tsp garlic powder
Combine beef, cooked rice, onion, catsup, Worcestershire sauce, salt, pepper and garlic. Mix lightly but thoroughly. Place 1/4 cup meat mixture on each cabbage leaf. Fold sides of leaf over mixture; roll tightly. Place 25 cabbage rolls seam side down in each pan. Spread shredded cabbage evenly over rolls in each pan.
5 tbsp soup and gravy base, beef
2 qts water
2 1/2 qts tomato paste, canned
3 1/2 cups sugar, granulated
2 cups lemon juice
Reconstitute soup and gravy base. Blend in tomato paste, sugar and lemon juice. Pour about 2
continued on page 82

series of Director, Naval Reactors interviews, after which he proceeds to a year of education in the Navy's reactor prototype schools. Such candidates came from three sources. The first and most common approach is from the US Naval Academy, located in Annapolis, Maryland. Secondly, potential officers of the submarine force may come from the ROTC (Reserve Officer Training Program) of many colleges and universities, which offer tuition and other financial assistance to the student who will be commissioned an ensign on his graduation. Finally, other college graduates may apply for admission to the Officers Candidate School (OCS), which is a short, three-month course leading to a commission as ensign. Officers taking this path are known in the Navy as "ninety-day wonders".

Regardless of the route taken by the new officer, if he is to continue in the submarine force he will spend the next three months in the Submarine Officers Basic Course at Groton, Connecticut, after which he will receive assignment to his first submarine, in which he will serve for between two and three years. During this period he will devote much of his time to learning on a practical level, and studying to qualify for his golden "dolphins". The Dolphins pin is the insignia of the US Navy Submarine Force.

In World War II Ernest J. King was Fleet Admiral and Commander-in-Chief, US Pacific Fleet. In June 1923 he was Captain E.J. King, Commander, Submarine Division Three, and it was then that he suggested a design for an insignia to distinguish qualified submariners in the US Navy. The pen-and-ink sketch he submitted to the Secretary of the Navy showed a shield mounted on the beam ends of a submarine, with dolphins forward of and abaft the conning tower. The Commander of Submarine Division Atlantic was enthusiastic about King's idea and the Bureau of Navigation solicited additional designs from several sources. A final design was a combination of two designs

from a Philadelphia company which had previously done class rings for the Naval Academy. It was a bow view of a submarine cruising on the surface, with its bow planes rigged for diving, and flanked by dolphins in a horizontal position with their heads resting on the upper edge of the bow planes. That design was accepted by the Navy in March 1924. The design of the present insignia worn by US Navy submariners is very similar, with dolphins flanking the bow and conning tower of a submarine. The version for officers is a bronze, gold-plated metal pin worn centred above the left breast pocket and above the ribbons and medals. Qualified enlisted personnel wear their bronze, silver-plated metal pin above the left breast pocket. Both pins signify completion of approximately one year of demanding qualification. The dolphins represent the traditional attendants of Poseidon, the Greek god of the sea.

Throughout his first tour the new officer will be scrutinized by his superior officers who will be evaluating his performance and estimating his propects for both advancement and possible command at some point in his career. He must also pass an engineer examination during this first tour. If he fails this make-or-break test, he is out of submarines.

Crewmen of US Navy nuclear submarines come from backgrounds as diverse as society itself. All have their own reasons for coming into the submarine force. There may be no typical example of a young entry-level sailor who is heading for submarines as a career, but there is a relatively common path they follow. For the young man who knows he wants duty aboard a nuclear sub, the path begins at his local Navy recruiting office where he applies for enlistment. After acceptance he will be transported to one of the Navy bases where basic training is conducted. On completion of basic several weeks later, our man must choose a specialty area such as electronics, sonar, or possibly nuclear power, and go on to the "A" school where that specialty is taught, to prepare him for his initial assignment on a submarine. If he is so inclined, there is ample motivation for him to select nuclear power as his career choice. Part of it is the money. The Navy demands a lot of its nuclear power specialists in the submarine service, and new recruits entering training in the specialty are immediately given the rank of petty officer (as opposed to seaman apprentice, the rank at which their surface ship counterparts begin). The difference in pay can make it easier for our boy to marry and begin a family at once if he wants. Submariners in the 2001 US Navy earn up to $350 dollars a month more than their peers on the surface; officers earn up to an additional $595 a month.

Even after he becomes a part of the crew of an American nuclear sub and begins his first tour of sea duty, this new sailor is not yet a qualified submariner. To achieve that status he will have to commit himself to a rigorous routine of work and study in preparation for the qualification boards examination. The promotion that goes with passing the boards and the award of the coveted "dolphins" pin signifies his membership in the élite submariner club. The best of his peers may be offered an opportunity to become a warrant officer, or to go to college and enter a programme to become a commissioned officer. Enlisted men who progress up the promotional ladder have a chance of rising to the rank of Master Chief and the job (and title) of Chief of the Boat (COB). The man in this role on an American nuclear sub today is often impressively qualified in terms of experience, judgement and education. He is of immeasurable value and importance to the man in command of the boat.

Ron Steed, skipper of the USS *Jefferson City*, SSN 759: "There is an aspect of the submarine which is unique. We go out and disappear and we're not heard from and we don't send mail back and

81

continued from page 80
1/2 cups sauce over cabbage in each pan. Cover. Bake 1 1/2 hours or until cabbage is tender and beef is done. Skim off excess fat.

Adapt yourself to the environment in which your lot has been cast, and show true love to the fellow mortals with whom destiny has surrounded you.
– from *Meditations* by Marcus Aurelius

No man can have society on his own terms. If he seek it, he must serve it too.
– from *Journals* by Ralph Waldo Emerson

preceding page—top: A brief time out of war for a submariner after months of Pacific patrol. preceding page-bottom: At the top of the hatch of USS *Marlin* (SS 205) in August 1943. above right: Executive Officer Stuart Munsch monitoring a weapons exercise on board the USS *Tucson* (SSN 770). right: The USS *Ashville* (SSN 753).

forth. For a period of time it's like we've fallen off the planet. That's something the families have to struggle with. One of the big changes we've had in the last five years is e-mail. We send e-mail all the time and I love it. The problem there though, and I've given a lot of thought to it, is finding the balance between the privacy of our sailors and their individual and personal lives, and the security need to be able to fight the ship. My XO reviews all the e-mail that comes in for the kind of content [bad or troubling news from home] where maybe I should be the guy to break the news to a fellow that something bad has happened. He also reviews every e-mail going out, for security concerns. There are not many cases though, where we have to censor e-mail. We try not to."

According to Commander Bill Hoeft of the USS *Salt Lake City*, SSN 716, "The traditional submarine game is cribbage, a very common Midwestern card and board game. My dad played like crazy growing up in Wisconsin and I played it as a kid. The highest-scoring hand you can be dealt is a 29. The odds against it being dealt are something like 216,000 to 1. In all the years I've been playing, I've never seen a 29 hand. My father has played cribbage all his life and he's never seen a 29 hand. Dudley 'Mush' Morton and Dick O'Kane, the CO and executive officer respectively of the USS *Wahoo* in World War II, used to play cribbage all the time. Twice within one week during the war, Morton dealt O'Kane a 29 hand."

Commander O'Kane was the leading American ace in terms of numbers of ships sunk when he was skipper of the USS *Tang*, which destroyed 24 enemy ships totalling 94,000 tons. Later, when his sub was sunk by a dud torpedo that it had fired, he was one of nine survivors from the crew of 87. After the ordeal of Japanese prison camp, O'Kane was awarded the Medal of Honor, one of only seven won by members of the submarine service. The citation for Commander O'Kane's Medal read:

"For conspicuous gallantry and intrepidity at the risk of his life above and beyond the call of duty as commanding officer of the USS *Tang* operating against two enemy Japanese convoys on 23 and 24 October 1944, during her fifth and last war patrol. Boldly manoeuvering on the surface into the midst of a heavily escorted convoy, CDR O'Kane stood in the fusillade of bullets and shells from all directions to launch smashing hits on three tankers, coolly swung his ship to fire at a freighter and, in a split-second decision, shot out of the path of an on-rushing transport, missing it by inches. Boxed in by blazing tankers, a freighter, transport, and several destroyers, he blasted two of the targets with his remaining torpedoes and, with pyrotechnics bursting on all sides, cleared the area. Twenty-four hours later, he again made contact with a heavily escorted convoy steaming to support the Leyte campaign with reinforcements and supplies and with crated planes piled high on each unit. In defiance of the enemy's relentless fire, he closed the concentration of ships and in quick succession sent two torpedoes each into the first and second transports and an adjacent tanker, finding his mark with each torpedo in a series of violent explosions at less than 1,000 yard range. With ships bearing down from all sides, he charged the enemy at high speed, exploding the tanker in a burst of flame, smashing the transport dead in the water, and blasting the destroyer with a mighty roar which rocked the *Tang* from stem to stern. Expending his last two torpedoes into the remnants of a once powerful convoy before his own ship went down, CDR O'Kane, aided by his gallant command, achieved an illustrious record of heroism in combat, enhancing the finest traditions of the U.S. Naval Service."

The sea speaks a language
polite people never repeat.
It is a colossal scavenger
slang and has no respect.
— from *Two Nocturnes*
by Carl Sandburg

I've had more fun at
funerals than I did at sea.
— Rev. J. W. S. Wilson

COMMAND

Submarine officers—filthy, oil-stained and often smelling of their cramped living quarters, unwashed chauffeurs and pirates to their elegant quarterdeck contemporaries. The strict class divisions that applied throughout the Royal Navy in Edwardian times fall by the wayside as submarine officers are required to learn trades unheard of for a gentleman and work side by side with their men. Withdrawing from their peers in the surface fleet, submariners form a special brotherhood of elite professionals in what is known as 'the trade.' Drawn closer by shared tasks, appalling living conditions and the very real dangers of service under the sea.
— an early Royal Navy view of submarine officers

right: Commander David C. White and a lookout on the bridge of the USS Cero (SS 225) in August 1943.

AFTER HIS FIRST TOUR a young submarine officer is normally sent to do a shore tour on the staff of a submarine squadron. In lieu of this, he may be made an instructor in one of the submarine specialty areas. On completion of this shore tour, he will be sent back to Groton for another six months study, this time in the Submarine Officers Advanced Course (SOAC), where he will be groomed to head a department such as weapons, navigation or engineering, on his next boat. If he continues to progress, and impress, his next step on the road to eventual command of a nuclear submarine is his second tour on one, this time as a department head for three years. Following this tour, the officer, who is by this time a senior lieutenant, may be screened for Executive Officer (XO), number two in command on a submarine, and, if approved, will head for the three-month training course called Prospective Executive Officers (PXOs). Completion here qualifies him to serve as an XO during his next submarine assignment. With successful completion of this tour, the officer will most likely serve another shore duty tour. He is now at the point of being selected for possible command of a submarine. Before that can happen, he must achieve promotion to the rank of commander and pass screening for command. Having done so, he will then go on to the Prospective Commanding Officers (PCO) course which will qualify him and lead to the command of his attack or missile submarine. The PCO course usually has an enrolment of about ten officers and, in six months, exposes them to the theory, method and specifics of tactical and operational command on a nuclear submarine. Here, these candidates for command are instructed in all aspects of a submarine mission, from intelligence gathering, to mining, to anti-submarine warfare, to strike warfare and more. Here they will conduct approaches and actually fire between five and seven live Mk 48 torpedoes, Tomahawk and Harpoon missiles. The very demanding nature of the course ensures that only the best of the best emerge to be awarded with their own command.

A graduate of the US Naval Academy in 1980, Commander William Hoeft, from Michigan, is skipper of the fast attack submarine USS *Salt Lake City,* SSN 716. Prior to this assignment, Hoeft served aboard the USS *Jacksonville*, SSN 699 and the USS *Hammerhead,* SSN 663. He was executive officer on the USS *Chicago,* SSN 721 from 1993 to 1995 and received command of the *Salt Lake City* in summer 1998. The *Salt Lake City* is homeported in San Diego.

"Every submarine commanding officer has spent four tours on submarines and they represent the four levels of seniority of an officer. First you are a division officer on one ship, then you are a department head on your second ship. On your third ship you are always the executive officer and on your fourth ship you are in command. There may be a little variation here and there. For instance, if we're short on officers you may spend four years as a department head instead of only three, and you may spend two years on one ship and two years on another, and in that case you may have been on five submarines during your tours. But one submarine each tour—four tours—is the norm.

"The mission of an attack submarine these days is just about everything. We do intelligence collection, we defend the battle group, we do surveillance of other ships, we can do anti-submarine warfare, anti-surface warfare, we can deliver special forces, we can operate under the ice, in shallow water, deep water, cold water and hot water. The biggest thing about a submarine that distinguishes it

from other platforms is that we are covert. You can be somewhere and no one knows you are there. It's useful when you don't want anyone to know you are there, and when you want them to know you are there, but not exactly where you are, as a kind of passive threat.

"The practical fact is that a submarine is virtually unfindable. We are a black hole. We can't be found. We really do operate with impunity in virtually any body of water we choose to go in. That's the truth.

"We strive for as much redundancy [back-up]as we can for combat readiness so that if a man gets injured someone else can step in and do his job. Confidence is essential. If you are operating on a ship that is already half-sunk, with a bunch of ordnance and a nuclear reactor on it, in a hostile environment, maybe with surface ships overhead, aircraft overhead, shallow water, you have to be confident that you know what you are doing and that the guy next to you knows exactly what he is doing. If you weren't confident, you might be looking over your shoulder to make sure that guy is doing his job, and maybe being distracted from your job, and we can't have that. One of the things about a submarine is that it is small and there is so much stuff to do, that you end up having to have each person do two or three jobs, which is why we need really super guys. And if you are doing two or three jobs, you can't afford to be distracted by a fourth or fifth job. You're really plenty burdened by your own stuff, so we emphasize cross-qualification very heavily.

"I'm married to a Naval Academy graduate, Class of 1980. She understands submarine business very well, not only from her time at the Academy, but also from all the years spent with me. She's got a pretty good handle on it. Right now it's Navy policy that we spend about half our time away from our home port, and that can include being here in San Diego but out at sea, as well as being far away. If we are in port on the other side of the ocean, that counts as being away from home even though we are tied up.

"Twenty years ago during the Cold War, when I started this business, we did not have a rule like that. Things were different then. In my first full year on a ship, when I started my first deployment, I spent 323 days out of 365 at sea. I had a six-month deployment, came back in for about two months, and we went right back out on deployment again because things were going on and that's just how it was back then. It's a lot nicer now. It's a much more reasonable approach, much more considerate of the fact that sailors and officers have lives to live and it gives them more time with their families. In my time in the Navy, I've spent a little more than six years underwater. That's a lot of time away from home.

"I think that the 50% number is a reasonable one, a good one. Less than that and we are probably not getting the right amount of practical experience and operational expertise. More than that, and it's maybe harder on everyone than it needs to be. When we started to 'build down', reduce the size of the submarine force, several years ago, there was some anxiety among submariners that, if the number of submarines decreased, but the missions didn't, we were going be very thinly stretched. It was with a great deal of satisfaction that we heard the Chief of Naval Operations say; 'I'm not going to cross the 50% Personnel Tempo Line [the percentage of time that a person is away from home]. Just because we are not willing to build ships, I am not going to put the burden on the backs of the sailors and make them spend 75% of their time at sea.' Those were the bad old days and we are not going back to them. I think we appreciate that greatly. We shoot for no more than 50%. Obviously, there are going to be times when it's a little above that, but it averages out. You go to any Navy Exchange and you see all the mugs that say THE HARDEST JOB IN THE WORLD IS NAVY WIFE! That certainly is

Tact in audacity is knowing how far you can go without going too far.
— from *Le Coq et l'Arlequin* by Jean Cocteau

The fate of the worm refutes the pretended ethical teaching of the proverb, which assumes to illustrate the advantage of early rising and does so by showing how extremely dangerous it is.
— from *Asides: Writers and Talkers, Ponkapog Papers* by Thomas Bailey Aldrich

left: The USS *Henry M. Jackson* (SSBN 730), the only one of eighteen US Navy ballistic missile submarines named after a distinguished person, the others being named after American states. Senator Jackson was a powerful supporter of the Navy's nuclear submarine programme.

above right: A gun crew in action aboard HMS *Orpheus* during World War II. right: Diving planes operators in the control room of the USS *Cero* (SS 225) during a dive off New London, Connecticut in the summer of 1943.

true, and we put an exclamation point on that in the submarine force because, not only are we away, but we are out of communication. For the most part wives can't talk to their husbands; they can't send them letters or get letters back, except very infrequently. They go in batches, three months' worth, as opposed to a constant trickle of mail on and off from a surface ship.

"We just got e-mail on our last deployment. It's been extremely well received. We have always had Familygrams, where a family could send a 25-word message to a sailor. You couldn't answer them, but at least you could get something from your family. E-mail actually allows a 'conversation' to take place. What a difference that has made, to be able to ask a question and get an answer, have a conversation instead of just a little one-way telegram-kind-of transmission. Of course, it's important to recognize that, for a submarine, e-mail is a transmission, and we only do transmitting when we are in an environment where we are not conducting a mission. When we are on a deployment, driving across the ocean to get to where we're going, we'll send e-mail back and forth. While we are moving between one port and another, we'll send e-mail back and forth. But once we begin operating on our mission, there are no more e-mails being sent or received. We stop all transmissions. We just disappear and conduct our job.

"There are rules about what a family member or a submariner can say in an e-mail, but we've found that submariners are very responsible about it. With respect to e-mails, we tell the wives in advance: 'Don't pass the guy some bad news on e-mail. Go to the Red Cross.' The message then gets sent to the ship. The guy's chain of command knows that if something bad happens, let's say a sailor's mother passes away while we are on deployment, they'll send a message to me. I'll bring the guy in and talk to him one on one and let him know in my stateroom in an appropriate way, and his chain of command will be informed

to support him in that situation. We don't want a guy finding out news like that without anyone knowing that he's going through a difficult situation. It's just not right. All you have to do is tell the wives and the families that, and tell the sailors that, and they all understand it. It's handled very professionally. I haven't seen any problems with it so far.

"Before the submarine is deployed, the submariners fill out a form that says what they want to be notified of and what they don't. Some folks may not want to know about a death in the family unless it's their spouse or a parent. They let us know that and we respect their wishes. They feel that, as long as they can't get back, as long as they can't do anything about it anyway, they don't want to know. Ten years ago, that was often the case. Nowadays though, if there is a death or a critical illness in the family, we will stop the ship's mission, bring it off station, go into the nearest port and put the sailor on the next flight home. We're not fighting a war. There is no reason to keep a guy away from home in a situation like that. That's submarine force policy. During the Cold War, if you were on a mission and something like that happened, you got off the ship only when the mission was over, but not so now."

Commander Hoeft continues: "One of the most memorable experiences that I have had was operating a submarine underneath the Arctic ice. It is completely unique. You can go and buy an airplane ticket now and some expedition company will take you up to the north pole, drop you off there and bring you back, but they can't put you underneath the ice on a nuclear submarine for days and days. It is a completely surreal environment. Just driving along for days, looking up at the bottom of the ice, big, heavy ice floes, open water, sunlight coming through, sea growth hanging from the bottom of the ice, crystal-clear water where you can actually see the deck and stern of the submarine, the kind of visibility that you just don't get in other kinds of water, the incredible sound of the ice grinding against itself. It's a sound that takes some getting used to because, along the ice edge where that grinding noise takes place, it sounds more like squealing, groaning and screaming, like a lot of women and children crying in anguish. You can hear it right through the hull. We like it when we get past the ice edge and under the ice where you don't hear that kind of stuff anymore. It's a very different environment.

"I have been operating in several different places where the water has been exactly the opposite. It has been very shallow, hot water where the depth was less than half the length of the submarine. We were sitting a little bit above the bottom in very silty water that you can't see through. You are not worried about people spotting you, but you are concerned about speedboats, fishing boats and other craft running around that you have to pay attention to and dodge. That's a completely different environment; one that requires continuous attention.

"This ship is nothing but equipment. It's jammed with wires and cables, pipes and electronics. The most challenging thing is to keep all that stuff running, keep it all fixed and repaired. With a ship this complicated, you might have ten or fifteen things on it that don't work at any given time, and the other 30,000 things do work, which is a real credit to the ingenuity of the sailors we have on board and the management of the officers. The officers do a good job of making sure that the sailors are spending their time on the most important things and getting them fixed. Without a doubt, we spend the bulk of our time managing equipment, maintenance and readiness. Personnel issues are a distant second. We spend an awful lot of time training. One of the ways we minimize the amount of equipment problems we have is to make sure our guys are very well trained. The

89

right: Officers Andy Duff and Rob Dunn in the wardroom of the nuclear-powered attack submarine HMS *Turbulent* at Devonport, Plymouth, England in February 2001.

single biggest thing we spend our time on is training. Drilling.

"I deal with most of the personnel things in port. They have to do with family issues, not problems that the sailors have on the ship: problems that a wife is having with housing, or that a guy is having with a credit card bill.

"I consider myself lucky that I have spent the last twenty years with such a high-class group of guys. They may not always be well-educated, but boy, they're smart and they're well-adjusted. They're balanced and professional. What a pleasure.

"You bring a bunch of kids in, they go through boot camp, but this is their first real job when they get to the ship. This is where they find out what the real standards are. When they get here they find out that nobody cares what kind of accent they have, or where they're from. They just care whether or not the guy pulls his share of the load. If he does his job and does it well, he's a shipmate. In terms of race and ethnicity, I think this is the best environment that I've seen as far as absolute merit standard is concerned. There are no hidden frictions going on; none of that business. It's just a bunch of guys who are real pros. There are guys who bring prejudices and pre-judgements from their home, their neighborhood, their city or part of the country, but they leave them at the door when they show up on the ship. They learn right away that that kind of stuff has no place here and they grow up real fast."

Commander Ron Steed of Atlanta is in charge of the fast attack submarine, USS *Jefferson City*, SSN 759, homeported in San Diego. "Training is the constant problem because of crew turnover. We just got back from a six-month deployment in July, and by the time we deploy again in 2002, only about 40 per cent of the people who were on the last deployment will still be here. The leadership changes. Both me and the XO will probably be gone by that time, so the way we fight the ship will

change. It's a constant struggle to train, re-train and train again. That's not a bad thing. It's just a problem that has to be solved. The guys train to do something in particular. Then they are ready for more responsibility and they go and do something else and someone comes in to fill their shoes. So, training is the biggest struggle we have.

"One of the most satisfying things about the Navy for me is that every job that I've had has been completely different. I've done teaching, and this is my fourth submarine. This is the only command that I've been on. I'm not sure what I am going to do after this, but I'm sure that, whatever it is, it will be different from command. My only regret is that I only get one command. I'd love to have another one, or stay here another five years.

"I have never been stationed on a boomer [missile submarine], and I'm unusual in that regard. Most [attack submarine] guys have, and are encouraged to do both, but I managed to dodge that bullet. I won't go from here to a boomer command because, formerly, full Captains were in command of Trident submarines and, typically, a Trident commander would have at some point, been commander of a fast attack sub before that. Nowadays, guys at my same level are in command of Tridents, and it's the first and only time they will be in command, so there is no chance that I would go from here to a Trident. But I've been pretty happy in the fast attack business."

In the matter of whether there will ever be women attached to US submarines: "Personally, I think it's inevitable. That's the way American society is going. If we do that, it probably won't be easy. To get women onto the submarine, we need to create the berthing and other facilities to support them, which actually means taking some combat power off the ship. I'm not sure that we are ready yet to remove any combat power from the ship. We don't have the money to do that now, so it remains to be seen whether or not we will go down that path. I'm sure that if we do, we will do it

The people who get on in this world are the people who get up and look for the circumstances they want, and, if they can't find them, make them.
– from *Mrs Warren's Profession*
by George Bernard Shaw

above: Mark Stanhope, as a young Lieutenant Commander aboard HMS *Orpheus*. right: HMS *Orpheus* under way.

the right way. We will introduce women, as we have done on the surface ships, at all levels of the chain [of command], officers, chiefs and enlisted, and we'll do it all at once, and there will be some struggles with it, as there have been in other parts of the Navy. Whether we can find the funding, and the willingness to take some capability away from the ship in order to put women on remains to be seen. Submarining is kind of an academic business. We're not infantry; we're not running around on combat fields, and there are some very smart women out there who could run this ship just fine. But we've got some hurdles to get through before we get to that point."

Royal Navy Rear Admiral Mark Stanhope: "The Perisher Course is a test that is unique to the submarine service. You don't have to have a test to drive a surface ship. You only have to grind your way up through the ranks, get yourself the required qualifications on moving forward and then at some stage, if you are lucky, somebody will recommend you for command. This is a six-month course that puts you through all of the procedures that are required of a commanding officer. It has changed now to be all in nuclear submarines, but when I did it it was only in conventional submarines, and in two phases. The first was an 'attacking' phase where they put me into a simulator and for five or six weeks they built up the number of ships that were attacking me, and this was in the days when we had torpedoes that only went a thousand yards and I had to therefore position myself to fire a straight runner or a gyro-angled torpedo at a ship and sink it. I started off with one ship and by the time I had finished with the simulator there were up to six or seven ships attacking and I was trying to manoeuvre myself through a screen to get to the tanker or the high-value unit. When I finished in the Attack Teacher [simulator] they took me to sea and I did the same for five or six weeks in a

92

conventional submarine where they built me up from one ship to about six ships, but this time it was 'for real.' It was all devised around mathematics—mental arithmetic—where I had a certain number of very clear rules that I had to use to make sure that my submarine was safe.

"I knew, for instance, that it took a conventional submarine one minute to get from periscope depth to 90 feet. At 90 feet all these warships would pass over the top of me. They wouldn't hit me. So if I could start the process of taking the submarine deep one minute before that warship was going to go over the top of me, then I would be safe. I knew that a warship at maximum speed does about 30 knots. I knew that my conventional submarine was doing six knots. Therefore, I had a 36-knot closing problem. If the warship was 2000 yards away, I knew that at 1000 yards [separation] I had to go deep, so I had 1000 yards of run. At 36 knots a ship does 100 yards in five seconds, so I was constantly working out, for all these ships around me, that if, when I put the periscope down, they turned towards me and came up to maximum speed, I had to look at that particular ship again in 50 seconds because he'd then be on the edge of my go-deep circle and I had to start the process of going deep. That is just one example of the mental gymnastics that we were forced through. It was hard and some people didn't meet the criteria, but it helped to build up this instinctive feel for the safety of the submarine and retain the mental picture of what's up and around you. This is the difference between being the commanding officer of a submarine and being the commanding officer of a surface ship. The CO of a surface ship has lots of people looking at the radar screens, lots of people looking at the picture around him. In a submarine, when things are difficult, the commanding officer is the only person who has got the picture clearly in his mind. This is situational awareness, not only of what's out there, but of what's going on inside

the submarine as well. In an attack scenario that can be constantly changing, it is how close your weapons system is to being ready to be used, and whether that system has set on it what you want, that counts. You've got to have all this awareness and it can be difficult. I think it can only be built up through experience. The average person going to Perisher now doesn't have as much experience looking through a periscope because nuclear submarines don't spend so much time at periscope depth. Actually, their ability to appreciate the situation at periscope depth is not as good as it used to be. Does it have to be? Sonars are better, the feed of information from the periscope to the computer systems is better, but in the end, when it all goes wrong, it's nice to have this ability.

"Once you have completed this first phase of Perisher, they take you back into a simulator and you do another five or six weeks of deep-ocean anti-submarine work on all the other skills that are required. Then you go back to sea again and do a lot of deep-sea work with other submarines, followed by an in-shore phase of taking your submarine into navigationally difficult places and getting it out again. In my Perisher, about 50 per cent of us passed. It's better than that now."

Co-author of the book *Command at Sea*, graduate of the US Naval Academy in 1966, a former commander of the submarine USS *Grayling* (SSN 646) and of Submarine Group Seven, Yokosuka, Japan, Rear Admiral Albert H. Konetzni, Jr., USN is the current Commander Submarine Force, US Pacific Fleet: "My job is to be the principal advisor to the Commander in Chief, US Pacific Fleet, for submarine matters. The Pacific Submarine Force includes attack, ballistic-missile, and auxiliary submarines, submarine tenders, floating submarine dry docks, deep-submergence vehicles, and submarine rescue vessels throughout the Pacific. The submarine force provides anti-submarine warfare, anti-surface warfare, precision

left: Ensign Aaron Keffler at the search periscope of the USS *Tucson* (SSN 770), a Los Angeles–class fast attack submarine deployed to the Persian Gulf in support of Operation Southern Watch, May 1998. below: HMS *Turbulent* alongside at Devonport, Plymouth, England.

Despair is the conclusion of fools.
– Benjamin Disraeli

Since the end of the Cold War we have three states of alert for SSBNs in the US Navy, Not Alert, Mod Alert and Alert. Not Alert means that the boat is at the pier, all torn up, not capable of executing its mission of launching missiles. Modified Alert means it is at sea, it has weapons aboard, it could, within a specified amount of time, go into an Alert posture. Mod Alert allows it to do things that it didn't do during the Cold War period like make noise, operate in a way that would be noisy and therefore detectable, participate with other ships in exercises such as playing the role of an aggressor submarine in a battle group exercise freeing up an attack submarine to go do other missions. The Alert mode means ready to actually conduct its strategic mission. It is within range of potential targets, it is capable of launching all its weapons within a specified amount of time, no one can locate it—US or foreign forces could not locate the submarine even if they wanted to, and it is in continual 24-hour passive communications with the National Command Authority, meaning it is never transmitting; it is not talking back; it is constantly listening for an order to launch its weapons. We think we are the most valuable portion of the Strategic Triad because we are undetectable. The bombers and the ICBMs are all in set locations. A very capable adversary with nuclear weapons and long-range missiles could

land strike, mine warfare, intelligence, surveillance and early warning, and special warfare capabilities to the US Pacific Fleet, and strategic deterrence capabilities to the US Strategic Command.

"I could not be prouder of the accomplishments and efforts of our submarine crews. If this position has shown me anything it's that everyone from the captains to the COBs (chiefs of the boats) to the junior man—top to bottom—have routinely demonstrated their ability to meet and exceed mission goals provided to them. For over a year and a half I've seen submarines conduct and successfully complete some operations that weren't only demanding and required the highest degree of professional expertise, but simply hadn't been tried before. That's the good news. That success comes at a cost, however.

"The unique capabilities of submarines are increasingly in higher demand. I've seen a steady increase not just in the number of missions, but also the diversification of tasking. I think word has gotten out on just how valuable submarines can be to a region. They afford theater commanders presence—overtly such as in port visits or exercises—or covertly, submerged and ready without any logistical train. That means commanding officers have to train their crews for any number of possible missions before they deploy.

"If you want an honest look at how you're treating the most important resource this or any other organization has, take a look at your retention and attrition numbers. It's no secret that people vote with their feet, and the Navy as a whole has been taking it in the shorts for a while now in retaining our younger folks. Last year retention of our nuclear-trained junior officers and first-term enlisted personnel was well below expectations. I am happy to say now, that thanks to an all-hands effort, our enlisted first-term retention on our submarines is at 60 percent over the last six months. Better yet, our

attrition of first-termers is at 10 percent. One hell of a lot better than the 25 percent we saw 18 months ago.

"This is a remarkable achievement and I attribute it to several reasons. First is having the commanding officers and boat leadership accountable in this most important area, including an effort with our junior officers, which is also paying dividends. The mentoring provided by submarine force senior officers to our junior officers is having a positive impact on their career decisions. Other things that certainly helped include the two pay raises this year, the increase in BAH (Basic Allowance for Housing), the improved duty section manning in port, the reduction in IDTC (Inter-deployment Training Cycle), the improvements in base MWR (Morale Welfare and Recreation) facilities around the Pacific, and the improvements in the BEQs (Bachelor Enlisted Quarters). It comes down to not just talking the talk, but walking the walk.

"The uncomfortable position in which I find myself as Commander of the Pacific Submarine Force, is being caught between two diverging paths. On one hand the desire for submarines continues to rise—in fact, national tasking requirements (as determined by the National Command Authority, among others) have more than doubled since 1992. I don't make up those requirements—they're given to us and we have to fulfill them. Concurrently, the number of submarines will have fallen by roughly 40 percent over that same period. My staff is working hard to reconcile the disparity, but we're already unable to satisfy valid mission requests from key agencies. And we're going to lose more submarines over the next few years.

[To those critics who argue that submarines are a relic of the Cold War] "I would say that we as a nation then were absolutely fixed on a monolithic adversary—and in my opinion appropriately so. As submariners, it was our primary mission to track their submarines. When the Berlin Wall fell, I think all of us were left scratching our heads without a firm idea on where the military needed to go. It's been about a decade now and we've had time to see what we as a nation will pursue with respect to security issues. I'd ask anyone who questions an increase in the number of submarines to simply look at the trends. I've already touched on the increased demand and diversity of missions. These are tangible, quantifiable demands placed on the submarine force from agencies outside the submarine force.

"Finally, I would invite everyone to study projections of our military and security needs of the future. The nature of warfare in the not-so-distant future is one that includes proliferation of missile technology and weapons of mass destruction. Couple this to quantum leaps in information technology, such as satellite imagery—available on the Internet already—and the appeal of submarines in the decade ahead becomes even greater. A popular term within strategic studies circles is 'asymmetric warfare', that is, to have the ability to strike your adversary without him having the ability to strike back. Recently a series of *Wall Street Journal* articles reported that the country was spending too much on defense, but did conclude that submarines were—in their research— a viable asset now and in the future.

"There are three basic ways to get the numbers up. The first is to refuel the seven Los Angeles–class submarines currently slated for premature inactivation. Each has, on average, about 13 years of life left. Aside from the immediate relief they'd provide in view of the alternative, the most appealing part of this idea is [that] it's risk-free. The crews are there, the platform is already together. It's a no-brainer. The second opportunity we have is to convert the four oldest SSBNs into SSGNs, or guided missile submarines. We'd like to think of them as underwater

battleships. We could have the opportunity to deploy these submarines with 154 Tomahawk missiles, which could relieve an entire battle group from this frequent requirement. You could also configure them to carry as many as 60 special warfare personnel, which provides this country with the ideal delivery platform. And again, it's risk-free immediate pay-back on your investment. There is an issue of START [treaty] requirements and configuration of the missile tubes, and I understand that is being reviewed.

"While these are both smart efficiencies, they are relatively short-term fixes. Ultimately, it comes down to how many submarines we need to build to maintain the right force structure. At the height of the Cold War we were building three or four submarines a year. What that means at the end of their life cycle is, they'll all go away at the same rate. Currently, we have a build-rate of roughly one submarine a year. In order to maintain a sufficient submarine force after the year 2015, we need to have a build-rate which exceeds two a year. Recognizing there are significant defense and national priorities competing for limited funds, I know it's a tall order."

US Navy Captain Michael King is Chief of Staff, Submarine Group Nine, Bangor, Washington, under the command of Admiral Charles Griffiths. Submarine Group Nine is responsible for water space management in the eastern Pacific, as well as operation of the eight Trident submarines located at Bangor. It is also responsible for communications and the maintenance of broadcasting, as well as the training of the sixteen Trident crews during their off-crew periods prior to their returning to sea on patrol. Captain King is a former commanding officer of the USS *Alabama* [SSBN] Gold Crew and prior to that, commanding officer of the USS *Albuquerque* [SSN]and is a 1974 US Naval Academy graduate. "Every commanding officer has different priorities. I led my commands and kept

conceivably destroy all of those systems before they would be able to launch, take them all out. But you could never destroy the at-sea Alert SSBN force because you can't find it. They are given huge bodies of water to operate in; they are undetectable when they are in those bodies of water by any reasonable means. Any such adversary has to recognize that, if they launch a strike against the United States or our Allies, even if they were to take out all our other forces, they would have to suffer the consequences of a retaliatory strike by our SSBN forces. That strike would be of such a devastating nature that they would find it unacceptable, and that's what we think equals strategic deterrence, that sure knowledge that they would face a retaliatory strike by SSBNs. That's why we don't consider our SSBN forces to be a deterrent when they are tied up at the pier. If you can find them, you can destroy them. If you can destroy them, they are not a deterrent. That's why we try to keep our forces at sea the vast majority of the time. The Trident submarine will stay at sea about 70 per cent of the time or more, and we have a number of means to ensure that we do that.
— Lieutenant Kevin Stephens, Public Affairs Officer Submarine Group Nine, US Navy

stress-handling problems at a very low level so that they didn't become big problems. If you are involved on a day-to-day basis with your troops and you understand what problems they are having at home, and you intercede early, then in most cases you can take care of them. In commands that don't work very well, you don't see that deck-plate interaction, small problems can become big problems to the point where the commanding officer and the executive officer and the Chief of the Boat have to get involved. When that happens, the system has broken down. It's not working.

"If you look at the number of people we retain in the submarine force, it's higher than the rest of the Navy. There is an emphasis on leadership and retaining people and helping them succeed. You see it every day in a submarine where you have a man who is having trouble with his qualification process, and you see the command doing everything it can to help him succeed, providing extra tutorial support, giving him extra time, whatever it takes. And after having exhausted all the tools in the bag of tricks, and that person is unable to make it, then we still have what is called a Second Chance programme where he may be sent to another submarine—the thinking being that maybe there is an environmental, or some interpersonal problem, or something on that command that prevented him from succeeding.

You send him to a completely new environment and give him a new set of leaders to work with, a new set of shipmates, and give him a second chance. We've been very successful in that programme in retaining people. The submarine force, as a whole, tends to be more involved; tends to retain people who in other situations would not be retained.

"Submariners tend to be similar in how they think. They tend to be analytical and introspective, just because the submarine attracts that kind of person. Therefore, although you see commanding officers who are different in their leadership styles, there's not that big a variance, and in the current environment the Captain Queeg type of leader just does not make it. A commanding officer who is leading outside the box is doing something really strange and unusual and that will become known to his superiors outside the ship, squadron commanders, group commanders, and if that abnormal leadership style is resulting in some substandard performance on part of the ship, then there will be some magnifying glasses put on the command. There will be people who ride the ship and look very closely at how things are working and it may result in counselling sessions for the CO, trying to help him improve his leadership skills, but that doesn't happen very often. And, especially in today's environment where we have fewer submarines, it's much harder to get to

Lieutenant Commander Malcolm D. Wanklyn VC conducted an unprecedented 25 patrols as commanding officer of HMS *Upholder* before she was lost with all her crew. The accepted maximum number of patrols for a war-weary Royal Navy submarine captain in World War II was fifteen.

My thought had rested day and night upon this awe-striking problem. At this time my sole and sure hope of victory depended upon our ability to wage a long and indefinite war until overwhelming air superiority was gained and probably other Great Powers were drawn in on our side. But this mortal danger to our life-lines gnawed at my bowels. Early in March exceptionally heavy sinkings were reported by Admiral Pound to the War Cabinet. I had already seen the figures, and after our meeting which was in the Prime Minister's room at the House of Commons, I said to Pound, 'We have got to lift this business to the highest plane, over everything else.

I am going to proclaim "the Battle of the Atlantic." ' This, like featuring 'the Battle of Britain' nine months earlier, was a signal intended to concentrate all minds and all departments concerned upon the U-boat war.
— from *The Second World War: The Grand Alliance* by Winston S. Churchill

right: In the control room of the World War II fleet submarine USS *Capelin* (SS 289) in the Pacific, August 1943.

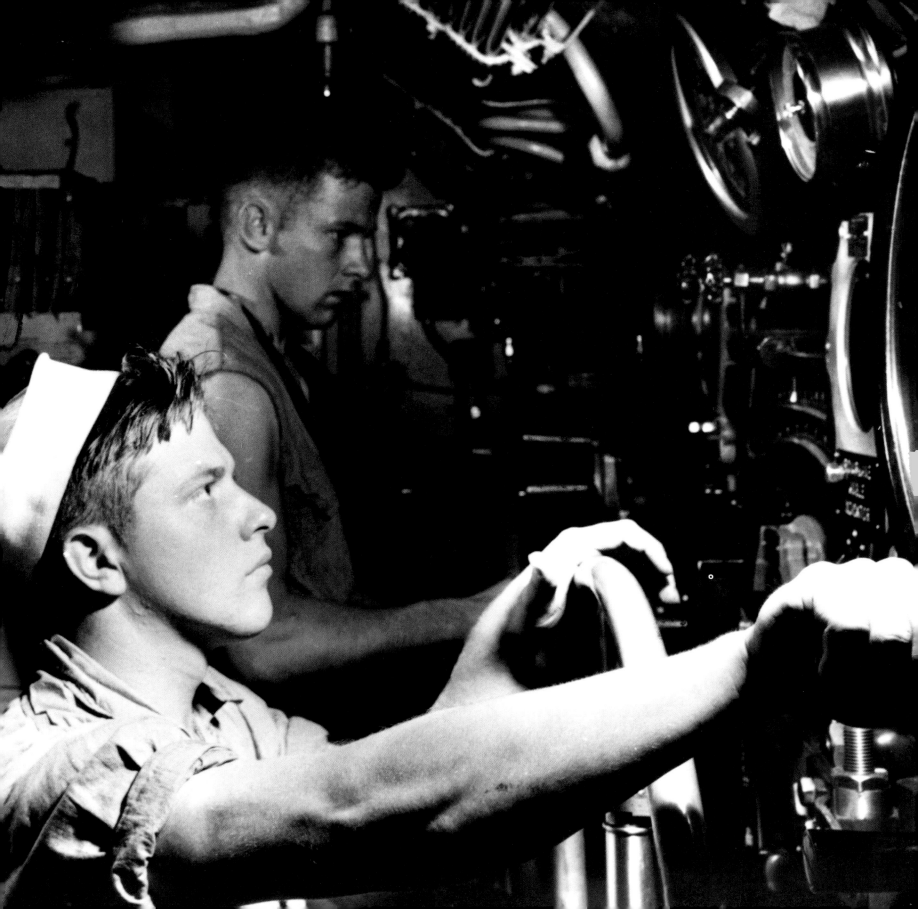

command. The command opportunity is less than it was in a growing Navy. So, the people who make it to that height are really the cream of the cream of the crop. They are very talented, extremely intelligent people who've been able to make their way through a very difficult labyrinth to get to that position."

O Captain! my captain! / Our fearful trip is done; / The ship has weathered every rack; the prize we sought is won.
— from *O Captain! My Captain!*
by Walt Whitman

left: *Ballast Point, San Diego* by John Charles Roach, 1986. above: The USS *Alabama* (SSBN 731) near her Bangor, Washington base.

AT 11.38 IN THE MORNING, Saturday, 12 August 2000, the first of two enormous explosions ripped through the forward hull of the Russian Oscar II class nuclear submarine *Kursk*, K-141, sending her to the bottom of the Barents Sea. Nearly two hours later, Lieutenant-Captain Dmitry Kolesnikov lay huddled with 22 other members of the *Kursk* crew who had survived the explosions. In the frigid darkness of the broken five-year-old boat, which lay listing 356 feet down on the seabed, the injured officer scribbled a note which began: "I am writing blind. It's 13:15. All personnel from sections six, seven and eight have moved to section nine. There are 23 people here. We have made the decision as a result of the accident. None of us can escape to the surface. . . Hello to everyone. It seems there is no chance." "The note is of a very private nature and will be passed on to his relatives, but it also gave us a lot of operational information," said Vice-Admiral Mikhail Motsak, Chief of Staff of the Russian Navy.

Twenty-one-year-old Gleb Lyachin, a Russian naval academy cadet, was about to join the crew of the *Kursk* just before the submarine left on what was supposed to be a three-day Barents Sea exercise. Then his orders were changed and he was sent off to another exercise. By sheer chance his life had been saved, but tragedy still struck his family that August morning when the *Kursk* went down. It was under the command of Gleb's father.

In Vidyayevo, the naval community in Northern Russia where the *Kursk* was based, the tearful wives of her crewmen gathered on Saturday, 19 August, knowing that the last shred of hope for their husbands' lives was now gone, replaced by the realization that they would never see their men alive again. In a televised message that night, Vice-Admiral Motsak had said that any survivors of the *Kursk* disaster had probably drowned as the submarine was flooded. Anatoli Safonov, the father

THE DOWNSIDE

Cheer up, the worst is yet to come.
— Philander Johnson

Valor is a gift. Those having it never know for sure whether they have it till the test comes. And those having it in one test never know for sure if they will have it when the next test comes.
— Carl Sandburg

We shall see, while above us the waves roar and whirl a ceiling of amber, a pavement of pearl.
— from *The Forsaken Merman* by Matthew Arnold

left: The greatest submarine disaster ever to befall the Royal Navy occurred in June 1939 when HMS *Thetis* sank during trials in Liverpool Bay with the loss of 99 men.

of a *Kursk* crewman, and himself a former naval captain said, "What has my son died for? I don't understand." Some of the villagers did understand how little chance the men of *Kursk* had had. "It was clear from the beginning of last week that they had all died," said one young sailor, and another submariner told reporters, "We wanted to hang on. Everyone wanted there to be survivors, but you have to be realistic. This didn't come as a surprise to anyone." That week several Russian doctors visited the homes of *Kursk* families, giving injections and tablets to the many suffering relatives.

It would be more than two months before divers from an international recovery team were able, in a five-day operation, to penetrate the inner hull of the submarine. There they located and retrieved the body of Lt-Capt. Kolesnikov. Of the twelve bodies of *Kursk* crewmen recovered in this effort, one other would yield a note: "There are 23 people in the ninth compartment. We feel bad . . . we're weakened by the effects of carbon monoxide from the fire . . . the pressure is increasing in the compartment . . . if we head for the surface we won't survive the compression." The rest of the contents of that note was not revealed by Russian Deputy Prime Minister Ilya Klebanov following a meeting in early November of the commission investigating the disaster.

The funeral of 27-year-old Dmitry Kolesnikov took place in St Petersburg on 3 November. Before leaving his wife of only a few months for the last time, he gave her his dog-tag and crucifix. "For some reason before he left, he left this. I don't know why. It seems to me my husband had a premonition of death. When I went to see him in the summer, not long before he went to sea, he wrote me this piece of poetry: 'And when the time comes to die, though I chase such thoughts away, I want time to whisper one thing: My darling, I love you.' "

The body of Viktor Kuznetsov, another member of the *Kursk* crew, was retrieved from the sub and lay in state in his hometown, Kursk, after which the submarine was named. According to his sister, Albina, their mother, Olga, "never lost hope that they would find Viktor and bury him in the Christian way, that we would return him to the earth." Olga Kuznetsov collapsed and died two hours before Albina received the phone call telling her that her brother's body had been identified.

It seems that most of the *Kursk* crew of 118 died instantly in the explosions as a massive fireball and shock wave tore through the five forward compartments of the sub, or in the next moments when torrents of sea water filled the spaces. The 23 men who survived the explosions had gathered in a compartment in the stern of the boat. Their hope was to get out through the rear escape hatch. Apparently, the end came slowly for some of them, through drowning, suffocation or hypothermia. Kolesnikov's widow: "I had a feeling that he didn't die immediately, and it turned out my feeling was right."

What caused the *Kursk* tragedy? From the first hours after it happened, Russian naval commanders insisted that they were "80 per cent certain" a collision with a foreign submarine was responsible for the sinking. Other possible causes, they said, included an internal explosion or contact with a Second World War mine. The governor of the Murmansk region, where the submarine's base is located, Yuri Yevdokimov stated: "There is no doubt that a powerful blast took place inside the *Kursk*. The explosion happened after the vessel sank to the bottom and crashed into the seabed. The blast was what destroyed the inside of the submarine, but it also wiped out the traces of the original cause of the catastrophe, which has not been established."

The Russian boat was torn apart by two great

explosions while participating in a large-scale military exercise. One Russian admiral of the Northern Fleet stated that a new type of torpedo had been forced on the Navy by arms industry officials amid fierce protest by the submarine fleet.

The official Russian military newspaper, Red Star, reported that *Kursk* had been re-fitted two years ago with new torpedoes which were believed to be difficult to store and dangerous to handle. The propellant used to power the new torpedoes was a highly flammable hydrogen dioxide liquid fuel, utilized because it was less expensive than the safer, battery-based solid fuel it had replaced, and the torpedoes were launched by gas triggers instead of by the safer compressed air method used previously. *Kursk* received the new weapons in January 1998 during her routine maintenance.

From the report of the Staff of the Northern Fleet to the Government Kursk Inquiry Commission: "On the port side of the submarine, at the binding frame of the first and second compartments, a rupture hole measuring of 2 x 3 metres was found. The edges of the rupture hole are *curled inside the boat and melted*."

The Russian naval representative to the torpedo manufacturer, Dagdisel: "Only a missile could have rammed the submarine. There are no explosives at

the binding frame between the first and second compartments. If the *Kursk* was rammed by another submarine, there would be only a hole there without signs of fire. A fire could lead to an explosion if a missile damaged the submarine's hull. But this explosion could not destroy the boat by itself. The cause of the terrible fire was [a] torpedo with [the] hydrogen dioxide propulsion system, which was on board *Kursk*. Those torpedoes can be compared to a barrel of gasoline burning in [a] garage."

Hydrogen dioxide is contained in a tank in these torpedoes. When fire heats the casing of the weapon, the liquid fuel boils leading to an explosion. Test data has shown that the torpedo will heat up enough for such an explosion to occur in about two minutes. The testing was conducted to show submarine crews how much time they have in the event of a fire breaking out in the torpedo room.

Many western military analysts take the view that an explosion in the forward weapons compartment of the 14,000-ton sub was the most likely cause of the accident. They believe that the second, more powerful blast which came two minutes later, destroyed and flooded the torpedo and control rooms, probably killing the estimated forty officers and crew in them. The surviving crew members in other compartments would have made their way back to section nine in the stern compartment, in the hope of escaping from a hatch there. As this proved impossible, they waited there in the cold and dark as their supply of oxygen rapidly depleted.

In a meeting with grieving relatives of the *Kursk* crewmen several days after the disaster, Russian President Vladimir Putin promised to recover the bodies from the wreck and, in the week after the *Kursk* sank, Russian submersibles made several unsuccessful attempts to make a secure connection with the sub's escape hatch. Then Norwegian divers were allowed to join the work. The diving teams

No more striking measure of the strong sense of security against U-boats which dominated all minds at Scapa Flow can be found than in the fact that, after one torpedo from the first volley had actually struck the *Royal Oak* none of the vigilant and experienced officers conceived that it could be a torpedo. The danger from the air was the one first apprehended, and large numbers of the crew took up their air-raid stations under the armour, and were thereby doomed, while at the same time the captain and admiral were examining the alternative possibilities of an internal explosion. It was in these conditions that the second volley of torpedoes was discharged. Thus the forfeit has been claimed, and we mourn the loss of eight hundred gallant officers and men, and of a ship which, although very old, was of undoubted military value.
— from the "loss of the HMS *Royal Oak*" speech by Winston S. Churchill, 8 November 1939

above: The cap badge of a Russian naval officer.
left: K-141, the *Kursk*.

finally managed to open the hatch and determine that none of the *Kursk* crew had survived.

In the weeks that followed, Russian and Norwegian divers faced extremes of weather which brought difficult and dangerous sea conditions in the area where the submarine sank. They had to contend with the currents, floating debris, darkness and confined spaces. There was also the danger of ripping pressure suits or cutting their air hoses on the jagged, mangled wreckage of the sub.

By late October they had been able to cut holes in the top of the *Kursk*. The divers did their work using state-of-the-art equipment including robots and mechanical arms, and an instrument that sprayed pressurized water mixed with diamond dust to cut through the 2-inch-thick inner steel hull of the boat.

The hazardous nature of the recovery effort caused two widows of the *Kursk* crewmen, visiting the ship being used by the diving team, to plead with the divers not to take excessive risks. The women had brought home-made pies to give the divers, and flowers to cast on the waters above the wreck. Russian officials meanwhile were warning that the body recovery attempts might be cancelled if it were decided that the divers' lives were in danger. Some Russian media at this point were declaring that by continuing the risky recovery effort, the government wanted to vindicate its confused response to the sinking of the *Kursk*. It had steadfastly resisted foreign offers of help for several days after the accident, while failing in its own rescue attempts.

The operating plan for the recovery operation called for work to begin, weather permitting, on 18 October. The platform would be provided by the Norwegian ship *Regalia* and two diving bells would be utilized. The *Regalia* can function even in a Force 5 gale.

First, templates for the holes to be drilled in the hull of *Kursk* would be brought to the *Regalia*. The templates were to be made by the Rubin design bureau, and before actual use they would be tested on the hull of another Oscar-II class submarine, the *Orel*, to determine precisely where the holes should be cut in order to avoid obstacles such as pipelines and ballast tanks.

Next, the diving bells would descend to the wreck of *Kursk*. Divers would mark the areas to be cut with the bright templates and would attach drilling equipment to the submarine's hull. They would then return to the bells to operate the drilling equipment by remote control. The size of the two holes to be cut was 1 x .7 metres. Initially, they would have to drill through the 40mm-thick outer hull, then the 200mm-thick inner hull. It was estimated that the drilling operation would take a minimum of fifteen hours. With completion of the first hole, and operating under a government order that only Russian divers were to enter the submarine, one of the Russians would go into the compartment, bringing a flashlight and video equipment on a twenty-metre cable. The other Russian diver would act as his back-up, while the Norwegian diver would remain in the bell about five metres from the submarine. The Russian divers would then gather and pack bodies and body parts into plastic containers to be sent up to the *Regalia*. When the divers had completed their work, the holes in the submarine hull were to be sealed.

After working for five days to cut through the inner hull of the *Kursk*, the diving teams finally succeeded. Initially, the bodies of four crew were recovered and further efforts resulted in the recovery of eight additional bodies.

It is known that both Britain and the United States had submarines in the Barents Sea at the time of the *Kursk* accident, and both countries have denied that their subs were in the vicinity of the Russian boat. In late October 2000, Russian officials persisted in the view that the *Kursk* sinking was most likely the result of a collision with a foreign military vessel in the area during the exercises in which she was participating. They conceded though, that other possible causes of the accident were still being considered and no final determination had yet been made. The two Russian submersibles, Mir-1 and Mir-2, that had been searching for fragments of a foreign submarine in the area of the *Kursk* wreck, had found no evidence in support of the collision theory. After the body recovery effort, the divers were expected to try to retrieve the ship's logs which might yield clues to the cause of the catastrophe. The *Kursk*'s two nuclear reactors are believed to be shut down and intact, and no abnormal radiation levels have been detected in the area of the wreck.

Among Russian Navy officers and participants in the rescue and recovery operations, two theories seem to have found strong support. The first involves a group of Russian nuclear submarines, including *Kursk*, that was supposedly carrying out a 12 August torpedo attack exercise against an opponent vessel, the nuclear cruiser *Peter the Great*, which was to defend itself by returning fire with missiles. This theory holds that one of the missiles from the cruiser malfunctioned at low altitude near where the *Kursk* was operating at periscope depth. Though unarmed, the missile then hit the *Kursk* in the forward torpedo section, causing one of the submarine's liquid-fuelled torpedoes to detonate. The captain may then have ordered the submarine to the surface, but sea water pouring into the boat's forward compartments sent it to the ocean floor instead, where other onboard torpedoes detonated in a second, much larger blast.

The other theoretical scenario, supported by many of the naval officers, suggests that, on the date of the accident, *Peter the Great* was conducting the firing of self-guided missiles at sea targets. These missiles were designed to penetrate their targets and then detonate, causing what is called a 'volume explosion'. During the launching of the missiles all other ships in the area were supposed to maintain radio silence. The launch period would have lasted for one hour, near the end of which, *Kursk* may have risen to periscope depth to fire its own torpedoes. In theory, if the submarine happened to radio for permission to begin firing its torpedoes at a moment when a self-guided missile from *Peter the Great* was already in the air, the missile may have received the radio signal from *Kursk*, changed its target designation and descended on the submarine.

In mid-November 2000 officials of the Russian Navy acknowledged for the first time that one of the two explosions on board the *Kursk* was that of a torpedo. The Russian government hoped to raise the *Kursk*, perhaps by summer 2001, and bring it to shore for a thorough inspection which might determine the actual cause of the accident.

In the aftermath of *Kursk* there was much pointed criticism of the Russian government, the Navy, and President Putin over their handling of the crisis. Controversy surrounded the lengthy delay before the government accepted offers of assistance from the British, among others, of assistance in an effort to save any survivors, causing indignation and bitterness among the relatives of the crew. Could any of the *Kursk* crew have been saved, with or without the help of another nation, or were these Russian submariners doomed from the moment of the first explosion in their ship? What do the experts think?

Veteran submariner Vice-Admiral Patrick Hannafin, USN (Ret): "My suspicion from the very beginning was that there was an internal explosion in the torpedo room, probably from one of their new experimental torpedoes. That set off the rest of it, and the rest of it was probably the cruise missiles which are in rows down each side. The forward ones are just forward of the bridge structure, and the first explosion could very well have set those off. The motors and the warheads, are of 600 to 1000 pounds, so it was one hell of an explosion.

We were heading back into Portsmouth. We'd been doing some training with Special Boat Section people [similar to the US Navy Seals] doing exit and re-entry through the escape hatch. All of a sudden we heard the announcement, 'Emergency stations. Stand by collision forward.' We knew that some ship or somebody had definitely made an error and it wasn't us because we were so used to these waters. We knew we would be in the right channel.

We had to shut everything down including all bulkhead doors, and some of these SBS guys were in the forward torpedo compartment and that had to be shut down quick. If you have to take a collision, you don't want to take it amidships, you want to take aft or forward.

I went to shut down the bulkhead of the forward torpedo compartment. I yelled at these guys to get out of the compartment and they wouldn't, so I finally slammed the door on them and just shut them in there. I'm sorry but in a situation like that, the thing is to protect as many men as possible. Even if it had been my own brother in there, I would have done what I was expected to do, to shut that compartment down and make the boat as safe as I possibly could.

That was the first really frightening thing that I had happen on a submarine. That 100,000-ton Liberian tanker, missed us by about 50 yards.
– Colin Watts-Tucker, former Royal Navy submariner

"I don't think any actual tapping was heard through the hull [as reported in some newspapers]. If anything like that was heard, I think it was just the metal working and the ship settling down into the mud. I expect that, from the size of the explosions, they may well have blown every watertight door all the way aft. Our own routine is that at 'battle stations' you put the watertight doors on the latch. You don't crack 'em down, but they're on the dogs. If the Russians were doing the same thing, even if the doors to the reactor compartments were shut and dogged—and I don't know how many of their bulkheads are really test-depth bulkheads—that explosion would have blown right on through. The only guys who could possibly have survived would be the ones in the after compartments. Even with the watertight doors shut, you've got ventilation pipes that go all the way through the ship. They have flappers on them that you can close off, but there wouldn't have been time to do that, and the flooding would have gone right on through.

"The *Kursk* is a double-hull submarine and is much larger than a Los Angeles–class boat. It has two reactors and is about 512 feet long and about 14,000 tons displacement. I understand that they have two very large torpedo tubes and use their new super-speed torpedoes which have liquid-powered engines. Liquid-powered torpedoes are scary in a submarine, as far as I am concerned. We know that they had two civilian torpedo technicians who were from the place where those torpedoes are made, and that they had permission to do some firing of those torpedoes. It all adds up for me that they had an internal explosion in the torpedo room, which set off everything else.

"I don't think that any other navy, finding itself in a similar situation to that of *Kursk*, would have delayed the way the Russians did before asking for help from another nation. As it turned out, though, there probably wasn't anybody alive to rescue. Our rescue vessels can match up with the submarines of every nation in the world except

Great deeds are done in the air and on the land, nevertheless there is no part to be compared to your exploits.
— Winston Churchill, to the men of His Majesty's submarines, 30 May 1943

There is no branch of His Majesty's forces which in this war has suffered the same proportion of fatal loss as our submarine service. It is the most dangerous of all the services.
— Winston Churchill, House of Commons, 9 September 1941

left: An emergency surfacing exercise, similar to that conducted by the USS *Greeneville* off Oahu, Hawaii on 9 February 2001. In the exercise the fast attack submarine accidentally collided with a Japanese fisheries boat, the *Ehime Maru*, resulting in the loss of nine men and boys from the Japanese vessel. In April 2001, Admiral Thomas Fargo, Commander of the US Pacific Fleet, issued a letter of reprimand to Commander Scott Waddle, skipper of the *Greeneville*, finding Waddle guilty of dereliction of his duty and negligent hazarding of a vessel. Waddle was relieved of his command, fined and forced to retire from the Navy.

111

The adrenalin was going, and I mean *going*. We had been down in the Falklands and were on our way back. We were somewhere to the west of Gibraltar and suddenly the general alarms went. I was actually turned in at the time, but I knew something had gone wrong. I knew we were doing an 'emergency surface' and, when you're off watch, you've got to get to your emergency station. I got out of my bunk and was fighting with everyone else to find my shirt, bunks were flying out of their supports, and before I got out of the bunk space we surfaced. We hit the roof.

All this happened within seconds and all of a sudden we rolled over at about 45 degrees. The guy who was on the planes said it was actually nearer to 50 degrees that we went over, and then we flew back up again. When you feel that you are going over, you think, 'what the hell?' The first thing that goes through your mind is 'we're turning over.' If you turn over in a submarine, if that was to happen, you're not gonna get out. But then we sprung back and we righted. Then the adrenalin was really going, but after that I calmed down like everybody else and we found out what had happened. The guy on the panel watchkeeping, who manned all the systems, he'd done everything right as soon as the flood alarm went. You just blow and go and that's it. The emergency blows were activated and we were on our way up. But what he

China and Russia, with whom we haven't had any co-operative work. I believe that the British system, which is built with the same sort of accommodation that we have, could match up with the Russian system. We've never done it with the Russians. We've done it with a lot of other nations, and we have joint specifications for the [escape] hatch, etcetera, so that we can match them. If there is any hope at all, you want to get stuff there as fast as possible, and frankly, it doesn't matter who owns it."

What do submariners fear most? According to Vice-Admiral Hannafin, "The greatest fear is having the ocean in the same compartment with you. In combat, of course, it was getting caught and being depth charged, or getting caught on the surface by aircraft and being bombed.

"You depend upon every one of your shipmates to do the right thing at the right time. Any one of them may be the guy who is on the spot when a casualty occurs. He may be the only one there, and he's got to know what to do—the right thing to do—and do it quickly, to save the ship. It's your confidence in yourself and in your shipmates that makes good submariners.

"Fire is a great fear. We are so careful to do the drills and have the fire equipment to make sure that we can keep a fire contained. Once you have a fire aboard the boat, you have to contain it, get to the surface and get the smoke out. It can eat up the oxygen very fast. It's especially [critical] if you are under attack and are constrained about what you can do to get to the surface. You've got to be able to contain it. In the design of the boat, we try to minimize the amount of stuff that can burn. Most fires that happen on a submarine are grease fires, galley fires. The cooks are very careful not to let grease accumulate on the hoods or where the ventilation is. Electrical fires can happen too, but those are things that you expect to happen and you drill to make sure you know how to isolate

the thing electrically and how to put out the fire.

"I think that flooding is probably the biggest terror you can have on a submarine. A ruptured pipe, particularly when you are deep, a salt-water pipe where you have an enormous amount of pressure . . . it doesn't take long for the salt water to come in and hit the electrical equipment and ground it out, which is probably what happened when we lost [the USS] *Thresher*. A salt-water pipe gave way back in the engineering spaces and knocked out power. There were other things that happened to *Thresher*, but that was probably the initiation of the problem."

"Surfacing off Sable Island—the graveyard of many a ship—to continue our surface passage to Halifax, Nova Scotia in 1958, we were agreeably surprised to find a calm if icy sea with a gentle long swell and took the opportunity to ditch the considerable amount of garbage that had accumulated after a lengthy period of submergence. This was normally done through the fin (sail) door, with a long chain of men through the boat handing it on via the control room and conning tower ladder to the casing (upper deck) where it was cast over the side. Suddenly, and to our horror, the garbage started to pile up outside the fin door and we found that the front man of the chain was missing; presumably he had fallen overboard unnoticed.

"Man Overboard drill was initiated immediately with the boat conducting a turn to bring us back down our track on a reciprocal course. In view of the calm sea state, the captain ordered a limited number of men onto the casing in order to have a closer look at the surface as, by this time, it was getting quite dark.

"I was stationed right forward with lifeline, life jacket and torch when, unexpectedly, the bow, caught in our own wake and, combining with the long, deceptive swell, broached and swept me over the side, with the lifeline parting under the strain. Fortunately, I hung onto the torch, had inflated my life jacket, and the shock of being immersed in a sea temperature of 0 degrees centigrade soon passed with the numbing of my lower body.

"I vaguely remember shining the torch in the general direction of the fast disappearing boat and singing 'Lloyd George knows my father' at the top of my voice as some inner sense told me to make some sort of noise, good or bad, to attract attention. It seemed an age (actually just twelve minutes) before the boat got close enough for me to be hauled back on board, whereupon I collapsed in a heap with no feeling in my legs.

"A tot of rum followed by the most excruciating attack of pins and needles all over and I was back on watch again, vainly looking for our missing shipmate, sadly to no avail after a very thorough search.

"The subsequent Board of Inquiry, quite apart from reprimanding me for losing a valuable pair of binoculars, property of Her Majesty the Queen, returned a verdict of misadventure and that no one could possibly have remained alive in that sea temperature for more than eight minutes. A very sobering thought indeed which caused me to thank my Maker for his infinite mercy, but gave little consolation for the tragic loss of our missing shipmate."
– Commander Mike Sizeland, RN (Ret)

Commander William Hoeth, skipper of the USS *Salt Lake City,* SSN 716: "I've never seen a real fire in a submarine in twenty years. I have seen water that I was uncomfortable about come into the ship once in twenty years. I'm always anxious when I tell a sea story about some kind of casualty, that whoever is listening doesn't get the impression that this is day-to-day stuff, that we go out there and we have these calamities happen on the ship. It isn't like that.

"We had a situation once on another ship where a sailor failed to do what he was supposed to do. It

was a great reminder for the crew of how important it is for everyone to do their job correctly. We had a significant amount of water come into the ship, and it was pretty exciting for a while. A bunch of water poured into the snorkel mast that we use to bring air into the diesel engine. It ended up raining down into the mess deck where the crew eats, pouring out of the overhead and down into the bottom of the ship where the diesel is. The diesel operator down there thought there was flooding. He called FLOODING, and shut off the diesel engine, which at the time was our source of power. There was a lot of smoke from the diesel shutting down and a lot of water everywhere.

"A chief petty officer looked through a watertight door into the space where the smoke and water was. Because of the angle of the deck, the water was just about up to the little window that he was looking through and he saw nothing but smoke and water. He clutched his chest and fell to the deck unconscious. The sailors nearby thought he was having a heart attack. It was pretty exciting.

"The ship got out of it fine. No one was hurt. It took us a few hours to clean things up and get everything fixed again, and for a few hours we were pretty well focused.

"A lot of people think that the biggest risk on a submarine must be the nuclear reactor. Far from it. We run that reactor very, very well. It's an extremely reliable power source. We don't have to worry about it. Other people think the biggest risk must be the torpedoes, the ordnance and all those explosives but they are very well designed and very safe. They have a number of features that keep us from worrying about them blowing up.

"The biggest threat, and we are always aware of it, is the ocean itself. The hull, of course, is constantly subjected to sea pressure. The hull of a submarine is thinner, relative to its diameter, than the shell of an egg relative to its diameter. The sea pressure is relentless; it's there all of the time. You have to be

should have done, he should have shut off the emergency blows [near the surface]. They can freeze up and you wouldn't be able to shut them down. Also, over the top of the fin there are shutters for all the major openings like the radar and everything else. What he hadn't done was open up these shutters, so all the water in the fin was still there. He hadn't drained down, and he couldn't drain down, so the balance was wrong, and it pulled us right over, and then back again. That was frightening.
– Colin Watts-Tucker, former Royal Navy submariner

Our last garment is made without pockets.
– Italian proverb

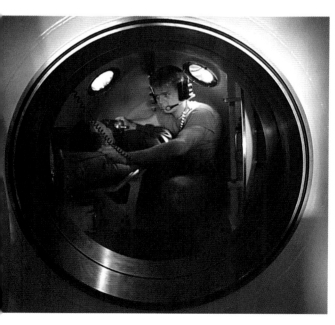

aware of it all the time. All of the pipes that carry sea water are always subject to sea pressure. If you get a leak through one of them—a big leak which we would call flooding—there is a long list of things that people have to do and they have to get them all right for you to be confident that the ship will be safe.

"We spend a lot of time teaching our junior sailors what they have to do in their different positions on the ship in the event of a casualty where there is water coming into the ship. We train the officers of the deck aggressively on what they have to do. We teach them the theory as well as the list of orders they have to give. They have to understand the orders. We do a lot of training, and on top of that, we drill like crazy. We run casualty drills like no other branch of the Navy and maybe like no other branch of the armed services. When we run a casualty drill, we have a number of people simulate flooding noises or air noises. We will have a whole team involved in simulating the different circumstances that might exist, such as smoke, fire, water, noise.

"We want to teach our guys to respond to real indications. The job of the drill monitors is to keep their mouths shut. They don't say anything. The guys don't get any verbal clues. They come in and they know by training that this is a fire. They know where it is and they will simulate doing the right stuff with their fire extinguishers, fire hoses, whatever they are supposed to do. They will make all the required reports. They'll don all the proper protective equipment. If there are some actions that they believe they need to take that we really don't want them to take because of limitations on the ship, we have someone stand by to prevent that sort of thing from happening. We do it all the time; every underway, and in every area of the ship. The crew never knows when it's going to happen. They never know if it's a drill or not. On surface ships you may hear THIS IS A DRILL, THIS IS A DRILL. We never say THIS IS A DRILL. We just say FIRE IN THE ENGINE ROOM, and sound the general alarm. Everyone goes back there and when they show up, that's when they find out that it's not really a fire, just a drill.

"More than 90 per cent of the oceans are so deep that this ship would not really have any chance of surviving if we sank. We wouldn't rest on the bottom intact. We are constantly aware of the threat of the ocean. We always have to be ready so that, if we ever get a little bit heavy and start sinking, we can put ourselves safely back up shallow or back up on the surface where we can sort things out.

"Throughout my career as a submariner, whenever there has been a casualty to some other country's submarine, I really felt I had a greater kinship with the other navy's submariners than I had, even with fellow US Navy members who aren't submariners. There is this bond among submariners because of the unique environment we operate in; the unique hazards we have to face on a daily basis; the unique separation from our families that we endure. I think we all share a similar outlook. It really strikes us in the heart when something bad happens to any submariner, regardless of nationality."

Writing in the [London] *Evening Standard* of 5 September 2000, columnist Brian Sewell commented in *Burial by bureaucracy*: "The tragedy of *Kursk* was, for me, one of particular horror and poignancy. Hundreds of submariners, thousands indeed, German and British for the most part, died in circumstances as terrifying during the Second World War, blown to smithereens by depth charges, waiting to drown in a punctured iron capsule, waiting for increasingly stale air to become, at last, unbreathable, waiting the worst part of a dreadful fate.

"I cannot imagine what goes through the minds of men waiting for inevitable death in darkness over days of bitter cold at the bottom of the sea;

Do not seek death. Death will find you. But seek the road which makes death a fulfilment.
— from *Markings*
by Dag Hammarskjöld

Man is the only animal that contemplates death, and also the only animal that shows any sign of doubt of its finality.
— from *The Meaning of Immortality in Human Experience*
by William Ernest Hocking

Death has but one terror, that it has no tomorrow.
— from *The Passionate State of Mind*
by Eric Hoffer

top left: The Deep Submergence Rescue Vehicle *Mystic* (DSRV-1) being readied for use in the *Kursk* tragedy. centre left: DSRV-1 on a transporter for loading aboard a USAF C-5. bottom left: Hospital Corpsman 3rd Class Larry Eddingfield demonstrates patient care in a transportable recompression chamber. left: The DSRV *Chiyoda* descends from her mother ship in a rescue docking exercise with the USS *Buffalo* (SSN 715) near Yokosuka Naval Base, Japan in the summer of 1999.

A depth charge must explode almost in contact with the tough pressure hull of a sub to get a kill. It takes some seconds for a depth charge to arch through the air and more seconds to sink through the water to its set depth, during which time a skillful sub skipper may maneuver out from under it. If he chooses to go down to say five hundred feet, he has quite a few seconds for his evasive maneuvering. If you miss him once he has that fifteen minutes reprieve during which he doesn't have to creep silently but can run at high speed while the ocean is reverberating and disturbed water conditions give your phony sonar echoes. . . .after a salvo of ashcans explodes all around him, maybe it takes the skipper's nerves that long to settle down too. While they are still agitated he *may* do something foolish.

So the standard procedure at this time was to fire a salvo of hedgehogs as you approached the sub and if you got no explosion as you continued your run, to plant a garden of ashcans around him. In perhaps half the sub killings during the Battle of the Atlantic, the whole action was fought without either side actually seeing the enemy. The battle begins with a radar blip or a sonar contact on the Allied side, and a hydrophone or Naxos warning on the German side. An hour or so later it ends with a blazing surface ship upending and sinking, or a

reason tells me that nothing in the cramped quarters of a submarine will be vertical or horizontal and thus that reconciling one's soul to circumstance or God cannot be done in the small comfort of a bunk; reason tells me that the emptying of bowels and bladders will add stench to the exhausted air; reason tells me that thirst and hunger will enhance the misery. Does one die sane, or mad and violent, screaming and scrabbling against the iron walls? And for those who believe in Him, what part can God, Eternal Father strong to save those in peril on the sea, play for them when they are committed to so lingering and terrible a death?

"I belong to a generation taught to perceive nobility in being a sailor, from the humblest stoker to the captain of the ship. Winston Churchill could pithily dismiss the historical navy with 'rum, sodomy and the lash', but to boys of my age the navy was the Senior Service, each ship of it a benign oligarchy utterly dependent on the loyal obedience of slaves, in which the ancient concepts of virtue, gravity, self-sacrifice and heroism were predominant in every action. And in every action all were expected to exceed the limits of human endeavour and even go down, achieving the classical ideal in honourable failure—and many ships' companies did both, to the last man. It is, however, one thing to go down in battle, quite another to go down in peace and for no immediately evident reason—which is exactly what happened to *Thetis* in June 1939, when Britain was on the brink of a war for which there could have been no more awful portent.

"*Thetis*, built at Birkenhead, was to have been the Royal Navy's prize submarine. On the fine first morning of the month, she nosed her way into the Irish Sea for her first diving trials, the mood on board confident, with as many civilian engineers, fitters, experts and observers as there were crew, 103 men in all. Accompanied only by a tug, *Thetis* reached her diving position 15 miles off the north

Welsh coast at 1.30 pm. When all the civilians had refused the chance to transfer to the tug, the captain ordered the conning tower closed, the ballast tanks flooded, the electric motors to replace the diesels, and the ship to dive. She dropped 20 feet but would not submerge, even with the weight of 50 extra men on board.

"She was light at the bow. Unarmed, her six torpedo tubes should have been flooded to match their weight and keep her on an even keel, but no one, not even Lieutenant Frederick Woods, the torpedo officer, was sure that this had been done. Woods began to check—a simple procedure aligning two tiny holes through which sea water would spurt if a tube were flooded, with the added precaution of pushing a thin rod through them to ensure that they had not been obstructed. This last he did with the first four tubes, which were indeed empty, but not the fifth, which was by mischance full, the essential spurt of water blocked by a neglected speck of paint. It was through the rear door of this tube that thousands of gallons of water suddenly flooded the nose of *Thetis* and took her to the shallow bottom at an angle steep enough to leave her stern projecting in the air.

"The marker tug did not immediately inform Submarine HQ and was swept off station by the tide. The first news bulletin, '*Thetis* has failed to surface', was issued at 11 p.m.; the projecting stern was not discovered until just before 8 a.m. the following day. At much the same time, inside the hull, the officers calculated that all air would be exhausted within seven hours and, with no sign of rescue, they had better attempt evacuation through the escape chamber, in spite of the angle, the total inexperience of half the men and only the benefit of level practice in a shallow tank of water for the crew.

"Of the first two men to escape, Woods was one, on the grounds that he could tell rescuers exactly what had happened; both were saved. Hoping to hasten the procedure, four men then entered the chamber but were drowned in it; reverting to a pair of men, the next two reached the surface. Then the exit hatch jammed. Exhausted by the struggle, dizzied and confused by the depleted air, at 3 p.m. a pair of men opened both the outer hatch and the door to the engine room; thus the sea claimed what the hymn describes as 'its appointed limits'.

"With 99 men drowned, the loss of *Thetis* was then the world's worst submarine disaster. The whole nation seemed to hold its breath in hope and prayer, reassured by reports of messages in Morse tapped from within the hull—but there was air aboard for little more than one full day and, as with *Kursk*, the rest was sheer incompetence.

"This vital diving exercise was monitored only from a tug; the tug sent the first message of distress by telegraph at least an hour late; the telegraph boy was mending a punctured tyre on his bicycle and did not deliver it to HQ in Gosport until 6.15 p.m.; the senior officer there, in the middle of the south coast, set off for north Wales by sea instead of in a car and arrived at the disaster many hours too late; HMS *Brazen*, the destroyer that discovered *Thetis*, carried no compressed air hoses, no oxyacetylene cutters, no engineers and no divers who might have sustained life in the sunken craft.

"My childhood recollection has always made the time between the first news bulletin and the final admission of disaster seem much longer than the bald facts—there was time to go to Mass and light a candle, time to hear news bulletins on the wireless, time to see people gathered in the street, singing 'Heavenly Father, strong to save . . .' —but it can only have been a day, as I know from the true bones of the terrible tale that was immediately rekindled in my mind by the protracted tragedy of *Kursk*.

"All those years ago off the coast of Wales, as it seemed this summer off Murmansk, officialdom was much more to blame than any single man, but at least we know the truth; shall we ever know the

truth of *Kursk*? We soon forgot *Thetis*. Within three months we were at war; in six, *Exeter*, *Ajax* and *Achilles* defeated *Graf Spee* and, exultant, we celebrated a great victory. Lieutenant Woods transferred to destroyers and, as befits the nobility of his profession, won the DSC."

"Any submariner will tell you that there is a brotherhood of submariners around the world. They care about one another, and understand each other and the dangers they face as no one else could."
— A Royal Navy submariner after the *Kursk* tragedy

"I am always a little nervous about my husband going out to sea. Deep down inside, I fear for his life just a little bit each time he leaves for sea. He always tries to quiet my fears by assuring me that the Navy is neurotic about safety.

"All of us wives of submariners were deeply affected when we heard about the *Kursk*. It is a horror we won't let ourselves think about. When

great puddle of oil spreading out across the ocean with pieces of submarine junk in the middle of it.
— from *Twenty Million Tons Under The Sea* by Rear Admiral Daniel V. Gallery, US Navy

below: A student and an instructor enter a diving bell at the US Navy Submarine Base, New London, Conn. in August 1943. The bell enables instructors to make 100-foot ascents with students and teach them the proper way to come up to the surface. The other students are wearing Momsen Lung submarine escape gear.

below: An underwater view of the sail and sensor masts of the USS *Florida* (SSBN 728). right: The USS *Ohio* at a submarine tender.

Full fathom five thy father lies; Of his bones are coral made: Those are pearls that were his eyes: / Nothing of him doth fade, / But doth suffer a sea-change / Into something rich and strange.
— from *The Tempest*, Act I, Scene II
by William Shakespeare

I heard the news, my heart stopped for a moment, then pounded. My throat tightened. I choked on my own breath, then my eyes overflowed with tears. It hit close to home and my heart. I felt so much compassion and empathy for the families of that Russian sub crew. Those men who died were husbands, fathers, sons and brothers. Each and every one of them had people back home that loved them. It could just as easily have happened to my husband or any of our men on one of our submarines. Any one of a thousand things could go terribly wrong and kill all on board or trap them.

"I feel deep sorrow for the friends and family members of the *Kursk* crew. Most will never even have their loved ones remains to put to rest. No one should ever have to endure such pain."
— Flo Garetson, submarine wife.

TRUE SUBMARINES

We're here to preserve democracy; not to practice it.
— Captain Ramsey in the film *Crimson Tide*

Submarines are like cats. They never tell "who they were with last night," and they sleep as much as they can. If you board a submarine off duty you generally see a perspective of fore-shortened fattish men laid all along. The men say that except at certain times it is rather an easy life, with relaxed regulations about smoking, calculated to make a man put on flesh. One requires well-padded nerves. Many of the men do not appear on deck throughout the whole trip. After all, why should they if they don't want to? They know that they are responsible in their department for their comrades' lives as their comrades are responsible for theirs. What's the use of flapping about? Better lay in some magazines and cigarettes.
— from *Sea Warfare* by Rudyard Kipling

WHAT DEFINES a true submarine? Since the First World War one definition has been: a vessel that can safely dive to and ascend from a depth greater than its own length. In fact, the generally accepted definition of a true submarine today is: a vessel that is capable of operating submerged, completely independently from the earth's atmosphere, for extended periods of time—the nuclear-powered submarine.

In January 1954 the world's first nuclear submarine, the *Nautilus* (SSN 571), was launched at Groton, Connecticut. The US Navy's Admiral Hyman G. Rickover, the champion and driving force of the Navy's nuclear propulsion programme, had overcome massive opposition before securing the support of the Navy for nuclear submarines. *Nautilus* was decommissioned in 1980 and is now on public display at Groton. The pioneering sub made headlines when she cruised beneath the polar ice cap to the North Pole in August 1958 in a dramatic example of nuclear submarine potential.

The first nuclear submarines, including *Nautilus*, *Seawolf* (SSN 575), *Skate* (SSN 578) and *Triton* (SSN 586) were all designed with conventional hull forms and thus were limited both by hull drag and early reactor horsepower to a maximum speed of around 20 knots. While these early nuclear-powered subs were in their infancy, the US Navy was also experimenting with an entirely new hull shape, the prototype teardrop, for its latest diesel-electric submarine, the USS *Albacore*. With the new hull shape, the *Albacore* was able to reach speeds in excess of 30 knots submerged, and the Navy immediately went to work developing a new class of hunter submarine called Skipjack. The six boats of this class combined the hull shape of *Albacore* with the then-Captain Rickover's nuclear reactor power plant, to become the fastest submarines in the world.

With nuclear submarines came greater knowledge of underwater acoustics and the effects of multi-layered deep water. New developments in electronics enabled substantial improvements in submarine detection and concealment, and greatly enhanced underwater weaponry, from torpedoes to mines to missiles. Through the design and deployment of elaborate new sensor arrays which could be extended from the sail/fairwater or from a pod attached to the hull, a submerged submarine crew could detect and listen to an enemy sub. Considerable effort was now being devoted to stealth and making submarines as quiet and undetectable as possible.

The quietness issue involved more than just the elimination or minimizing of obvious sources of noise on and in a submarine. The British solved much of the noise problem by putting all noise-making or vibrating machinery on insulated platforms, damping out the vibrations and isolating the machinery from the hull (a noise-monitoring system with sensors throughout the boat is fitted on current subs to alert crewmen to sounds emitted by any loose or malfunctioning equipment). The main problem, however, was propeller cavitation noise. Submarine designers tried to reduce it by slowing the propeller rotation speed, but this required a larger-diameter propeller which caused intermittent vibrations and an unacceptable low-frequency noise. A new propeller design employing scythe-shaped blades finally minimized the problem.

Among the most important features of current submarines, such as the highly-effective US Los Angeles-class fast attack vessel, are their sensor capabilities. These include radar, communications, the search and attack periscopes and Electronic Support Measures, a passive receiver system designed to detect radar emissions from surface ships and aircraft. All are represented by masts mounted in the sail/fairwater, providing the submarine crew with vital information connections to the outside world. Additionally, a Very Low Frequency (VLF) and Extremely Low Frequency

(ELF) communications capability is afforded through the use of a trailing antenna which floats several thousand feet behind the submerged sub.

The Type 18 search periscope is the workhorse of the two control room periscopes. It provides a colour television image that can be projected throughout the boat, a 70mm camera for periscope image photography, and readouts for the Electronic Support Measures (ESM) receiver. It also supports the antenna for the Global Positioning System (GPS) navigational equipment. The masts of the two periscopes project up through the sail/ fairwater structure and are coated with a radar-absorbing material to minimize their radar signature.

Forward of the control room of a Los Angeles boat is the communications shack containing cryptographic and radio transmission equipment. Located here are communications gear from ultra-high frequency to extremely low frequency capabilities, links to communications satellites, as well as underwater telephone equipment. The message traffic is encrypted through processors called Crypto. Through the VLF/ELF trailing antenna, submerged submarines can be signalled to come up to periscope depth and raise one of their communications masts to receive a signal from a satellite or UHF channel. Actual radio transmission from submarines is absolutely minimal.

Silence is key in submarine operation and all noise, electronic or acoustic, is guarded against. Another way in which a submarine is put at risk is by allowing its own magnetic field or "signature" to become strong enough to produce detectable, measurable distortions, or anomalies against a constant background pattern. Such anomalies are detectable, from below by a magnetic mine, or above by an aircraft fitted with MAD (Magnetic Anomaly Detection) equipment. To counter this threat, a submarine undergoes a procedure called "deperming" in which it is positioned in a Magnetic Silencing Facility which electrically reduces the magnetic signature of the hull in a few hours of treatment.

BSY-1 (Busy One) is the core of the Los Angeles submarine combat system, connecting the boat to the underwater world through four manned consoles in the sonar room forward of the control room.

The main sonar system of the boat is actually a combination of systems. It begins with the great spherical sonar array occupying much of the teardrop-shaped bow. The 15-foot diameter sphere offers both active (echo ranging) and passive (listening) modes and is extremely powerful. Mounted around the bow, is a low-frequency passive sonar conformal array, and there is a high-frequency array which incorporates a mine-detection and under-ice capability. A large tubular shroud on the starboard side of the hull/deck surface contains the basic towed array passive sonar which is designed for medium-range low-frequency noise detection. It pays out a 3 1/2"- thick 2600-foot cable fitted with hydrophones along a 240-foot array at the end of the cable. An additional passive towed array sonar, the TB-23 "thin-line", can be extended farther from the noise of the towing sub to detect very low frequency noise at long ranges. Additional to these devices is an acoustic intercept receiver which alerts the crew to the use of an active sonar such as that of the large array of another submarine, or the sonar of an incoming weapon. The data from all of these systems is processed and translated through other equipment into display data on the four BSY-1 sonar consoles. The sonar technicians "read" their displays of data from the various systems, looking for unusual indications that stick out from the random background noise patterns on their screens. When such an indication is spotted, it must be identified and classified, and given a contact designation from

Navy Bean Soup
Yield: 100 one-cup portions
3 1/2 qts beans, white, dry
Pick over and wash beans.
7 gals ham stock
8 ham bones
Add ham stock and ham bones. Heat to boiling point; cover and simmer 2 to 3 hours or until beans are tender. If necessary, add hot water. Remove ham bones.
2 3/4 cups carrots, shredded
4 1/2 cups onions, finely chopped
2 tsp pepper
Add carrots, onions and pepper. Simmer for 30 minutes.
2 cups flour, hard wheat, sifted
3/4 qt water, cold
Blend flour and water to a smooth paste. Stir into soup, cook 10 minutes longer.

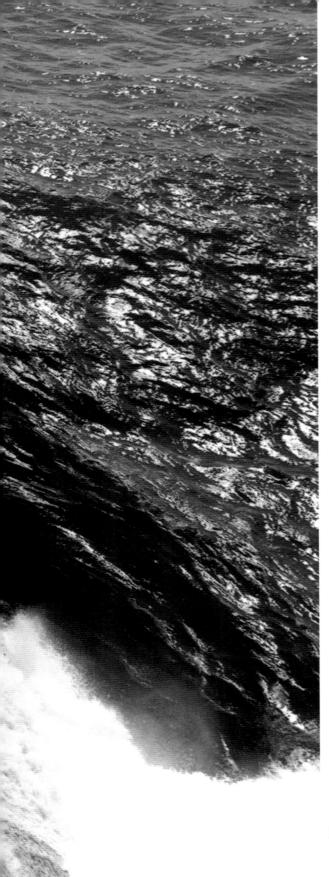

the following: Sierra=a sonar contact, Victor=a visual contact, Romeo=a radar contact and Mike=a combined contact of one or more signals from different sensors. A contact that has been identified and classified as a threat results in an exchange of information between the sonar room and the fire control console, through the BSY-1 system. This initiates a Target Motion Analysis (TMA) leading to a fire control solution, target speed, course and range. The fire control technician then continues the attack process, inputting the required data into the selected weapon, whether it be a Mk 48 torpedo, Harpoon or Tomahawk missile.

The best nuclear deterrent the United States has is the Trident missile submarine, the SSBN. It is seen as the most credible and survivable of the US nuclear delivery systems. The massive and very capable SSBN transports and maintains a load of 24 Trident missiles which are stationed in two vertical rows aft of the sail. Each Trident I missile has a warhead estimated to pack greater destructive power than the combined force of both atomic bombs dropped on Japan in World War II.

The United States Strategic Command issues orders to all Ohio-class Trident submarines of the US Navy from its headquarters at Offutt Air Force Base in Nebraska. Trident nuclear submarines are big business. They provide the key sea-based element of the American strategic force triad. The Tridents, also known as boomers, are highly survivable, flexible and able to re-target their missiles rapidly, if necessary. They utilize secure, constant at-sea communications links.

The first of these impressive ships, the USS *Ohio*, SSBN 726, sailed on her initial operational patrol in late 1982, and the Navy took delivery of the final ship of the class in 1997. Trident submarines carry either Trident I (C-4) or Trident II (D-5) missiles, and are also fitted with four torpedo tubes for launching Mk 48 torpedoes as a defence against

Lord thou commanded us saying 'thou shalt not kill'. Thou knowest that we prepare ourselves constantly to kill, not one but thousands, and that by this preparation we believe we help to preserve peace among nations. Do thou, who gave man the knowledge to fashion this terrible weapon, give him also the sense of responsibility to control its use. So that fear for the consequences may indeed maintain peace until that day when love not fear shall control men's actions. Give us the will, but never the wish, to obey the order to fire, O God, if it is thy will that order may never need be given.
Amen.
– an early Polaris submarine commanding officer

left: The Seawolf-class USS *Connecticut* (SSN 22) during her sea trials.

That terrible war we feared never came. America's leaders place special trust and confidence in the Submarine Force, who went to sea entrusted with weapons of incredible destructive power, propelled by power plants of unbelievable sophisitication, armed for Armageddon, while charged with the solemn responsibility of preventing it.

U.S. strategy during the Cold War relied on our ability to dominate the seas. This required naval forces capable of projecting power to deter and prevent conflict, and when required, to fight and win. Undersea superiority was a vital aspect of this strategy, and for this reason our submarines were key elements of U.S. forces.

Throughout the Cold War, a cornerstone of national security was deterrence. SSBNs were the preeminent and survivable leg of the strategic triad that was instrumental in deterring global nuclear war for half a century. Lurking in the ocean depth, anyplace around the globe, and capable of retaliation to an enemy attack on America, SSBNs carried over half of our nation's strategic warheads at less than 20% of the total costs.

Deterrence of war has been the sole mission for the SSBN since its inception in 1960. It was on a November day in 1960 that the *George Washington* left Charleston on that first patrol—at the height of the Cold War. We were all on guard against a belligerent,

hostile anti-submarine forces. These stealthy subs are among the quietest ever built. Through careful maintenance, updating and some modification, the Navy plans to keep its Trident subs in operation for a lifespan of up to 44 years.

Few organizational units at the start of the 21st century surpass that of the US Navy nuclear submarine in self-sufficiency, complexity and efficient operation. The Commanding Officer, or Captain of the ship, is key in the successful running of the organization, having the ultimate responsibility for every aspect of the submarine's operation. His remit: to successfully carry out the missions assigned, utilizing whatever measures are required, in his judgement, to accomplish the task. His second-in-command is the Executive Officer, who is always the next senior in rank to the Captain and is directly in line to attain his own submarine command. Informally referred to as the XO, his wide-ranging experience contributes greatly to the organization through his coordination of the ship's administrative and training activities. His role also requires him to become involved in every aspect of submarining.

The nuclear missile submarine organization is made up of six primary departments: Navigation/Operations, Strategic Weapons, Engineering, Tactical Systems, Supply, and Medical. Of these, the first four departments are headed by senior officers who rank immediately below the XO. The departments are composed of divisions which are run by junior officers and comprise enlisted men skilled in their division specialty field.

A second and essential element of the nuclear sub organization is the Watch system, which is established to conduct and coordinate the actual daily operation of the ship. It is divided into three separate groups called sections and one of these sections "has the watch" at any given time. A watch section is supervised by the Officer of the Deck, who carries out the commanding officer's orders during the hours of his watch. The OD

orders the submarine's course, speed and depth. He operates with the aid of the Engineering Officer of the Watch, who controls the nuclear reactor plant and propulsion. Each watch is made up of the helmsmen who steer the boat, the throttlemen who control the steam turbine engines, sonarmen who monitor the sea around the ship, reactor operators who control the vessel's energy source, missile technicians to service and launch the submarine's missiles, radio operators who maintain constant communications with command centres ashore, and electricians who supply reactor power for nearly every service on the ship.

At roughly three billion dollars each (on-the-road price, complete with missiles) a Trident submarine is not something you leave lying around the pier for a year or more between patrols. The US Navy (and the nation) need and demand more utility than that of the submarine-based strategic deterrent, which is why these ballistic missile subs are operated by two separate complete crews, the 'Blue' and 'Gold' (for the Navy colours). Each crew is made up of 16 officers and 156 enlisted men. The Blue and Gold crews alternate manning the sub, with one crew taking it to sea for a routine 77-day patrol which is followed by a 35-day turnover, replenishment and refit period. The other crew, meanwhile, is ashore combining a period of rest and relaxation with additional training as well as evaluation in simulators in preparation for their next patrol. In this way, the Navy gets maximum utility from the boat, being able to keep it at sea for over two-thirds of its operational life. The crews are given maximum relief and the "off" crew is provided a regular programme of refresher training on equipment exactly like that found on the sub, which keeps the "off" crew sharp. The intensive instruction serves to continually upgrade their knowledge.

The ship's crew is defined as: all the officers (wardroom) and enlisted members assigned to a ship or shore command. On a fleet ballistic missile submarine the enlisted crew is comprised of technical experts from various occupational fields who ensure that the ship is safe and self-sufficient while at sea.

The enlisted component of a fleet ballistic missile submarine crew breaks down as follows:

Electrician's Mate (EM): are responsible for all electrical systems throughout the ship and must continually monitor, troubleshoot and repair electrical equipment.

Electronics Technician (ET): are responsible for all electronic equipment on board the ship. Some of these personnel are trained to operate and maintain the nuclear power plant, while others specialize in navigation/electronic support equipment. The ET rating has recently absorbed the Interior Communications Electrician (IC), Quartermaster (QM) and Radioman (RM) ratings. The former IC personnel specialized in the maintenance and repair of interior communications and sensor circuits aboard the submarine. Their area of expertise also includes alarm and control circuits. The former QMs monitor the ship's position while at sea, providing the navigational data to the Officer of the Deck to support the safe navigation of the submarine. The former RMs operate, maintain and troubleshoot the complex communication system of the ship. The capacity to maintain continuous communication with headquarters is a critical element of the nuclear deterrent force.

Fire Control Technicians (FT): specialize in the operation of the ship's tactical weapons control system. They are responsible for ensuring that the tactical weapons are ready to fire at a moment's notice.

Hospital Corpsman (HM): the on-board doctor responsible for the physical readiness of the crew. He constantly monitors the atmosphere and water systems to ensure their proper sanitary operation. He monitors the sanitation of food preparation,

and is capable of handling most minor medical emergencies that might occur at sea.

Machinist Mates (MM): the personnel in this field specialize in the operation, maintenance and repair of mechanical systems. Due to the complexity of the nuclear propulsion plant, and submarines in general, MMs assigned to subs further specialize in Auxiliary, Propulsion and Engineering Laboratory Technician occupational fields.

Mess Management Specialist (MS): they are responsible for providing properly prepared food for the subsistence of the crew. In addition, they ensure that a sufficient stock of rations are on board prior to deployment.

Missile Technicians (MT): perform preventive and corrective maintenance on the mechanical and electrical systems supporting the Trident missiles in their stowage tubes. They specialize in the operation of the ship's strategic weapons control system.

Storekeeper (SK): ensures that adequate supplies of repair parts and consumables are carried on board and orders replacement parts as required.

Seaman/Fireman (SN/FN): these are non-rated personnel just reporting aboard for their first at-sea tour. They are exposed to the different occupational fields aboard the submarine to help them decide which career path to take. They are responsible for the topside maintenance of the ship in port.

Sonar Technician (ST): they are the underwater "eyes" of the submarine. Using the complex passive and active sonar systems, they listen to the sounds from the ocean and provide information on activity outside the ship.

Torpedoman's Mate (TM): they operate and maintain the torpedo tubes and associated tube-launched weapons. They ensure proper operation of the torpedo tube system in combat operations, and supervise the movement and reloading of weapons into the torpedo tubes.

Yeoman (YN): the administrative experts of the

nuclear-armed Soviet Union.

Attack submarines, SSs and SSNs, deployed to every region of the world during the Cold War, operating in the open ocean, in choke points and narrow waterways, and under the arctic ice. The U.S. clearly dominated the undersea environment and the Soviets knew it—such that the attack boats were also a deterrent force.

Cold War submarines made over 3500 strategic deterrent patrols and uncounted surveillance and barrier patrols. In addition, during the major campaigns in this war such as Korea and Vietnam, submarines made many offensive, defensive, and special operations patrols.
— The Cold War Submarine Memorial Foundation

A man who is not afraid of the sea will soon be drownded, for he will be going out on a day he shouldn't. But we do be afraid of the sea, so we do only be drownded now and again.
— John Millington Synge

ship, ensuring that all correspondence received by the command is properly replied to, and that all personnel records are properly updated and maintained.

In actuality, everyone on a submarine, whether a boomer or fast attack, is required to perform many other tasks in addition to those of his own specialty field.

Key to successful implementation of the two-crew system on a ballistic missile submarine is the procedure wherein the returning crew works with the next crew, briefing them on the status of all systems on the boat. It is an especially demanding time for the new crew, during which repairs must be made, systems tested, and every aspect of the submarine checked to ensure safe and proper operation on its next patrol. The crew turnover and replenishment time is minimized by such boat features as the three logistics hatches fitted to provide large-diameter repair and resupply openings. They make possible rapid transfer of equipment replacement modules and supply pallets, greatly reducing the time needed for maintenance and replenishment. Such capabilities allow the boomers to operate for up to twelve years between major shipyard refits.

The large, Ohio-class Trident submarines are considered a prime duty assignment by those who serve in them. With substantial working and living spaces, habitability is good and the ample crew provisions normally eliminate any need for "hot-bunking". The crews also appreciate the relatively short 75 to 90-day patrols of the SSBNs, compared to the six-month deployments of their fast attack counterparts.

While the Los Angeles-class fast attack submarines of the US Navy often appear in foreign ports, the boomers do not. The great ballistic missile boats normally remain submerged and invisible for the duration of their patrols. They rarely even transmit radio messages, preferring to listen rather than

127

HMS *Turbulent*, menu for Friday, 9 February 2001

Breakfast
Bacon, sausage, beans, tomatoes, fried egg, fruit juice, fried bread.

Lunch
Soup of the day, deep-fried cod in batter, chipped potatoes, processed peas and curry sauce, cheese and pickle Ploughman's.

Supper
Stir-fried beef in black bean sauce, egg fried rice, omelets to order, baked potato, strawberry cheesecake.

left: Displacing 18,750 tons submerged, 566 feet long with a 42-foot hull diameter and a 36-foot draft, the enormous bulk of the ballistic missile submarine USS *Alabama* is mostly hidden from view, like that of an iceberg.

talk. Their communication with USSTRATCOM is highly classified and encrypted. They operate with stealth, undetected. The torpedoes they carry are for defensive situations only. They never chase other targets. The fast attack boats chase the noise of target submarines. The boomers run away from the noise. In that respect they are like the Lancaster bombers of Britain's Royal Air Force in World War II, whose role was to transport a massive load of explosives for delivery on a target. If attacked or threatened and forced to defend themselves, they fought, but in general, they tried to avoid such situations and prudently fled from them whenever possible.

The Trident missiles of the boomers are supported by strategic weapons facilities at both the King's Bay, Georgia and Bangor, Washington SSBN bases. Lockheed, the prime contractor for the Trident missile, is responsible for building approximately 95 per cent of the weapon, with the Navy building the key final 5 per cent. In an interesting client/contractor arrangement that is informally referred to as "you fly 'em, you buy 'em", the missiles are leased from the contractor and are not actually purchased until the Navy fires them.

The Trident submarine is propelled by a nuclear reactor, two geared turbines and one shaft with a power capability of 60,000 horsepower. The sub is 560 feet long with a draught of 36 feet and a beam of 42 feet. Her displacement submerged is 18,700 tons loaded. Her performance is classified, but the estimated top speed submerged is 25+ knots and her estimated maximum diving depth is 900+ feet.

The fast attack submarines of the US Navy's Los Angeles-class are designed to attack, subdue or destroy an adversary surface ship or submarine. They combine quietness, speed and a powerful arsenal of torpedoes and cruise missiles, with the ability to follow the noise made by their target vessels, much as a sniffer dog follows a scent to its prey. The mission of the fast attack sub includes peacetime engagement, surveillance and intelligence gathering, special operations, precision strikes, sea denial, sea control and deterrence. The Navy intends to operate the Los Angeles-class subs over a 33-year lifespan.

In peacetime, the fast attack submarines provide a high-visibility presence in support of America's interests throughout the world. Through their many port calls they clearly demonstrate their country's determination and ability to navigate the entire world, on or under the sea. They are able to go into an area without giving away their presence, to conduct surveillance and gather intelligence for America's military. The fast attack subs deploy with a lethal load of Tomahawk land attack missiles (TLAM), whose long-range conventional strike capability was convincingly displayed during the 1990-91 Gulf War. The boats can carry commandos, reconnaissance teams, special agents or US Navy SEAL teams to locations where they may be needed for special operations. Another important aspect of the mission of these potent ships is denial of certain ports, sea lanes or specific areas at sea to hostile surface ships or submarines. They also serve in the essential role of keeping the sea lanes open for national security.

The attack submarines of the US Navy Pacific Fleet are based at Pearl Harbor, Hawaii and Ballast Point, San Diego, California. In the Atlantic Fleet, they are based at Groton, Connecticut and Norfolk, Virginia. Normally, they deploy on six-month patrols, either as part of an aircraft carrier battle group, or on independent operations throughout the world. Through their port calls, the crews are able to communicate with family and loved ones, see the sights of the local area and breathe fresh air for a brief while.

The crews of the attack submarines work mainly in isolation. They are cut off from access to fresh air and sunshine for weeks at a time, during which their only contact with the world is through their instruments. They work hard. Their recreation is limited to reading, playing cards and other games, writing letters, studying or watching movies, all in the one relatively large communal area on the boat, the mess room. It is also where they eat.

These attack and missile submarines are able to operate independently of the earth's atmosphere thanks to their primary power source, the nuclear reactor. In operation, the reactor is referred to as "running critical". The fission process produces radiation as well as heat, and substantial shielding is placed around the reactor for the protection of the crew.

A nuclear propulsion system in current American submarines uses a pressurized water reactor design with primary and secondary basic systems. In the primary system, ordinary water is circulated. The system is made up of the reactor, pumps, piping loops and steam generators. The reactor produces the heat which is transferred to the water, kept under pressure so that it does not boil. This water is then pumped through the steam generators and back into the reactor where it is reheated. In the steam generators, the heat from the primary system water is transferred to the secondary system where steam is created. The water in the two systems does not intermix, as the systems are isolated from each other. The steam now flows from the secondary system generators to drive the turbine generators which supply the submarine with electricity. It also feeds the main propulsion turbines to drive the ship's propeller. The steam is then condensed into water which is fed back into the steam generators by feed pumps. Both the primary and secondary systems are closed. The water is recirculated and reused. At no point in the power generation process is the presence of air or oxygen required.

Electric Boat Division of General Dynamics in

The man does better who runs from disaster than he who is caught by it.
—from *Iliad* by Homer

left: Of the many movies that have featured one or more submarines, one of the strangest is *Mysterious Island*.

above: Commander
Doug Prince, CO of the
fast attack submarine
USS *Helena* in San Diego,
September 2000. right:
The USS *Seawolf*
conducting sea trials in
September 1996.

Connecticut received an order in January 1989 to
build a new class of submarine intended to
replace the Los Angeles-class nuclear attack subs
as they neared the end of their operational
lifespan. The first boat of the new class was to be
called *Seawolf*. She would be the first of 29 such
vessels. The Seawolf-class submarine was to be
quieter and faster than the Los Angeles-class sub
and it would have more torpedo tubes and carry
up to 50 weapons—torpedoes, missiles, or up to
100 mines. It would operate an advanced combat
system that included a larger spherical sonar array,
a wide-aperture array and a new towed-array
sonar. But the end of the Cold War, and the
resultant budget constraints, meant a radical
change in Seawolf planning. Only three boats of
the class are now expected to be built: *Seawolf*,
SSN 21, which was commissioned in July 1997,
Connecticut, SSN 22, commissioned in December
1998 and *Jimmy Carter*, SSN 23, which is planned
for delivery in June 2004. The design of the latter
is being modified for improved payload carrying
capability, underwater manoeuvrability and other
features.

The Cold War requirement for the Seawolf-class
stemmed from the Navy's determination to
maintain an acoustic advantage over the Soviet
submarines. With the end of the Cold War, and the
Navy's changing emphasis to littoral (shallow water)
operations, the cost of the Seawolf submarines was
deemed prohibitive and the programme was
curtailed in favour of new, smaller and cheaper fast
attack submarines, the Virginia-class.

The redefined requirement for the Los Angeles-
class fast attack boat replacement calls for an
advanced-stealth, multi-mission nuclear-powered
submarine highly capable in both deep ocean anti-
submarine warfare and littoral operational
environments. It also has to be a smaller and less
costly package than the Seawolf-class.

To reduce the acquisition and life-cycle costs of
the Virginia-class design and engineering process, a

These machines [submarines] are made with large amounts of margin for safety. They are over-built. If you require two inches of metal thickness, we make it with four inches of metal thickness. They are made to exacting standards; they are maintained and repaired to exacting standards. The loss of the *Thresher* specifically in the mid-sixties caused the submarine force to review how it built its seawater systems and how it conducted its corrective maintenance, and that resulted in what we call the Sub-Safe programme. It resulted in braised piping systems for our seawater systems as opposed to mechanically bolting them, and in very very tight controls on the materials that we use to build parts, the manufacturing of those parts, and the control of those parts from inception to installation.

The whole Sub-Safe programme is built upon being able to go to a component on a Sub-Safe system, which are the critical systems in a submarine that are subjected to sea pressure or are associated with control surfaces on a submarine, and being able to point to a part and find the paperwork that will lead you to the manufacturer and even the batch number of the metal that was used to make that part. That's how meticulously detailed it is, and it's worked. Our Sub-Safe systems are phenomenally built, phenomenally maintained,

whole range of state-of-the-art methods are being employed. These include concurrent engineering design/build teams, computer-aided design and electronic visualization tools, system simplification, parts standardization and component elimination. These innovations help to keep the new submarine affordable in sufficient numbers to meet the Navy's future nuclear attack submarine force level need.

Electric Boat is the lead design authority for the Virginia class and is constructing the first boat of the class, *Virginia* (SSN 774) which is to commission in 2006 and the third of the class, to commission in 2008. Newport News Shipbuilding will construct the second and fourth boats of the class, which will commission in 2007 and 2009 respectively. The Navy's total requirement for the class is thirty submarines.

The Virginia-class submarine is similar in size to her Los Angeles-class predessessor, at 377 feet long and a 34-foot beam, but her submerged displacement is greater, at 7,800 tons. She is fast (28 knots dived) and has a published depth capability of 800+ feet. She comes with four 21" torpedo tubes and twelve vertical launch system tubes for Tomahawk cruise missiles. She can also deliver advanced mobile mines and unmanned undersea vehicles. Her command centre will be installed as one single unit which rests on cushioned mounting points. Her control suite is equipped with computer touch screens and her steering and diving control is via a four-button two-axis joystick.

The new sub features an Advanced Swimmer Delivery Vehicle which is a mini-submarine atop the hull for delivering special warfare forces such as SEAL teams or Marine reconnaissance units for counter-terrorism or localised conflict operations. At 65 feet in length, the ASDV is nearly twelve feet longer than the *Holland*, the US Navy's first submarine.

Acoustically, *Virginia* has about the same noise

level as that of *Seawolf* and lower than that of the Russian Improved Akula-class and fourth-generation attack submarines. This is achieved through the use of a newly designed anechoic coating, isolated deck structures and a new-design propulsor.

The Command, Control, Communications and Intelligence system of the *Virginia* integrates all of the boat systems (sensors, navigation, weapon control and countermeasures). The vertical launch system is capable of firing sixteen Tomahawk cruise missiles in a single salvo. A 3500-pound Tomahawk can deliver 1000 pounds of high explosive within inches of its target over a distance of 1500 miles. Capacity for 26 Mk 48 heavyweight ADCAP torpedoes and Sub Harpoon anti-ship

missiles is provided. The Mk 48 can bring 650-pounds of high explosive a distance of more than five miles. Mk 60 CAPTOR mines may also be carried.

Virginia-class sensors include bow-mounted active and passive array, wide aperture passive array on flank, high-frequency active arrays on keel and fin, and towed arrays. Her propulsion unit is the General Electric Pressure Water Reactor S9G which is designed to last as long as the submarine itself, two turbine engines with one shaft and a pump-jet propulsor. The reactor will not need refuelling during the entire lifetime of the boat.

Operated by a crew of 113 officers and men, the military performance of the Virginia-class submarine is at least comparable to that of *Seawolf* and is significantly better in littoral warfare operation, at considerably less cost. *Virginia* is stealthier than *Seawolf* and, according to the US Navy, surpasses the performance of any current projected threat submarine, ensuring US undersea dominance well into the next century.

The Royal Naval Base at Faslane, Scotland is home to Britain's four Vanguard-class SSBNs, the largest submarines ever built in the United Kingdom. The Vanguard vessels displace 15,900 tons submerged, twice that of the Resolution-class subs that they replaced. The Vanguards were constructed by Vickers Shipbuilding at Barrow-in-Furness. HMS *Vanguard*, the first of the class, was commissioned in 1993 and was followed in 1995 by HMS *Victorious*, in 1996 by HMS *Vigilant* and in 1999 by HMS *Vengeance*. The US Navy calls their Trident subs boomers; the Royal Navy calls theirs bombers. As the construction of a massive new refit complex built specially to handle the Vanguard submarines nears completion at the Devonport Dockyard facility, Plymouth, England, the Royal Navy has announced that HMS *Vanguard*, their first Trident missile SSBN, will be arriving at the Plymouth yard in 2002.

The *Vanguard* carries sixteen Trident II (D5) submarine-launched ballistic missiles (SLBM). The missiles are fitted with a number of multiple independently targetted re-entry vehicles (MIRVs), each armed with a destructive yield of 100 to 120 kilotons. The Trident II missile can carry up to twelve MIRVs.

Trident II is a supersonic, three-stage solid fuel missile with a range of more than 11,000 kilometres. This highly-accurate missile is ejected from the submarine by high-pressure gas. When the Trident reaches the surface, the first rocket stage fires automatically. The inertial guidance system then determines the flight behaviour and guidance characteristics. With the exhaustion and separation of the third rocket stage, a star-sighting is taken by the warhead carrier to confirm the missile's position. It then manoeuvres to the point where the warheads are released to free-fall onto the target.

Vanguard submarines are fitted with four torpedo tubes for the wire-guided Tigerfish and Spearfish torpedoes they carry. They are equipped with a very effective range of sensors and electronic warfare devices. Nuclear propulsion comes from a second-generation Rolls-Royce PWR 2 that was developed specifically for the Vanguard-class vessel. This pressurized water reactor was designed to allow the boat to circumnavigate the world forty times before needing refuelling. It produces a maximum speed of 25 knots submerged.

The front line attack submarine of the Royal Navy in 2000 is the Trafalgar-class SSN built by Vickers Shipbuilding. These boats bring a powerful threat wherever they go. They are extremely quiet and quite fast, and may well be the best attack sub Britain has ever made. The year 2000 was not a good one for the Trafalgars though. In May one of them, HMS *Tireless*, suffered a serious reactor accident while at sea. The boat put into port at Gibraltar and promptly became embroiled in

and they provide us the kind of assurance we need.
— Captain Michael King, Chief of Staff, Submarine Group Nine, US Navy

All these tidal gatherings, growth and decay
Shining and darkening are forever Renewed; and the whole cycle impenitently Revolves, and all the past is future: Make it a difficult world . . . for practical people.
— from *Practical People* by Robinson Jeffers

left: The USS *Nautilus* (SSN 571) during her sea trials off Groton, Conn. This first American nuclear sub made her maiden voyage in 1955. above: Admiral Hyman G. Rickover, champion and father of the US nuclear submarine force.

right: The forward control station of a typical US Navy nuclear-powered submarine of the Cold War era. Here are the ballast control panel and the helm and bow plane controls. It is displayed as part of the 2000 US Submarine Centennial Exhibition at the Smithsonian's National Museum of American History in Washington DC.

controversy over British plans to repair her there, much to the displeasure of the locals. Subsequent investigation of the other ships of the Trafalgar-class has revealed evidence of a similar potential fault on at least four of them. In October all the ships of the class were withdrawn from service. By mid-April 2001 the repair of *Tireless* was completed.

The Trafalgar-class nuclear attack submarine is powered by one pressurized water reactor with steam turbines driving one pumpjet propulsor producing 15,000 horsepower. The top speed is 30 knots submerged and the displacement is 5208 tons submerged. The length is 280 feet with a beam of 32 feet and a draught of 27 feet. Her armament consists of five torpedo tubes and an arsenal of 25 weapons.

Intended to enter service in 2006, the Royal Navy's newest submarine is the Astute SSN. The first of an initial order of three is HMS *Astute* which was to begin construction in January 2001. Her first sister ships will be HMS *Ambush* and HMS *Artful*. Their power will come from the Rolls-Royce PWR 2 second generation nuclear reactor (originally developed for the Vanguard-class Trident submarines), two GEC turbines and a single shaft with a pumpjet propulsor. There will also be two diesel alternators as well as one emergency drive motor and one auxiliary retractable propeller. They will have a digital, integrated control and instrumentation system for steering, diving, depth control and platform management. There is capacity for a total of 38 torpedoes and missiles. It is expected that the wire-guided Spearfish torpedo will be used on the Astute boats, which will also be equipped with the Tomahawk Block III cruise missile, and the Submarine Harpoon missile. Astute-class boats will be manned by a crew of 98. The hull will be 298 feet long with a beam of 34 feet, a draught of 32 feet and a displacement of 7200 tons submerged. The top speed will be 32 knots dived. The Astute-class subs will replace the ageing Swiftsure-class vessels as they near the end of their operational service.

At the time of the keel-laying of the initial Astute-class submarine in late-January 2001, there was speculation in the British press about the possibility of adapting the new class of boats for the inclusion of female crew members. A Royal Navy officer, Lieutenant Debbie Hutchings, reported on a special trial in which she spent two weeks aboard HMS *Triumph*, a Trafalgar-class submarine, at the request of the Flag Officer Submarines. She indicated that she did not see gender as a problem; that it was just a question of common sense. She felt that the main problem was coping with the claustrophobic atmosphere.

The Royal Navy ban on women in submarines has been maintained primarily due to concerns about the possibly harmful effects on foetuses of pregnant submariners. According to Royal Navy sources: "There is no medical evidence to guarantee that the level of contaminants that exist in the atmosphere [aboard a submarine] will not have a damaging effect on a foetus."

The prey in a US or British fast attack submarine mission, may be a Russian fleet ballistic missile submarine, a Delta or Typhoon, and the situation may be one in which an international conflict develops, whereupon the attack sub is directed to destroy the Russian boomer before it can launch its missiles at American or British targets. Up to this point the role of the SSN has been to stalk the movements of the boomer, having "picked it up" on its departure from base on the Kola Peninsula. As a part of their NATO mission, the SSNs need to watch the activity of their Russian counterparts too, which often accompany the Russian missile subs in a guardian role. The US or British attack submarine skipper is interested in the routine operation of the Russian subs and, especially, in any variations of their operating patterns. He must conduct tracking and surveillance of both the boomer and its guardian SSN, without being detected by them. It comes down to a game of wits, silence and stealth.

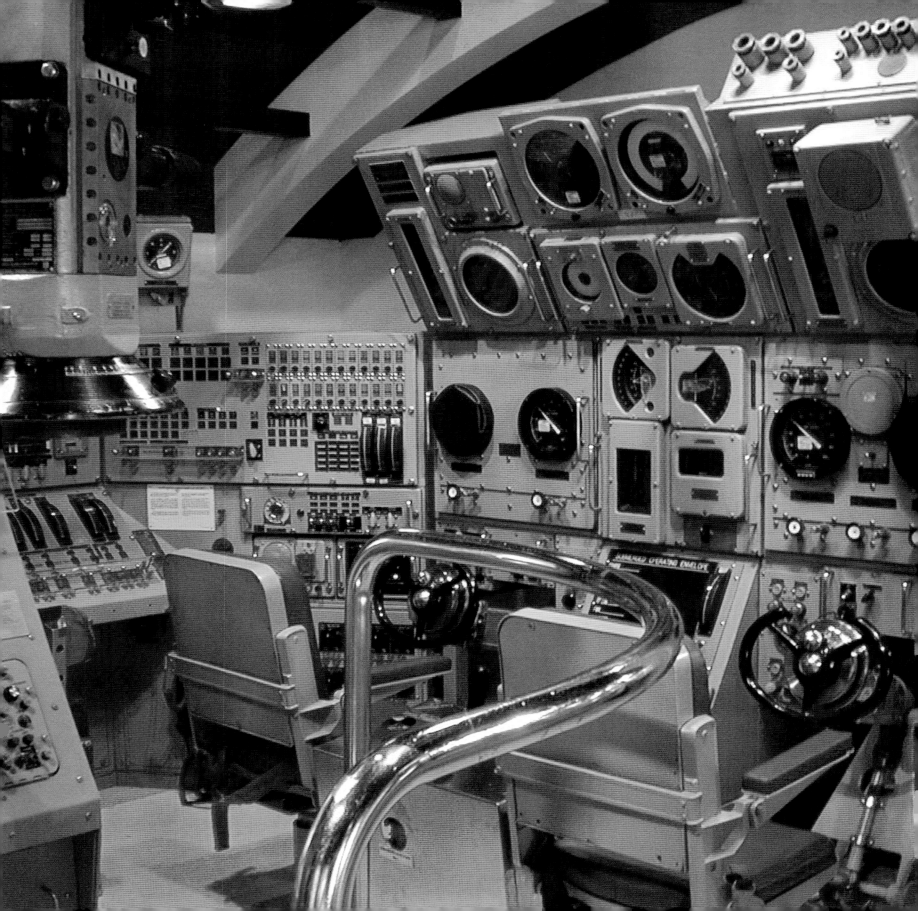

RUSSIANS AND OTHERS

Despite the most rigid checks by the Gestapo on the French shipyard workers, underground agents actually wormed their way into the yards where the U-boats were readied for their next cruises. These seeming collaborators, ostensibly working for the Germans, slipped little bags of sugar into the lubricating oil tanks and those U-boats came limping back into Lorient with their engines in sad shape. The underground agents made sound-looking welds on pressure fittings that would give way when the boat went deep. Some skippers who didn't take their boats down to maximum depth on trial runs, are on the bottom of the ocean now with their whole crews because these welds gave way under attack. Workmen drilled small holes in the tops of fuel tanks and plugged the holes with stuff that was soluble in salt water. A few days after this boat went to sea, the plug would dissolve and the boat would leave a tell-tale oil streak behind her when

ALL OF THE nuclear-powered submarines in Russia's Northern Fleet are older than the *Kursk*, whose tragic story is told in an earlier chapter, The Downside. These boats rarely go to sea any more owing to the lack of funds available to the Russian military. Many western naval experts believe this has led to shoddy and minimal maintenance, severe cost-cutting, greatly reduced training and rock-bottom crew morale; in short, other disasters waiting to happen. Some noted submarine specialists believe that, until Russia can afford to maintain her subs properly and operate them safely, her entire fleet should be shut down. Failing that, they fear that more Russian submarine accidents are inevitable.

A gigantic graveyard of decommissioned and rusting Soviet warships, the world's highest concentration of old nuclear reactors, nestles on the Kola Peninsula today. In the past ten years, 138 Russian nuclear subs have been decommissioned, many of them left to rust at Kola.

Just days before the *Kursk* sailed on her final patrol, financial constraints caused a decision to leave batteries on shore that might have provided back-up power for the doomed ship when her reactors were shut down following the accident that sent her to the bottom of the Barents Sea on 12 August 2000. It was only to be a three-day cruise and officials evidently believed that the expense involved in taking the batteries along was not justifiable, a decision that would not have found favour with the 23 crew members who survived the blasts and sought shelter in a stern compartment for their remaining hours.

When a Russian submarine returns from an exercise, it is generally believed that its arsenal of weaponry is removed and placed in ammunition storage. An unofficial report from the Northern Fleet though, indicates that the cruise missiles and torpedoes of *Kursk* were not offloaded when the boat returned to her base prior to her final sailing. Apparently, the Russian Technical Register had

banned the use of the lifting cranes normally employed in such operations because the cranes were worn out. Thus, *Kursk* was required to put to sea with armed weapons. According to one naval official: ". . . at the moment the Russian Navy operates fourteen 100-ton, and 63 40-ton cranes. Only three 100-ton and seventeen 40-ton cranes are in good order. [The]others are in need of immediate repair. As a result, loading of torpedoes and missiles cannot be conducted in the Northern Fleet." The Russian Duma immediately requested that an allotment of 516 million rubles be added to the state defence budget of 2000 for the repair of the cranes. The request was ignored.

Nearly half a century ago, few people thought much about how the nuclear reactors in the brand new submarines of the day could or would be disposed of at the end of their operational lifespan. In recent times, as many of the world's older nuclear subs reached the end of their service lives, the governments that operated them had to face the challenge of getting rid of them in a safe and environmentally acceptable manner.

In the early days of submarine reactor disposal, the United States believed that such reactors could be safely dumped at sea, and they did just that with the original powerplant of the old *Seawolf*, SSN 575. In that era the Soviet Union was using the same method to get rid of its clapped-out submarine reactors. Other examples from the world's nuclear sub fleets were simply being laid up in reserve, their reactors still in position, until a time when someone, somewhere would come up with an appropriate method of disposal. Eventually the United States developed a viable and comprehensive programme for dealing with the problem, which had gradually become a worldwide concern.

Until 1992, the US Navy was still decommissioning its nuclear subs and laying them up to await disposal. While many of them were stricken from the Naval Vessel Register, they were still kept in the reserve status. Then, at the end of 1992, the Navy started the Nuclear Powered Ship and Submarine Recycling Program (NPSSRP) at the Puget Sound (Washington) Naval Shipyard. It will ultimately include the scrapping of all discarded US nuclear-powered ships and submarines. The procedure is in two phases. The first phase involves putting the vessel in drydock, stripping it of all sensors, weapons, electronics, reusable equipment and materials, radioactive and hazardous materials, and the removal of the nuclear fuel. The work is carried out at either the Pudget Sound facility, the Portsmouth (New Hampshire) Naval Shipyard, or the Norfolk (Virginia) Naval Shipyard. In phase two, the reactor compartment is cut out of the boat and the rest of the hull is cut up. The metal is sold as scrap, unless it is excessively radioactive, in which case it is buried. The reactor compartment is then shipped to the Hanford (Washington) Reservation where it is buried. All phase two work is done at the Puget Sound facility. The US Navy nuclear submarines that were decommissioned prior to the start-up to the NPSSRP programme are being included in it as scheduling permits.

The discarded nuclear submarines of the Russian Navy are being stored in varying degrees of non-maintenance and await scrapping and the disposal of their reactors, as funding and facilities become available. The scrapping is proceeding slowly. Through an agreement with the United States, the scrapping of some of Russia's giant Typhoon-class SSBN subs is being undertaken with US aid. There were more than 100 former Soviet, and Russian submarines awaiting scrapping in the year 2000.

The United Kingdom stores several discarded SSN and SSBN nuclear subs at the Rosyth and Devonport facilities pending disposal. France is believed to have several SSBNs awaiting disposal, and India, whose nuclear subs were based on Soviet submarine designs, returns them to Russia for disposal.

At the end of 2000, the Russian Navy was operating 25 strategic nuclear submarines, 50 general purpose submarines, 80 diesel submarines and approximately 100 surface vessels. Russian Navy Headquarters is said to believe that, to ensure the country's security in the 21st century, it requires twelve strategic nuclear submarines, twenty general purpose submarines, 35 diesel subs and about 70 surface vessels. Western authorities believe that a total of 183 nuclear-powered submarines are being taken out of service in Russia's Pacific and Northern Fleets. To achieve its operational needs, the Russian Navy believes that it must get a 25 percent share of the country's defence budget. Currently, it receives between eleven and twelve percent.

Of the 25 strategic nuclear subs the Russian Navy says it is operating, five are Typhoon-class, seven are Delta IV-class, and thirteen are Delta III-class. In total, they are carrying 2272 nuclear warheads on 440 ballistic missiles. The planned operational lifetime of these submarines is twenty to twenty-five years. The youngest of the Delta IIIs is, in the year 2000, nineteen years old.

The Start-2 Treaty, which was ratified by the lower house of the Russian Parliament in 1999, specifically prohibits the use of multiple reentry vehicle missiles. Plans to extend the operational life of the Typhoons have had to be scrapped as no treaty-legal substitute for the multiple-warheaded SS-N-20 missiles, which currently arm the giant subs, is available. In July 1999, the first of the world's largest submarines arrived in the Sevmash shipyard for decommissioning, a task which is being financed by the American Cooperative Threat Reduction Program (CTR).

A new, fourth-generation submarine, the Borey-class *Uriy Dolgoruky*, is being built at Sevmash currently. Construction began in 1996, but delays due to insufficient financing make commissioning unlikely before 2010. Sevmash and Zvezdochka shipyards are both located in the city of Severodvinsk in the Arkhangelsk region. The region has established a limit of no more than 32

below: A French SSBN, the Triomphant-class submarine. bottom: A Russian Akula in port for weapons replenishment.

above right: A Russian Typhoon-class SSBN with her acoustic tiles removed, being moved by tugs into the Sevmash shipyard at Arkhangelsk. She will be dismantled under the Cooperative Threat Reduction Program. right: A rotting Russian sub awaiting final disposition.

far left: Another Russian Typhoon entering the Sevmash yard. left: A Swedish Gotland-type sub under way. below: A Russian Kilo-class diesel submarine being towed by a support vessel in the central Mediterranean Sea in 1995. She had been purchased by Iran.

reactor cores in the city's harbour at one time, but in late 2000, 44 such cores, which contain spent nuclear fuel, occupy space in the area of the shipyards. Both yards are involved in the repair and decommissioning of nuclear-powered submarines. Local politicians and environmentalists are quite concerned about the presence of the reactors. "We should not continue transforming the city into a nuclear dump, posing a threat to people's health," said Anatoly Shushkanov of the Envirocommittee, which estimates that it may take up to three years to reduce the number of reactor cores from 44 to 32.

Delta-class Russian nuclear subs, meanwhile, are slowly being decommissioned at the Nerpa shipyard on the Kola Peninsula, also under the Cooperative Threat Reduction Program. Nerpa began work decommissioning second-generation nuclear subs in 1992. The CTR support is essential to the implementation of the Start-2 agreement and the Nerpa operation appears to be well-structured and productive. Additional decommissioning of Delta-class nuclear submarines is being carried out at the Zvezda shipyard in the Russian far east. The CTR objective is to dismantle 32 Russian strategic missile submarines: one Yankee-class, 26 Deltas and five Typhoons. Contrary to the CTR plans, however, was an announcement in early November 2000 by Russian Rear-Admiral Vladimir Makeev, head of the Northern Fleet rocket test site at Nenoska, Arkhangelsk County. He stated that media reports about the Typhoons being taken out of operation were groundless, and that three of the six Typhoons will remain in active service in order to test the new Bark strategic missiles; this in contradiction of earlier reports that the Bark missiles were to be cancelled due to design failures. Russian plans seem to call for the installation of the Bark missiles in the new Borey-class strategic submarines. Thus, it now seems that three Typhoons will continue in service and have their active life extended, possibly through 2010.

The remaining three boats of the class will either be scrapped in accordance with CTR planning, or placed in reserve status. The eldest Typhoon, *TK-208*, began her service life in 1981, but has been under repair at the Sevmash yard for nine years and may now be nearing a return to operations.

The massive and formidable Typhoon-class SSBN submarine displaces 26,500 tons submerged. Fully loaded, she displaces 48,000 tons submerged. She is the largest submarine ever built and is manned by a crew of 160. Powered by two nuclear PWR reactors and two turbogear assemblies, she is 562 feet long with a beam of 80 feet and a draught of 42 feet. She can run surfaced at 12 knots and make 25 knots submerged. Typhoon's armament consists of twenty launchers with RSM-52 ballistic missiles and twenty anti-submarine missiles and torpedoes which can be launched from six tubes. Maximum diving depth is believed to be 1200 feet and her sea endurance is 120 days.

Armed with eight torpedo tubes, twelve cruise missiles and a mix of Mk 40 torpedoes, Stallion and Starfish missiles, the Akula-class SSN nuclear attack sub has a crew of 73 and an at-sea endurance of 100 days. Her maximum diving depth is reported to be in excess of 1800 feet. She can run at a surface speed of 10 knots and up to 33 knots submerged. Her displacement when fully-loaded and submerged is 12,770 tons.

The Oscar II-class submarines, including *Kursk*, were designed specifically to attack the NATO aircraft carrier battle groups, mainly with cruise missiles. When submerged the Oscar displaces 14,000 tons. It is powered by two nuclear PWR, two turbines and two shafts. With unlimited range, this submarine can run at 22 knots on the surface and 30 knots when submerged. The armament consists of eight torpedo tubes and 24 Ganit anti-ship cruise missiles.

Key in the Russian submarine inventory are the Delta-class SSBNs, in particular the Delta IV-class, largest of the Delta boats. The Delta IV is the newest of the type and is based with the Northern Fleet at

Saida Guba, and at Rybachy in the Pacific. The Delta IV is 547 feet long and has a fully-loaded submerged displacement of 18,200 tons. This large submarine's power comes from two water reactors, two turbines and two propellers. Her maximum diving depth is at least 1300 feet and she can run on the surface at 14 knots and 24 knots when she is submerged. She carries a crew of 135 and has an at-sea endurance of 80 days.

Since 1949 when the Communists gained power in China under the leadership of Mao Tse-Tung, they have been determined to build a powerful naval force with submarines as a key component. Their priorities include control of the seas bordering China's coasts, regaining control of Taiwan from the Nationalists who took refuge there and, not least, establishing China as a Great Power.

The Chinese Navy is steadily bringing its submarine fleet up to modern standards after decades of being saddled with obsolete Romeo- and Ming-class boats. While adding Russian Kilo-class vessels, as well as the indigenous Song-class boats to the inventory, the Chinese are at work on their next generation fast attack and missile subs as they continue their nuclear submarine fleet development. It appears that their interest in developing a powerful blue water submarine force continues, as does their war of nerves with Taiwan, providing ample motivation for China's stepped-up naval modernisation.

At present the majority of the Chinese submarine force is obsolete, but this is changing rapidly. Her current inventory is believed to consist of four or five Han-class nuclear attack submarines, one or two Xia-class nuclear ballistic missile subs, two Song-class cruise subs (with two or three more being built) and two exceptionally quiet Kilo-class boats (with twelve more being built).

Based on the design of the USS *Albacore*, but without much of the high-technology of the American and British attack submarines, the Han-class attack boats represent the Chinese Navy's great leap forward from their previous submarine design and performance level. The Han subs were developed in the 1970s as a relatively spartan version of the attack submarine concept and have been the basis for China's modern submarine evolution leading to the Xia-class nuclear ballistic missile sub. Operated by a crew of 120, the Han displaces slightly over 5000 tons submerged; is armed with six torpedo tubes and is powered by a single-screw, pressurized water nuclear reactor. With unlimited range, the Han has a maximum surface speed of 20 knots and a submerged top of 28 knots.

Similar to the Russian Yankee II missile sub, the Xia-class boat is the first nuclear ballistic missile submarine of the People's Republic of China. With a crew of 140, and a submerged displacement of 6500 tons, the Xia is armed with six torpedo tubes and twelve SLBMs. Her power comes from a PWR with a single-shaft turbo-electric drive. With unlimited range, Xia can cruise submerged at a top rate of 22 knots.

China's Kilo-class diesel-electric submarines are a Russian design dating from 1980. The rather small boats have the western-style 'teardrop' hull displacing 3143 tons submerged. They carry a crew of between 45 and 50 and have a 6000 nautical mile range at a 7-knot cruise speed. The surface top is 15 knots with a maximum 24-knot submerged speed. The armament is six torpedo tubes.

India apparently plans a future fleet to dominate the Indian Ocean. It is based around two carrier groups with a total force of 125 ships and at least 24 submarines. She is establishing a submarine-construction capability at Bombay and an SSN programme is under way with the first keel expected to be laid by 2005. The design is believed to be based on the Russian Charlie I class boat. Additionally, India's new nuclear triad doctrine may include nuclear-tipped cruise missiles to be

A sampling of names given to British submarines over the years, these being the S-class:
Safari, Saga, Sahib, Salmon, Sanguine, Saracen, Satyr, Sceptre, Scorcher, Scotsman, Scythian, Sea Devil, Sea Nymph, Sea Rover, Sea Scout, Sea Wolf, Sea Dog, Sea Horse, Seal, Sealion, Selene, Senechal, Sentinel, Seraph, Severn, Shakespeare, Shalimar, Shark, Shrimp, Sibyl, Sickle, Sidon, Simoom, Sirdar, Sleuth, Snapper, Solent, Sovereign, Spark, Spearfish, Spearhead, Spirit, Spiteful, Splendid, Sportsman, Sprat, Springer, Spur, Starfish, Statesman, Stickleback, Stoic, Stonehenge, Storm, Stratagem, Strongbow, Stubborn, Sturdy, Sturgeon, Stygian, Subtle, Sunfish, Superb, Supreme, Surf, Swordfish, Swiftsure, Syrtis.

Views of the Soviet Foxtrot-class hunter killer sub *Scorpion* (B-427) now on display next to the *Queen Mary* at Long Beach, California. *Scorpion* operated in the Soviet Pacific Fleet from 1972 to 1994. Displacing 2475 tons submerged, she had a 20,000-mile surface range; 11,000 miles snorting. She did 16 knots surfaced and 15 knots submerged. She went to sea with a load of ten torpedoes, a 78-man crew, three toilets and two showers.

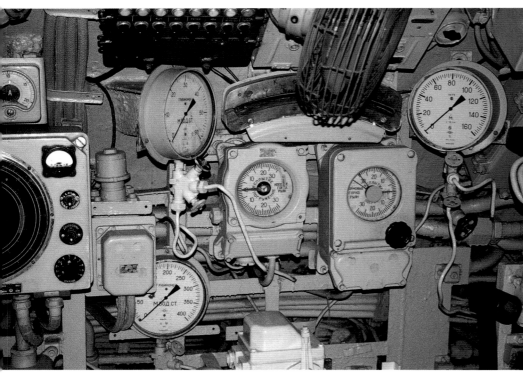

fitted to modified Kilo-class SSK subs. She is strengthening her fleet with the likely addition of more aircraft carriers, strategic maritime bombers, cruise missiles, the aforementioned SSN programme and probably an SSBN force as well.

The submarine force of North Korea is comprised mainly of ex-USSR Whiskey- and Romeo-class boats. They appear to have placed more emphasis on their air force and missile programmes in recent years than on their Navy. South Korea operates a smaller force of submarines and seems intent on maintaining it as such, while emphasizing the development of her frigate and destroyer force. She does not seem particularly interested in being, or being perceived as, a substantial naval power in the region.

Locked in a very uneven arms race with her arch foe India, Pakistan cannot afford the level of

The London *Sunday Times* reported on 18 June 2000 that Israel had test-fired domestically-produced cruise missiles from its newly acquired Dolphin-class submarine off Sri Lanka in May. The US National Air Intelligence Center warned the US Congress in July 1998 that Israel was developing a cruise missile—believed to be the Raphael-produced Popeye Turbo missile— with a range of 215 miles that was expected to be operational by 2002. Although the Popeye Turbo is promoted as an air-launched weapon, it may be adapted for submarine launch.

Number One, this is quite a moment. We have never seen the enemy before. They don't look very different from us, do they? – from *The Cruel Sea* by Nicholas Monsarrat

There is a phenomenon in underwater propulsion called supercavitation. As the hull of a vessel moves through water, friction creates drag, slowing the ship. Streamlined hull design and increased engine power can only do so much to counteract the effect of the drag. But scientists now believe there is a new way of defeating the effect of this drag.

When an object, such as a torpedo, can be made to move through water at speeds greater than 50 metres per second, the supercavitation effect comes into play. When this occurs, the movement of the object causes the pressure of the surrounding water to greatly decrease; enough for the water molecules to separate from each other and become a gas. The gas bubble, or cavity, formed at this point, trails behind the object like the wake of a boat. At speeds approaching 3000 mph, the cavity surrounds the object, closes up and becomes a supercavity. The development of such

defence expenditure that India is committed to. India is currently on a $10.5 billion USD defence budget, which is increasing. Pakistan is unlikely to be able to increase her spending in that area beyond the current $3.75 billion USD. Her naval force is based mainly on frigates, patrol boats and submarines, including the French SSK Agosta 90B type. She will probably maintain and upgrade her navy on a relatively modest scale.

Singapore may not normally spring to mind as a significant sea power, but her near-term purchase of three Challenger-class SSK submarines (ex-Swedish *Sjoormen*) may well signal the start of something important. The 1960s-era *Sjoormen* boats resemble the US Navy Albacore hull design built for speed, manoeuvrability and silent-running capability. Upgraded in the 1980s with new Ericsson combat data/fire control systems, they are effective as offensive anti-submarine hunter-killer vessels, with a surface speed of 15 knots and a submerged top speed of 20 knots. The armament is six torpedo tubes. As recently as 1997 Singapore was budgetting approximately $4 billion USD for defence and an extensive army and air force modernization programme is under way there currently. With some of her neighbours deploying a variety of large warships of formidable capability, Singapore may well elect to place new emphasis on naval procurement, especially submarines.

The mission of the Taiwanese Navy is to defend Taiwan and the offshore islands of Quemoy, Tachen and Matsu from invasion or attack by sea. With a reasonably effective surface fleet, and the on-going threat from China, Taiwan seems a likely candidate for developing a more substantial submarine force beyond the two Hai Lung-class subs she purchased from the Netherlands in the 1980s. Taiwan wants to purchase up to eight diesel submarines from the Americans and, in late April

2000, US President George W. Bush agreed to the sale as part of a larger arms package. The Dutch diesel-electric Hai Lungs were modified Zwaardvis-class vessels that had been based on the American Barbel-class submarine. China had vigorously protested their sale to Taiwan, so much, in fact, that a Taiwanese order for two additional Hai Lung subs was quashed by the Dutch government. China was equally insistent that the US not provide the new weaponry to Taiwan.

In the last financial year Japan spent $43.5 billion USD on defence despite the recent financial hiccups experienced there and elsewhere in Asia. The expenditure is more than seven times that of Australia, for example. It seems probable that Japan, through its Japanese Maritime Self Defense Force, will become more pro-active in the region, in part to help ease the American military burden there. With significant expansion of her naval capability in general, Japan, along with China and India, is becoming a sizeable naval power in Asia with the potential ability to project that power beyond the local area. In submarines, Japan is on course with her front line Oyashio-class programme of five boats. Construction is shared between the Kawasaki and Mitsubishi yards at Kobe. The fifth boat of the class is to commission in March 2002. Operated by a crew of 69 the Oyashio subs have a submerged displacement of 3000 tons and are powered by a single shaft, diesel-electric system. The surface speed capability is 12 knots and submerged performance is 20 knots. The armament is six torpedo tubes as well as Sub Harpoon SSMs.

Australian interest in the use of submarines in naval defence began with her development of a submarine component in 1913. Her involvement with the vessels was relatively minimal until the 1960s when she purchased six Oxley (Oberon) class subs from Britain, which have since been modernized to dramatically extend their service lives.

Designed by the Swedish shipbuilders, Kockums, for the Royal Australian Navy, the Collins-class SSK (Type 471) is a diesel-electric submarine built in Adelaide, South Australia, although some structural components have been produced in Sweden. There are six boats in the Collins class, the first being HMAS *Collins* which was commissioned in 1996. These submarines have been the subject of considerable controversy and a June 1999 government report identified a number of shortcomings in the type relating to the diesel engines, noise, the propellers, periscopes, masts and the combat system. Since publication of the report, the Australian Ministry of Defence has announced plans to upgrade two of the Collins subs, HMAS *Dechaineux* and *Sheean*. The weapons systems are to be upgraded, there will be improvements to the sonar system and the combat system, the tactical data handling system and weapons control system, and operational fixes to reduce the acoustic signature. Completion of these modifications is to coincide with the retirement of Australia's last Oxley-class submarines in 2001. A new combat system is being planned for future use in the Collins boats.

The Collins-class submarine can carry up to 22 Sub Harpoon missiles and torpedoes, or up to 44 mines in place of torpedoes. Crew for the type is 42 including six officers. The dived displacement is 3350 tons. Performance is 10 knots surfaced and 20 knots submerged and the range is 11,500 miles at 10 knots surfaced. The Collins hull is 253 feet long with a beam of 26 feet.

According to the government report on the vessels: "The Collins class submarines are well designed for Australia's special requirements and have generally been soundly built. They are, however, bedevilled by a myriad of design deficiencies, many of which should not have occurred, and most of which are taking far too long to remedy. Together, they are seriously restricting the operational usefulness of the boats. Apparently sensible remedies for nearly all defects have been presented to us, which gives us confidence in the ultimate performance of the boats. The main issue is to improve the managerial and contractual structures so that the deficiencies are addressed much more quickly and robustly."

Prior to the beginning of World War II, France saw her navy as the defender of her colonial territories, protector of her trade routes and a partner with the British in English Channel, North Sea, Atlantic and Mediterranean operations. In the late 1950s President de Gaulle decided to create an independent nuclear deterrent capability for the country and committed the largest share of his arms expenditure to a sea-based delivery system. France then became the only major nation to develop a ballistic missile submarine as her first nuclear-powered sub—a huge, complex, demanding and expensive challenge to her industry.

Today the French Navy operates the Triomphant-class ballistic missile nuclear-powered submarine (SSBN). *Le Triomphant,* S616, is the first of the class and entered service in 1997, followed in January 2000 by *Le Temeraire,* S617. *Le Vigilant,* S618, is under construction and due to enter service in 2004, while a fourth such vessel is planned for commissioning in 2008.

Triomphant-class boats carry the M45 ballistic missile, a three-stage solid-fuel rocket of hypersonic speed. It lifts a thermonuclear warhead with six multiple re-entry vehicles over a range of 6000 km. For surface-to-surface attack, the submarine utilises the SM39 Exocet missile which is launched in a capsule from the torpedo tubes. It is propelled away from the sub and clear of the sea surface by a solid-fuel motor; it then separates from the capsule and flies to the target on a booster motor just above sea level.

supersonic torpedoes is the goal of scientists in America and, it is believed, Russia. These supercavitating weapons would be fitted with nuclear warheads and travel so quickly that they would reach their targets before the enemy could react.

At the start of the 21st century, research is being conducted in the United States by Lockheed Martin, Florida State and Pennsylvania State universities, under the direction of the US Office of Naval Research, into the possibility of developing small, supercavitating projectile weapons.

Some western experts believe that Russia may be well along in her effort to develop supercavitating weapons. The magazine *Scientific American* has reported that Russia has already developed a 27-foot-long rocket-powered torpedo called *Shkval* (Squall), which she may have sold to China and Iran. Equally fascinating is the rumour that Russia is working on a super-cavitating submarine.

above: Lieutenant-Commander Greg Sammut, CO of the Australian Collins-class submarine HMAS *Farncomb* which sank the old destroyer-escort *Torrens* in a trial of her Mk 48 torpedoes. right: Other views of the *Farncomb*.

above: A sequence showing the awesome power of the Mk 48 war-shot torpedo fired at the destroyer-escort *Torrens*. The plume of water rose 150 metres as the blast cut the old ship in two. *Farncomb* was over the horizon and submerged when she fired the torpedo.

In June 2001, Russia's newest submarine, the *Gephardt*, left the Sevmash construction yard near Archangel to begin her sea trials prior to deployment with the Northern Fleet. Her significance lies in the claim that she is the quietest and most undetectable submarine in the world. The Russians say that the Akula 2-class sub cannot be detected from beyond a distance of seven miles by even the most sophisticated listening devices of the US and Royal navies. They claim that the *Gephardt* surpasses her US counterpart, the Los Angeles-class fast attack submarine, in quietness, speed, firepower and maximum diving depth. Western experts consider the *Gephardt* to be more the result of espionage than of Russian technical achievement, as important aspects of her technology were stolen in the 1980s by KGB moles in the US Navy.

The disasters of the world are due to its inhabitants not being able to grow old simultaneously. There is always a raw and intolerant nation eager to destroy the tolerant and mellow.
– from *The Unquiet Grave* by Cyril Connolly

The submarine is powered by a pressurized water reactor driving a turbo-electric propulsion system. It has an auxiliary diesel-electric propulsion system as well. The submerged speed of the submarine is in excess of 25 knots with a surface speed of 20 knots. She can dive to a depth in excess of 975 feet. Her submerged displacement is 14,120 tons and her endurance is 60+ days. The crew is 110.

The primary attack submarine of the French Navy is the SSN Rubis Amethyste-class, six of which are operated from the Toulon naval base. They are nuclear-powered and can carry a mix of fourteen missiles and torpedoes for anti-surface and anti-submarine warfare. The dived speed of this boat is 25 knots. A derivative of the Rubis Amethyste-class is the Turquoise SSK which has been developed for export. It is capable of anti-surface and anti-submarine missions, as well as mine-laying, intelligence gathering and commando landing and recovery operations. Endurance is 60+ days.

A new attack submarine developed by France is the SSK Agosta 90B class, currently serving with the French, Spanish and Pakistani navies. Operated by a crew of only 36, the Agosta is highly automated. She can dive to 1100+ feet and has a range of 10,000 nautical miles. Agosta is armed with torpedo tube-launched Exocet SM39 missiles as well as wire-guided torpedoes.

Israel has acquired three German Dolphin-class submarines for operation in the Mediterranean, primarily in interdiction, surveillance and special operations roles. They are replacing her Gal-class subs which have been in service since 1977. The first two Dolphins were partially financed by the Germans and Israel has financed the third, *Tekuma*. According to *Jane's International Defense Review*, September 1999, Israel plans to fit Dolphins with a nuclear land-attack capability using a modified US Sub-Harpoon missile with a newly-developed nuclear warhead and guidance kit. Each Dolphin is believed to be able to carry five modified Sub-

Harpoons, with a range of 80 miles, as well as 16 torpedoes.

Israel's interest in land missiles was highlighted in March 2000 when Washington rejected her request to purchase 50 Tomahawk land-attack cruise missiles to enhance her deep-strike capabilities under her wide-ranging strategic defence programme. Shortly after the rejection, an Israeli official was quoted as saying, "History has taught us that we cannot wait indefinitely for Washington to satisfy our military requirements. If this weapon system is denied to us, we will have little choice but to activate our own defence industry in pursuit of this needed capability." The creation by Israel of her own submarine-launched nuclear-tipped cruise missiles would mean a major step-up in her nuclear capability and tip the balance of power further in her favour. Her concern is that the Middle East crisis situation has the potential to pull in surrounding Arab nations and blow up into a regional war.

The Dolphin submarines have been designed by a subsidiary of Howaldtswerke-Deutsche Werft AG (HDW) of Lubeck, Germany. Construction was at Kiel and Emden. The first Dolphin boat was launched in 1996, the second in 1998 and the third was intended to enter service in 2000. Their weaponry is up to sixteen surface-to-surface Harpoon missiles or torpedoes. They have ten bow tubes and can also be armed with mines and have a wet-and-dry compartment for deploying underwater swimmers.

Power is supplied by three diesel engines, three alternators and a Siemens 2.85 MW sustained power motor. They are operated by a crew of 30, and are 186 feet long with a beam of 22 feet. Their dived speed is 20 knots and they have a surface range at 8 knots of 8000 miles. Their dive depth is 1100+ feet with endurance of 30 days.

Commissioned over the period 1996-97, Sweden's three SSK Gotland-class submarines are diesel-powered boats of 1490 tons dived displacement. As a neutral nation, Sweden is mainly interested in keeping foreign submarines out of her local seas, and the protection of her neutrality. The design specifications of the Gotland sub are tailored to that role. With a length of 200 a 20-foot beam, the Gotland carries a crew of 33 including five officers. The power is provided by two MTU diesels and two Kockums V4-275R Stirling Air Independent Propulsion systems. The surface speed is 11 knots and the submerged speed is 20 knots. They have six torpedo tubes and can carry up to sixteen of the new Torpedo 2000 weapon.

With the largest population in the southern hemisphere, Brazil maintains a big military capability. At the beginning of the 20th century she was wealthy from her control of the world's coffee and rubber supplies, and was ambitious to become a world power through the development of her navy. A decade later her economy collapsed, as did her designs on power. In World War II, she operated four submarines in her home waters on the side of the Allies. Her interest in submarines reignited in the 1970s with a new fleet expansion programme. She now has subs designed by Howaldtswerke-Deutsche Werft. By 2002 the Brazilian Navy will operate four Tupi-class and two Improved Tupi-class subs. The Improved Tupi can carry sixteen torpedoes including the British BAE Systems Mark 24 Tigerfish Mod 1 or Mod 27. The wire-guided Tigerfish has an acoustic seeker in the nose. Data is downloaded from the submarine weapon control station to the torpedo's onboard computer. As the torpedo nears the target a magnetic proximity fuse and an impact fuse detonate the warhead. The weapon achieves 25 knots in the passive mode and between 35 and 50 knots in the active-seeker mode. Tupis are powered by four MTU diesel engines, four Siemens alternators and a Siemens 3.4 MW motor. The surface speed is 10+ knots and the submerged

speed is 24 knots. The Improved Tupi will have an 11,000-mile range at a surface speed of 8 knots. The crew numbers 40 and the dived displacement is 2425 tons.

Designed specifically for operation in the Baltic, the North Sea and the Mediterranean, the U212 is the principal new submarine under construction for the German and Italian navies. The German Navy, with primary patrolling duties for NATO in the Baltic and North Sea, has four of the vessels on order with the first to be commissioned in 2003. Two U212 subs are being built for the Italians by Fincantieri. The first of these is expected to commission in 2005. They will be homeported at Taranto, site of the historic World War II attack by Royal Navy Swordfish torpedo/bomber aircraft on warships of the Italian fleet in November 1940.
  With a crew of 27, the new boat has a range of 8000 miles at 8 knots surfaced. Her performance will be 12 knots surfaced with 20 knots dived. The dived displacement is 1830 tons; propulsion is diesel/electric. Her weapons include 24 torpedoes from six tubes. An advanced submarine class called the U214 is also under development. It will have increased diving depth (1300+ feet), greater overall performance, better stealth characteristics, low frequency detection sonar and an integrated torpedo countermeasures system. The range will be 12,000 nautical miles; the mission endurance twelve weeks.

It took an eight-year war and the intervention of the British, French and Russian navies at the Battle of Navarino in October 1827, to defeat the Turkish-Egyptian fleet and bring Greece independence from the Turkish Ottoman Empire. The Greek Navy has kept a watchful eye on Turkey ever since.
  In their recent submarine upgrading programme, three of the German Type 214 boats have been ordered by the Greek Navy with the initial delivery scheduled for 2006.

top: A Russian Yankee 10 under way. above: A Yankee 10 shown being scrapped.

SSN 645
JAMES K. POLK

USS SUNFISH
SSN 649

SSN 660
USS SAND LANCE

USS NEVADA
SSBN 733
SILENT SENTRY

USS LOUISVILLE
SSN 724
Best of the Breed

U
TRE
SSN

grayling
646

USS POGY
FROM YESTERDAY
TO TOMORROW
SSN 647
NO KA OI

USS FINBACK
SSN - 670

USS
SSN

USS SPADEFISH
SSN 668

SPIRIT OF 76
USS BILLFISH SSN6761

USS PINTADO
ALMASPINTADO

USS ALBUQUERQUE
SILENTUM EXCUBITOR
SSN 706

SSN 678
USS ARCHERFISH

**A SELECTION
OF US NAVY
SUBMARINE
PATCHES**

U.S.S. WILLIAM H. BATES
SSN 680
A SPIRIT UNQUELL'D

UNITED STATES SHIP BOSTON
FREEDOM'S BIRTHPLACE
SSN - 703

USS Minneapolis
Saint Paul
SSN 708

BATFISH
SSN 681

U.S.S. SSN 282

USS
LOS ANGELES
SSN 688

SSBN 737

DEPLOYMENT

THE NAVY EXPECTS both nothing and everything of its wives. In the summer of 1998 Tami Calhoun, the wife of a US Navy submariner, Sonar Technician First-Class Willis Calhoun, learned that her husband was going to be re-assigned from his shore job to sea duty on one of the Navy's fast attack submarines. Knowing of the stresses associated with being the wife of a submariner who is away on six-month deployment, she searched the internet for a submarine wives support group. There were none, so Tami started the Submarine Wives Club. By the end of 2000 it had more than 300 members. The Club also welcomes the girlfriends of submariners and includes women whose men serve in the navies of other nations, including Canada, the United Kingdom and Australia. "As long as their husband or boyfriend is on a submarine, they're more than welcome to join us." The website is www.submarinewivesclub.org.

Tami spends at least twenty hours a week answering e-mails, updating information on the site and processing new memberships which are coming in at the rate of about twenty a week. "It's a lot easier to get through a deployment if there are other people you can talk to, people who are going through the same thing you're going through," she says. The Club website fills a vital need in helping to prepare women for life as the wives of submariners, an experience that can be quite demanding and rather strange. Navy wives have to cope with some unfamiliar issues owing to the extended nature of their husband's "business trips". Such issues are exacerbated by the routine of submarining which involves highly-classified missions where the boats virtually disappear and can be out of contact for months at a time. According to Tami, "Most surface ships have e-mail these days and most of the wives know where their husbands are most of the time. With submarines, you might not know where your husband has been until he comes home." She offers her webpage as "a

support group for wives, girlfriends and family members of all submariners, past, present and future. Share your thoughts, vent your anger or ask for help. We are all in the same 'boat' and are here to offer support and advice. It lets the other wives know they're not the only ones going through it [depression, anxiety and anger at being left alone], that it's a normal thing to feel that way when their husbands leave."

Among the many Submarine Wives Club website items of specific interest and importance to the family members of submariners are: information on ombudsmen, bulletin boards, advice on helping children to remember daddy, submarine pictures that can be downloaded for kids to colour, discussion groups for girlfriends, fiancées and wives of retired submariners, a book club, feedback surveys, and links to hundreds of official and unofficial Navy sites. Most importantly, there are diaries of how other wives have gotten through deployments.

The wife of a submariner shares some of the journal she kept of her husband's deployment.
19 MAY 2000 "My husband will be deploying soon and I find myself feeling a little 'odd'. This will be my first deployment. I'm not sure what to expect. I don't really feel any anxiety right now but I am sure I will once we get a little bit closer to his departure date.

"I think maybe I am starting at the Detachment stage. I feel kind of indifferent. I 'know' I will be upset when he leaves but I don't feel that way now. I just want to enjoy the time I have with him while he is still here. I can feel myself pulling away from him just a little bit. I don't think he has noticed because I am trying to be my usual self. I don't want him to worry about me and the kids. I want him to believe that I will be fully capable of taking care of everything while he is gone. I want to believe that too.

"I start thinking about how long six months is and

The wives and girls they watch in the rain / For a ship as won't come home again.
"I reckon it's them head-winds," they say. / "She'll be home to-morrow, if not to-day. / I'll just nip home 'n I'll air the sheets / 'N' buy the fixins 'n' cook the meats As my man likes 'n' as my man eats."
– from *The Yarn of the Loch Achray*
by John Masefield

right: Familes and loved ones of the attack submarine USS *Groton* await her arrival at New London, Conn. in 1980.

below: Ed might catch a glimpse of his girl and the sign she is holding, if the television camera in the search periscope of his submarine focuses on her as they depart the Ballast Point US Naval Submarine Base at San Diego.

that scares me. When my daughter turned six months old, I said to my husband, 'Do you realize you will be gone for as long as she is old?' and he just chuckled. I was being serious.

"And he has his own fears. He is afraid I may find someone else to fill his shoes while he is gone. I reassure him the best I can. I don't want anyone else. He is the only one for me. I don't think six months is too long to wait for the man that you love . . . in our beginning, I waited even longer for him than that."

27 MAY 2000 "I had the most incredible week with my husband and this weekend looks to be very promising also. I think we are at that stage where we want to spend as much time together as possible. I think we should be like this regardless of the upcoming deployment.

"Earlier in the week I started feeling stressed about him leaving. I am going to miss him so much. We have such a good time together that the thought of him not being here is upsetting to say the least. I think he knew what I was going through and we had a long talk. He is always very straightforward with me so there are no surprises. He wanted me to know what he expected from me while he was gone and what I could expect from him. We discussed our budget and all of that other boring stuff. But most of all, we shared our feelings. We let each other know that the other would be missed. I understand how busy he is going to be but I just wanted to know that he would take time out of his day to think about us."

3 JUNE 2000 "It's starting to hit me! I have had a couple of really bad days because I can't get the thought of six months out of my head. Six months, six months, six months. Ahhhhhhhhhh.

"I feel like I just want to cry and cry on his shoulder but I think I am afraid to. I am trying to put on this 'brave face' for him and the kids but I need to get this out. I don't want him to say, 'You know I have to go.' That isn't what this is about for me. I do know that he has to go. I just need

his comfort."

7 JUNE 2000 "I'm scared. I don't know what I am going to do without him. I will get up every morning and get on with life but a big part of it will be missing. A part of me says I can't stop living when he is gone but moving on without him is a scary notion. It scares him too. He thinks that I may realize I don't need him anymore. I don't think that will happen.

"I am trying to stay positive. I know I have some really great friends I can turn to when I need them. It will make life a whole lot easier."

16 JUNE 2000 "Well, my Deployment Day came and went and I am still alive. When I woke up this morning, the birds were still singing and the sun was still shining. I survived my first day without him!

"It was a nice send-off, if there is such a thing. It was sad to see him go but I know he had to go and I can deal with that.

"The last several days were GREAT! We spent as much time together as we possibly could and we grew very close once again. Now, I have to deal with life without him. My first encounter . . . the light bulb in my kitchen blew out and my first thought was that he can fix it when he comes home and then I remembered he wasn't coming home any time soon. It may seem like a simple thing but I have never changed the light bulb in the kitchen. Do I have to unscrew the light fixture? Where are the light bulbs anyway? After looking around I did find some but they weren't the right kind. What are the right kind anyway? I guess I will find out when I take the old ones out. I suppose I need to buy more light bulbs since they blow so fast in these houses. What does tomorrow hold?"

22 JULY 2000 "Wow . . . I can't believe a month has gone by already. Time has just flown.

"His first port call was short but we talked every day that he didn't have duty. It was really nice talking to him. He seemed to be sadder than I was. He reminded me that I am the lucky one. I just have one person to say goodbye to while he has four very important people to say goodbye to. Missing the kids is just tearing him up.

"I got a really nice letter from him today that he sent while he was in port. I really do miss him but we are functioning without him. I kind of feel guilty about that. I am sad without him because a part of me is missing but I don't sit around and think about it all day long and cry over it. I have too much to do. I have to make sure my family is taken care of. I can't let the children see me upset or it will make them upset.

"So far, the kids are taking it pretty well. They are still young but they know where he is and what he is doing. They seem to understand that he has a very important job to do and when the job is done Daddy will be able to come home. We have had a couple of rough moments with our oldest daughter but I helped her through it. I let her know that Daddy is missing her just as much as she misses him. I told her that Daddy gave me some very special hugs and kisses to give her whenever she feels sad and all she has to do is ask me for them. She has asked for her 'special hugs and kisses' a few times. Makes her feel so much better."

24 JULY 2000 "I was able to talk to my husband today but only for a few minutes. They had an unexpected port call and I got a surprise phone call. I was very disappointed that I only got to talk to him for a very short time. I had so much I wanted to say to him. I guess I did get to tell him the important things like I love him and I miss him. I am trying to think of it as a positive thing but I'm not sure it didn't make things worse for me. I was doing really well until this morning. It has just thrown off my whole day. I feel blessed that I was able to hear his voice and he was able to tell me that he loves me and misses me but . . . I just don't know."

22 SEPTEMBER 2000 "We hit Halfway last week. That definitely feels great to know that we are halfway

done with this deployment. Three more months still feels like a very long time though.

"I've had lots of emails, letters and phone calls from my husband, which has been great. I don't feel as bad saying goodbye to him each time like I did the first time. He seems to be more sad than I am. Maybe I just have so much to do that I don't have time to be sad.

"I have already started to get ready for homecoming. I ordered some new lingerie—by his request. The kids and I are talking about what kind of banners we want to do for him. My husband and I have talked about what to expect when he gets home . . . one thing is for certain, I will be driving and we more than likely will be having pizza for dinner. He doesn't want to wait for me to cook dinner. I am also trying not to get too excited about our homecoming night because more than likely our kids will end up in bed with us. Won't that be romantic!

"I have learned a lot of things so far. Patience, patience, patience. I have to be patient with the kids, with the Navy and with all of the other stuff going on in my life. I have also realized how deep our love is."

28 SEPTEMBER 2000 "Break my heart. My husband just called. He misses me and the kids very much. He was able to talk to our son and baby daughter but our oldest one was still in school. The baby said, 'Da Da', (the first time she has said it to him). That really broke him up. I just let him know that I love him and miss him very much. I told him that I still need him and can't wait for him to come home. He said how much he misses my kisses and hugs. He misses holding all of his babies. I think this was his real low point. I told him we don't have all that much longer and he would be home before we knew it. I tried to lift his spirits by telling him about the new lingerie I got today. I think that made him more homesick.

"I don't worry about him when he is out to sea because he has so much work to do to keep him

The *Resolution*, in making the first dive of her patrol into the waters of a troubled world, will be taking out on behalf of the nation the best insurance policy it has ever had.
— *The Daily Telegraph*, London 1968

busy. It is the in port periods when I worry about him. He has too much free time to think about all that he is missing and it upsets him. Luckily, this is a brief port call and he will be back out to sea soon. I just wish I could be there to give him the hugs he needs."

9 OCTOBER 2000 "The kids are so ready for this deployment to be over. My oldest daughter, almost five, keeps asking when Daddy is coming home. I tell her how many months and she says, 'Don't say months. Say days!' I tell her it won't be too much longer and she has done such a good job with him being gone. I let her know how much I appreciate her help with the housework and taking care of the other kids. That always makes her feel good.

"The other kids are doing well too. My husband was afraid that our baby would forget him. I don't think she has. I just showed her a picture of him last night and she got very excited, pointed to him and said, 'Da Da'. She remembers even at such a young age. I made sure I e-mailed him about that.

"I can't wait for homecoming! Some days I get so excited knowing that we have made it this far with no major problems (knock on wood) and that I can see the light at the end of the tunnel.

"I am getting tired of doing everything by myself. I am going to try not to dump everything on him when he gets home, but by then I will be so ready for a break! Heck, I'm ready for a break now but I just know I have to keep going just a little bit longer. I am off work today so I'm going to spend the day cleaning."

15 OCTOBER 2000 "There are some days that I just don't want to go on. Some days that I don't want him to be in the Navy. Some days I just want to lie down and cry all day long. This is one of those days. Not hearing from him is making things worse for me. This is definitely my low point. I think four months is enough. I'm tired. I need a rest. I just don't know what I'm doing anymore. How do I get past this time? What can I do to make things better

Jefferson Deviled Fried Chicken

Yield: 100 portions
40 lbs chicken, boneless, raw, thawed
Wash chicken thoroughly and set aside.
1 1/2 qts milk, nonfat, dry
1 7/8 gals water, warm
2 cups vinegar
Make buttermilk by combining the nonfat dry milk, water and vinegar.
3 cups Dijon mustard
1/2 cup onion powder
3 1/4 cups salt
1/4 cup dry mustard
1/4 cup cayenne pepper
4 tbsp black pepper
1/4 cup parsley
In a large insert, combine the buttermilk mixture, Dijon mustard, onion powder, salt, dry mustard, cayenne pepper, black pepper and parsley.
Place chicken in deep inserts. Cover chicken with mixture and marinade overnight.
9 1/4 qts flour, wheat, bread
3/4 cup baking powder
3/4 cup garlic powder
1/2 cup onion powder
3/4 cup salt
3/4 cup dry mustard
3/4 cup cayenne pepper
1/2 cup black pepper
3/4 cup parsley
Whisk flour, baking powder, garlic, onion powder, salt, dry mustard, cayenne pepper, black pepper and parsley. Dip marinated chicken into flour mixture until thickly coated. Deep fat fry @ 350° F until golden brown.

left: USS *Salt Lake City* crewmen sporting facial hair while out on their six-month deployment.

157

When I was first in submarines, the very first time I went away, I was away for eight weeks and most of the patrols I used to do were about eight weeks. The operations I was doing would have me diving the submarine off the Eddystone Lighthouse and eight weeks later we would surface again. During that period of time my wife had no correspondence with me whatsoever other than her ability to send two 25-word familygrams which may or may not have got through. The flow of mail and communication, once a submarine is at sea, is very limited.
— Rear Admiral Mark Stanhope, Royal Navy

for me? The kids are driving me nuts and I am going to put them to bed extra early tonight so I can have some time by myself. They are basically good kids but I have had them for four months straight with hardly a break, and they are just getting on my last nerve. They don't understand why I need them to be extra good for me. All they know is that they want to take every toy out of the toy box and not have to put it back. I don't want my house looking like a tornado hit a toy store anymore. I want my house to look nice but I also want them to learn that I'm not going to pick up after them all the time. I want them to learn that they have to clean up their mess."

2 NOVEMBER 2000 "I was able to talk to my husband recently and it was wonderful. We talked quite a bit and he is growing anxious. Time is starting to get short for us and we both just can't wait for this to be over.

"I haven't had a horrible time (I actually feel pretty lucky because I didn't have any major troubles) but I just want my husband home. I'm ready to sleep in the same bed with him, hold hands, cook dinner together. Just all the stuff that civilian couples do.

"I got five envelopes full of his deployment journal today. It was nice to read his thoughts over these past four months. He even commented on the *Kursk* accident. He said, 'My submariner heart cries for them.' It seemed to affect him deeply since an accident could happen to any of the boats at any time. He was hoping that I wasn't worried about him.

"We have been talking about him not re-enlisting in the Navy next year. He has been in for almost fifteen years and he feels that he is done. Fifteen years is a long time to be doing the same thing. He is ready for a change but yet he is afraid to take the risk. I think that is where I come in, to reassure him. We aren't kidding ourselves. We don't expect that he is going to get a real high-paying job just because he has been in the Navy and is an expert at his job. We also don't think 'the grass is greener

on the other side' either. We know what we will be giving up. The job security and medical benefits issue will be the big hurdle to get over. If it was just 'us' that would be one thing, but we have kids now. We have to make sure we can afford to take them to the doctor when they are sick. Those are scary issues."

Susan Bergquist is the wife of John Bergquist of the USS *Nevada*, a Trident submarine based at Bangor, Washington. "The first time I saw my husband's boat on the pier, I was dropping him off for a routine shift prior to his first patrol. I had seen subs before and had even been aboard several, but had never seen HIS boat. The moment I saw it, I burst into tears. It was completely unexpected. I was just dropping him off for a day at work. Seeing the thing that would take him away and carry him to the bottom of the ocean though, released this huge emotional response.

"I had such anger and sadness toward this inanimate monster. When I told my boss (who was also a sub wife) about it, she said that the same exact thing had happened to her.

"I'm going to attempt to explain, with limited whining, how my life has changed since marrying a submariner. I am not the same person I was four years ago. I was a Civics teacher at a small Minneapolis high school. I paid my own bills and made my own choices based on a set of goals and plans I'd been working toward for years, fairly successfully. I was surrounded by family, friends, and familiar activities. I had never seen an ocean and couldn't fathom why any intelligent and sane person would choose to take orders for a living. I also had a boyfriend, a fellow political science student at the U of MN, who occasionally told stories about the time when he was in NROTC and was a nuclear engineering major at MIT. I viewed these stories as an eccentric part of his past and didn't give them much weight.

"That past came sneaking up on me and changed

my life. I had dated John for about six months when he explained that he'd gotten a letter from the Navy asking that the $60,000 NROTC scholarship they'd given him be repaid. He could also have the option of repaying the debt by enlisting for two years. John didn't want to chip paint (the job that would get him back to the real world in two years), he wanted to run the nuclear reactor on a submarine. So he signed up for six years instead. At that point we had a few months to figure out if we wanted to spend our lives together or not. We had been dating for just over a year when I shipped him off to boot camp knowing that if the initial separation worked out, we would get married soon after.

"Fast forward to today. I live far from my entire support system. I have missed births, graduations, illnesses and deaths. I have been transplanted from middle America to places that have been a tremendous culture shock for me. I never thought of myself as a Minnesotan, or a Midwesterner, or a Yankee, until I found myself on foreign territory in Florida, South Carolina and Washington. Our frequent moves, combined with being stationed on bases where post-Cold War military cutbacks have slashed the local enonomy, have meant the end of my career. I worked as a substitute teacher in three different states and in four different short term/part-time teaching jobs before finally giving up and taking a job outside education. I've been working as a glorified secretary for a little over a month now. This was the best job I could find with my MA in Political Science and eight years of teaching experience. It has been a blow to both my pride and income.

"We have not had children yet. My only dependent is a 65-pound black Lab mix named Liberty, who is both my baby and my security system. I've argued from the beginning that a child shouldn't be without a father eleven weeks at a time, twice a year. John used to think I was being overly sensitive, but after witnessing what

left: USS *Ohio*. above: *Michigan* crewmen on return to their Bangor base. below: Crewmen on the USS *Florida* tied up at Bangor.

159

other guys in his department have gone through, he's come around. Still, the decision continues to be an agonizing one for me. I'm now past my peak childbearing years and entering the zone marked by infertility and high-risk pregnancies, and I hope this choice, made in our future children's best interests, doesn't end up negating their existence.

"The patrol cycle puts a tremendous emotional stress on our marriage. There is a progression of emotions (similar to the grief cycle) that most people go through, both leading up to separation and following being reunited. There is a great deal of sadness, anger and denial both partners have to go through before reaching a state of independence after separation. We've found our most difficult time is after a patrol, when, after 48 hours or so of blissful honeymoon time, we have to once again share space and responsibilities while learning to get to know one another again. We've both had to become more patient, open, understanding and mature, rather than giving in to the emotional frustrations of the situation and lashing out at one another. We've learned to respect and live through the cycle as peacefully as possible, because there is no avoiding the pain.

"In many ways my life has been on hold. So many things are in limbo, just waiting for the day that my husband will not go underwater anymore. In many ways I feel I too am sacrificing for the good of the country. I am doing my part to support my husband who is right now sleeping with his feet against a missile tube. He will walk to his next shift down a passageway flanked by enough firepower to annihilate a society. And because of what he does, in part, most Americans have never really questioned why it is they feel safe from foreign aggression within their borders. I am proud of the role my husband plays and the sacrifices he has made. I don't love the situation it puts us in, but I accept that it is necessary.

"I often feel like there is a well-developed support system in place to help the men through each patrol, but the wives are alone to fend for themselves. The submariners are in a different world, gray and metallic and male. They've got their mission and their duties and their shipmates (the level of bonding is incredible to see after a patrol). They get Familygrams, Halfway Night surprises, holiday celebrations, etc. Their news from home is monitored and censored for happy content in an incredibly patronizing but well-meaning way. They can completely separate themselves from life above the water and focus on getting their jobs done. I have to sleep in our bed alone every night. If I forget to pay the bills, the phone is turned off. I cannot escape reality. And nobody is checking to see that I'm holding it together, or setting up little surprises for me. Two weeks ago my grandmother was diagnosed with aggressive melanoma in her lymph nodes. I can't turn to my husband for support. I'm not even allowed to tell him about it. The news is too depressing to be allowed in a Familygram, but not serious enough to warrant official action. So I'm on my own. The Navy expects both nothing and everything of its wives."

"To be fair to the Navy, I think there would have been support if we'd needed it. There was a telephone number you could ring and I think there was a welfare unit. As for the officer's wives, the vast majority of us kept in touch with each other, but we heard nothing from the Navy. As I say, if we'd had a problem, we could have rung up, but I don't ever recall anybody [from the Navy] ringing up. They made it quite clear that, when they were out on patrol, there was probably no way they were going to come home. If one of us had died, I suspect that something might have been done, but certainly, it was made quite clear that, if parents died, nobody was going to suddenly pop back."
— Jan Stanhope, wife of Royal Navy Rear Admiral Mark Stanhope

Good company in a journey makes the way seem shorter.
— from *The Compleat Angler*
by Izaak Walton

left: Members of the USS *Corvina* (SS 226) crew relaxing in the torpedo room, August 1943.

Douglas Cushman is a sonarman on the USS *Jefferson City*, SSN 759, a fast attack submarine. "I'm in the process of a divorce. Second marriage. We just got back in from a six-month deployment. How the heck can you hold a marriage and family together, being separated like that? It takes a hell of a woman to be able to put up with it. She'd done it for five years. I saw her for just 42 days out of the whole first year I was attached to the boat. After that it was better. I leave the house at 5.30 am to make it here by 6.30 and I don't leave here 'til 7 at night, so you're putting in a twelve-hour day. Then you have duty days on top of that where you are on 24-hours. You only sleep for three or four hours out of a duty day. You come home tired the next day. It's kind of hard. If you have collateral duties besides your basic duties, I don't see how some people do it. I know fifteen people that have been divorced; five of them who are going through it right now. The life style has a lot to do with it. The fact that you're gone, you're back, you find somebody who you think you'll hang with and they'll hang with you, and the next thing you know, you've married the wrong one. Each time I've gotten married, shortly thereafter she'd be pregnant. I was scared to get out of the submarine force. I needed the job."

Sarrah Malone is in the US Navy, serving on a sub tender, the USS *Emory S. Land*. Her boyfriend, Shane Swenson, is on the USS *Albany*, SSN 753. He is a Machinist Mate. "Being a sailor myself I understand the stresses of being underway; lack of sleep, standing watches, the lack of privacy, and missing home and loved ones. Sometimes I just want to scream with the loneliness, but that is when I stop and think about the pride that being part of the 'silent service' brings my Shane. When he comes back from a deployment he spends most of the first few days and nights lying in a hammock on the patio, staring at the sky and stars. The submariners are so deprived of nature, going as

they sometimes do months at a time without sunshine, rain, fresh air and breezes.

"On our last date we went to dinner and then out for drinks. As always, he treated me like it was our first date and did all the things that men tend to forget after years in a relationship. As we were walking along the beach, it began to rain. My first instinct was to run inside, but he stopped me, told me he loved me, and how wonderful the rain felt on his skin and how lucky I was to be able see and feel things like that every day.

"Some days are harder than others when the guys are gone. The little things are what keep you going; surprise letters and gifts. E-mail has made life a lot easier for us. Now we can 'talk' all the time and it makes the distance seem smaller. He says it shines a little light into his dark world."

Twenty-three-year-old Heather Walders has been a Navy wife for two years. Her husband Billy, a Fire Control Technician, is serving aboard the USS *Salt Lake City*, SSN 716, a fast attack submarine that is homeported in San Diego. "My husband has been on active duty for three and a half years. I would not trade the last two years for anything, although like any other relationship, it has had its vicissitudes. Nevertheless, unlike every other relationship, I have learned never to take my husband or the love that we share for granted. He is my oxygen and my soulmate and I have immense pride in his job. I went on a Dependent's Cruise a year ago and gained a whole new understanding and a deepened respect for what he endures as part of his job's daily routine—tiny racks (my husband is over six feet tall), narrow spaces, limited facilities (such as showers, heads, and a single clothes washer for 130 men), and the general stresses of protecting the United States.

"I do not represent the status quo for the typical Navy wife. I have a college degree, work full-time and have no plans for children in the near future. Personally, I do not feel that bringing a child into

above: US Navy torpedoman David Noel aboard the fast attack submarine *Jefferson City* in September 2000.
right: The homecoming of the ballistic missile submarine USS *Nevada* to her Bangor base.

this crazy and completely unstable life that my husband and I share would be fair. We are too busy enjoying what precious little time we have together and saving our money for the future. We do everything together. We are each other's best friends. He has to count on me at home, as much as I have to count on him while he is out to sea.

"Billy is gone on deployment for six months of every eighteen. We don't make enough money for a second car, much less for me to fly out and visit him in ports with the off-chance that the boat will be delayed, deterred, or that the schedule will change. Therefore, I stay home. I work overtime, go to the gym, teach craft classes and coach girl's middle school soccer. I do whatever it takes to stay busy. Some days it is all I can do not to stay in bed and cry. Everything depends on me. The bills have to be paid, the car serviced, the checkbook balanced and the house maintained. Often I watch holidays and significant days go by without even a phone call. Gifts are opened alone with thousands of miles of ocean between us. I live for my phone calls only to fake a cheery attitude during the call and then cry afterwards until my body hurts out of longing for him. Only his presence can ease the aching in my heart. The calls that come at all hours, because of the time difference, are welcomed. Sleepless nights, talking on the phone, then quickly dressing to head off to work make me happier than words can say. I learn to live without the sleep just to simply hear his voice and hear him tell me he loves and misses me as I do him. Our photo albums are worn with constant viewing. We send audio tapes back and forth to hear each other's voice when he can't be near a phone. These periods can last sixty days. Sixty days of nothing.

"There are many benefits as well. Medical is covered and dental is based on co-pays. We have commissaries and shopping benefits on base. There is Navy housing, VA home loans and scholarships. My husband travels and has made

Absence lessens ordinary passions and augments great ones, as the wind blows out a candle and makes a fire blaze.
— from *Maxims* by La Rochefoucauld

If there is a desire to put women in submarines, and this is the one I'd like answered clearly by the politicians, and a desire by women to serve in submarines, then, in the society we now live in, we've got to make it possible for them to do so. I don't think it would affect combat capability in regard to inter-human relationships.
— Rear Admiral Mark Stanhope, Royal Navy

left: Happy families greet the arriving nuclear-powered attack submarine USS *Groton* (SSN 694) on her return from an around-the-world patrol in 1980.

invaluable lifelong friends. They share a bond like no other group in the military. He is able to take college courses through the boat and is gaining priceless training and real-world skills.

"I am a happy woman. I love my life. My husband sees to it. It takes a very special man to be a submariner. My husband is the best man I know and I would stand by him come hell or high water because that is what he does for me and for every other person in this country."

"My wife hates it. She hates the separation, but she has never once asked me to quit my job, because she knows I love it. I'm gone more days than anyone else on the planet. It's just a way of life that isn't normal, but it's a way of life that I like. I like what I do. I like going to sea. I like shooting torpedoes. I like doing things that nobody else in the world has any concept about. She knows that my time is getting shorter, and pretty soon it's gonna be just the five of us. I'm looking forward to that. I retire in three years. That will be my twenty-year mark. I think I'll start my own business building furniture. There's not much call for a torpedo tech in the outside world."
– David Noel, torpedoman, USS *Jefferson City*, SSN 759.

"My wife gets by just fine. She does not like the deployments. I just finished my sixth deployment and she's managed to weather all six with me. She says, 'They never get any easier.' But we've had a very satisfying time together in the submarine business. We have thirteen-year-old daughters and I had both my wife and daughters out to Singapore to meet me on this last deployment, and she has met me at several other ports on previous deployments. We try to make the best of it. We do just fine. I know that a lot of the troops and officers struggle with that question. Many of them come in as bachelors, looking to start families somewhere along the way, and in many of their minds the idea

that you can have a satisfying career in the Navy and a family seems incompatible. In my mind though, they're not. You can do both. It may be a struggle. You've got to find the right woman, but it can be done. I'm a testament to that."
– Commander Ron Steed, skipper of the USS *Jefferson City*, SSN 759.

Liz Campbell has been a submariner's wife for four years. "My husband is an Electronic Technician First Class on the USS *Philadelphia,* a fast attack submarine. I am a stay-at-home mom of two children. I have 'done' only one six-month deployment so far, but I'm not very far off from another one. When I first married my husband (we were married just before he got to a boat) I found the short deployments hard. Even though they were only two or three weeks. Just before the boat left for its WestPac, its schedule picked up and, in a three-month period, they were only home for a week or two. That was really tough since I knew he was leaving soon [for six months] and I wanted to spend as much time with him as I could. Then came D-Day, deployment day.

"The day started very early in the morning. We had some last-minute packing to do. I tried to get very into the packing so I wouldn't think about what was going to happen in a short time. It came time to leave and I managed to drive to the base by going through my checklist with him. I call it the 'mommy checklist' and it consists of things like 'did you bring enough underwear?, do you have enough soap until I send your next care package?' etcetera. We got to the base and they were having a barbeque on the pier for the boat next to ours. I was so busy talking with everyone that I lost myself in conversation and wasn't thinking that in less than a few hours the boat was leaving for six months and taking my husband with it. Things started winding down about an hour and a half before the boat was due to leave and when the guys from the tender came out to get the boat

Peace and rest at length have come, / All the day's long toil is past; / And each heart is whispering "Home, Home at last!"
– from *Home At Last* by Thomas Hood

below and left: The return from patrol of the USS *Nevada*.

ready to leave everything went silent. Not many people were talking and a lot of us new wives had our eyes locked on the boat and all the things going on over there. I started feeling really sorry for myself and really sad that my husband was leaving. All I could think of was our three-month-old baby, a major 'daddy's boy', and how was I going to handle him during his afternoon 'where-is-my-daddy' fits? I was thinking that I would never make it and that someone was going to lock me in a padded cell in less than a month. Then I saw another wife, a bit older than me. She had just come home from the hospital the day before with her brand new baby, only four days old. I gave myself a mental kick in the butt and stopped feeling sorry for myself. I told myself, it could be worse; he could have been gone when I'd had my son.

"The time had come for the boat to leave. The guys all started saying their goodbyes to their families and I don't know if I started panicking or what, but my heart kicked into overdrive and I started breathing really fast. Jim came over and said he had to go now. He took our son and gave him a kiss and a hug and said a few words to him. Then he did the same to me. The whole time I tried not to cry. I didn't want him to see that because I knew he would worry about me when he was gone and I didn't want to give him anything else to add to his stress. He climbed onto the boat, climbed down the hatch and gave me a little wave and blew a kiss at me. The minute his head disappeared, I lost it. The captain's wife came over and gave me some tissues and a hug. His friend, who hadn't gotten on the boat yet, came over and gave me a hug and tried to build me up saying it would be okay and I would be fine. I made him swear not to tell Jim I had lost it. By this time nearly everyone was on the boat. I had to leave. I couldn't stand there and watch it. I didn't want to see them taking up the lines and removing everything so the boat could leave. I went over to the end of the

base and parked along the sea wall so I could see the boat leave the harbor. I grabbed my camera, checked on the sleeping baby and hopped in the bed of my truck ready to snap some pictures for my son's memory book. The boat came by me and I took two rolls of pictures. I stayed until I couldn't see the boat anymore.

"I went home and a few minutes after I walked in the door my mom called. She asked how I was doing and I couldn't even speak. She asked if I wanted my mommy and I said yes and broke down in tears again. She said she was going to get off work early and come home. I hung up the phone and had a sob fest. Then my grandma called. She asked how I was doing and told me her experience with six-month deployments. Her dad was in the Navy for thirty-plus years, and her late husband was also in the Navy. I'm really glad I have my grandma. At that time our boat didn't have much of a support group, but I had my family in the same town. My grandma nailed everything. She told me how long I would be in a certain mood and the order the moods would come in. Love that woman.

"The first three days were the worst. Then I got over it and stayed as busy as I could get. I found that the more time I spent doing something, no matter how small, the faster the days went and homecoming came closer.

"Every mistake we could have made during that first deployment, we made. I now feel very confident about this coming six-monther. I know what not to do. I know what worked for me. On this boat, we have e-mail. A few weeks ago my husband went on a short run and one day during it I opened my e-mail and found one from him. I was thrilled. He was only gone a couple of weeks so there were no moody feelings that went along with it. I now accept the deployments as part of his job and I don't get so emotional when he leaves for a couple of weeks. I do miss him though, so when I get an e-mail from him I am walking on cloud nine. I know I will be able to send and receive e-mails

We didn't get any medals, Number One. And we only sank two U-boats. Two in five years. It seemed a lot at the time.
— from *The Cruel Sea* by Nicholas Monsarrat

left: US Navy Lieutenants John Ditewig and Gerson Berman playing Acey Ducey aboard the USS *Batfish*)SS 310) in May 1945. Berman is wearing night-adapter goggles as he is about to go on night watch.

from him on the big one, as many as they will allow anyway.

"My perspective on the submarine community is a good one. It is very tight-knit. The good thing about living in housing here is you are pretty much surrounded by people who can help you. I think it is a relief to our husbands when they leave, to know that there is another wife next door who knows exactly what we are going through. There is also a lot of help from the wives whose husbands are home. One of the times my husband left, my car started making funny noises. My neighbor sent her husband over to look at it and make sure it wouldn't break down on me. There are times when a wife is moving into housing and her husband is already deployed, so she is doing it all by herself. We call them moving parties and we all go over there and help her unpack. We drag any available husbands with us to move the furniture in the house. There is a lot of support here and I am very glad I am a part of this community."

Flo Garetson is the wife of David E. Garetson of the USS *Ohio*, Gold crew. "The submarine universe is a very different world from anything else you can imagine. Sometimes I feel as though I am living in Catch-22. I am a 38-year-old local girl. Born in Seattle, I grew up here on the Kitsap Peninsula. I'm not your typical Navy wife. I have had a career and lived on my own for eight years before I met and married into Navy life. Most of the wives are in their 20s and have never known anything but their parents' house and their husband's bed in Navy housing.

"David has been in the Navy for thirteen years and this September he was frocked Chief Petty Officer. He has served on the *Ohio* for four years and on two other subs before that. We have a close, loving relationship. We have a three-year-old son. All we ever want is to be together as a family. For over half of our son's life, I have been the sole parent.

"Wives of men on surface ships and sub wives often argue about which of them has it harder. Surface ships are gone for six-month deployments. Their sailors are allowed to use the telephone to call home whenever they wish and can receive calls. They are allowed to receive and can send letters and packages of almost any size. They have, when the ship's system is working, almost unlimited access to uncensored e-mail. Trident submarines go to sea for eleven to fourteen weeks. The fast attack boats have an erratic schedule. We have no telephone contact with them unless they happen to pull into a port and call us. We cannot call them. If we are lucky, sometime during the patrol, we have a mail drop. If we do, there is no guarantee the mail will go both ways. Sometimes it comes off the boat with an ill sailor. We are never told the circumstances until our husbands tell us when they arrive home. Letters are usually limited to one business-size envelope. I have stuffed them so full that I have to reinforce the seams with strong tape.

"Our e-mail is experimental, screened, censored and sometimes critiqued before it reaches our husbands—that is, if it has passed the screenings. We do have Familygrams. Each sailor is allowed to receive a total of eight Familygrams during a patrol. If more are sent, the extras are handed to the sailor as he leaves the sub at the end of the patrol. Familygrams are sent through a general radio broadcast to the entire Pacific fleet. The messages for a specific boat are recorded and distributed to the crew. The truth is, everybody reads all of them. There is no privacy. They make copies of the juicy ones and pass them around. There is a maximum of 50 words (actually 48. The first is the sailor's name and rank; the last is the sender's name). Any mention of the ship's location, port visits or time schedules are strictly prohibited. Any news that might be considered depressing or upsetting to the sailor is not allowed. We cannot mention births, deaths or

all: Children eagerly anticipating the arrival of their daddies with the returning USS *Nevada* to the Bangor base.

illnesses. We cannot use anything that might be considered a code for something else. I got called once because I sent 'the blue fish is still alive'. They were sure it was a secret code for something. I had to explain that we had a blue Saimese fighting fish in our aquarium and I haven't been having very good luck with this breed in our fish tank. When David left for sea, he said, jokingly, [to the fish]: 'Well, I'd better say goodbye to you. You be dead by the time I get home.' I explained that I have this blue fish and I haven't managed to kill it yet.

"I hate writing Familygrams. They all end up sounding the same. It seems I can never tell him anything real. I can't, for example, tell him that I am proud of myself for fixing the van because he was not aware it was broken. I can't ask him a question because he cannot answer. So, it boils down to some cute thing that his son did that week, followed by a 'We love and miss you very much.'

"Sure, we ballistic missile sub wives have a much shorter deployment time, but it seems so much longer when you can't communicate.

"The best way to make the deployment time not seem like it is standing still is to keep as busy as possible. This is not as easy as it sounds. Schedules are extremely important. To young children and the elderly, schedules are a vital part of life. They are what we cling to, however mundane the task. The simple chores of life become milestones. I rejoice in the fact that I only have to take the garbage out to the curb two more times in this deployment. I change the linens on the beds three more times and water the plants once more.

"The silent waiting for husband to return is hard. It is so hard that, almost every deployment, there is at least one wife waiting for her husband at the pier with divorce papers for him to sign. There are those who say, 'If you can't handle the separation, you shouldn't have married a sailor.' I don't see it that way. I married the kindest, most loving, best

Conversation, n. A fair for the display of the minor mental commodities, each exhibitor being too intent upon the arrangement of his own wares to observe those of his neighbor.
— from *The Devil's Dictionary* by Ambrose Bierce

left: The end of an around-the-world patrol for the USS *Groton* in 1980.

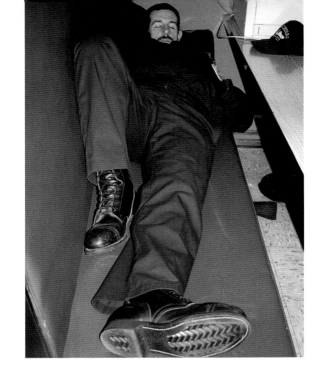

friend I ever had, and I couldn't possibly imagine my life without him. In short, I married my husband to spend the rest of my life with him, and I'm still waiting for him to show up.

"I can imagine that it must be so much harder for the guys. I know it is not possible for David to see, let alone be, with any other women while out to sea. On the other hand, the wives have the possibility of encountering all sorts of temptation. Husbands, and I know mine does, must believe very hard in trust and marriage. He has no other choice, isolated out there deep in the ocean. If he believed otherwise, even for a moment, it would drive him mad.

"I do everything I can think of to keep busy. I invented Movie Night. The first Friday of every month at 7 pm, about twenty of my closest friends come over for a pot luck supper and a movie. We take turns picking a video or DVD to watch. Some movie nights we have a crazy party theme. Every June we have a 'Trailer Trash Night'. We all dress up, in this case way down. The food is Midwest junk food pot luck—Spam casserole, anything involving Velveeta or hot dogs, a menu that, any other day of the year, would make your skin crawl. There is the Best of the Worst Night, when we all bring our very favorite bad movie and groan together.

"Other things I do to keep busy are garage sales, my son's play group, a lot of field trips to places like the zoo, the fire station and anywhere else I can think of. I have a stack of books piled up to read that is over four feet high. I bake and make candy. I bake whenever I feel anxious or depressed. I bake a lot. I make cookies, cakes and sweet breads. I had all my Christmas baking done by the first week of November. My freezer is full. I have developed a reputation for making the best cookies in the Pacific fleet. David's division is always begging me to send cookies. Before they pulled out on this last deployment, they gave me the name and number of a new

174

guy who was coming aboard the sub a week into the patrol. I got hold of him and he agreed to take cookies to the boat for me. I baked 278 cookies, enough for the whole crew, half peanut butter and half chocolate chip. The whole crew did not receive them. David's division hoarded, traded and rationed them out for special favors.

"I keep a daily journal. This helps both of us. It helps me to pass the time and it helps Husband not to feel so disconnected from his life here. If kept informed, he won't feel too confused when he arrives home [from deployment], and I won't hear things like 'When did that happen?', 'When did we get this?', 'Where did that come from?' and 'When did we start doing that?' I still hear 'Where's my . . .' and 'Have you seen my (fill in the blank)?'

"When I hear news of a mail drop, I add a few lines to my daily journal about how much I love and miss him, and slip it in an envelope. If I can, I also send him pictures of our son and the things we have been doing to keep busy while he is away. I have to be careful what I write in his letters for several reasons. The Navy has the right to censor mail to sailors, and with the subs the right is exercised more often than with surface ships. News that might affect his morale at work is not permitted. All bad news is better left for when he returns home. After all, unless it is a serious illness or a death in the family (in which case the Red Cross can intervene) there is nothing he can do about it except worry. There is another reason why I must be careful about what I write. The guys [on the submarine] are so starved for outside contact that they let each other read their letters. The unwritten rule is: keep it light, keep it upbeat, no bad news and never write anything that you don't want other people to read.

"The anticipation of Homecoming starts long before Homecoming Week itself. I have several calendars in the house, one in my son's room, one in my bedroom, one in the kitchen and one in the

right: Aboard the USS *Batfish* (SS 310) at the end of a 17-month patrol in the western Pacific, May 1945.

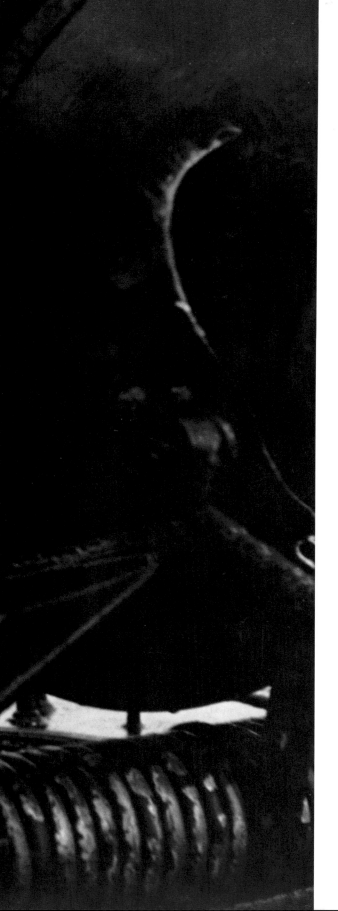

geek (computer) room. All of them are scarred with big black Xs on the days of the deployment that have passed. Within three to five days of Homecoming the phone rings and it is the call I have been waiting for. The phone tree caller relays information on where and when to meet to catch a ride down to the pier where the sub will tie up. We are never told which pier we are going to, just where to catch the bus to that pier. She reminds us to bring our military ID and asks if any other family members will be with us as they will need ID too. The night before Homecoming is the worst of all. Merchant Marines and sailors call it 'channel fever'. You are excited, tired and anxious. You know you need sleep, you try to get to sleep, but your mind won't let you. You are too hot, too cold, can't relax. Thousands of thoughts run endlessly through your head, some meaningful, some so obscure you wonder why you are thinking of this garbage. 'If I go to sleep right now, I can get four hours of sleep.' It doesn't happen. You don't fall asleep until the hour before you are supposed to get up. You awake exhausted.

"It is D-day. The first thing my son and I do—before breakfast, before coffee—is hang the big red, white and blue 'Welcome Home Daddy' banner on the dining room wall. After that, it is the longest day of the deployment. The wait is worse than Christmas Eve is to a seven-year-old. After a very long day, all of us wives, girlfriends and children are on the pier awaiting sight of the submarine way off in the distance. The fleet admiral believes it is good for morale for the family and loved ones to be waiting on the pier while the sub pulls up. Obviously, the admiral has never waited for three hours in 30-degree weather.

"We wait for an hour and a half as the submarine is slowly inched into tie-up position by the guide tugs. It is at least another hour before they get it tied up and rigged for shore. Another hour before all garbage is hauled off the boat, chores are done and liberty is called, and our husbands are allowed

Come, lay thy head upon my breast, / And I will kiss thee into rest.
— from *The Bride of Abydos*
by George Gordon, Lord Byron

We know, Mr Weller—we, who are men of the world— that a good uniform must work its way with the women, sooner or later.
— from *Pickwick Papers*
by Charles Dickens

Bug Juice was originally called Bugs Bunny. In the 1960s, when powdered flavoured drinks were first coming out, a company that made them put a picture of Bugs on the packages. Over time, submarine cooks were no longer allowed to buy such supplies from civilian sources. Around this time the drink powder began arriving in typical military brown paper wrapping, and Bugs became Bug.

to leave. All told, it is four hours before I can get my husband in the van to bring him home.

"The first thing I do when he arrives home is start washing everything in his sea bag. Submarines use a chemical, amine, to retrieve breathing oxygen from seawater and the smell of this chemical permeates everything. It smells like ammonia, and if he leaves the sea bag unattended on the living room floor the cats will sniff it and mark it with a stream of urine.

"By this time, my husband has been awake for almost 36 hours. He is part of the pilot team that brings the sub through the home stretch into the channel. After a hot shower and a home-cooked meal, he tries so hard to stay awake and talk with us. He wants so badly to catch up on hugs and being a part of the family again. But fatigue always wins.

"My favorite part of Homecoming is when we are in bed and he is fast asleep. I lie there listening to him breathing. I have decided this is my favorite sound in the world. I know I sure miss it when he is gone. It reminds me of our wedding night. At about two o'clock in the morning, he wakes up, gently kisses me and whispers the word 'wife', then rolls over and goes back to sleep. It is one of my most treasured memories and I know he didn't even realize I was awake."

Like the destroyer, the submarine has created its own type of officer and man—with language and traditions apart from the rest of the Service, and yet at heart unchangingly of the Service.
– Rudyard Kipling

FISH
DON'T VOTE

THE BACKBONE of the American nuclear-powered attack submarine force going into the 21st century is the Los Angeles-class, SSN 688 and 688 I (improved) fast attack submarine. This proven, reliable vessel is indeed fast with a better than 25-knot submerged speed. 360 feet long, with a 33-foot beam and a 32-foot draught, the Los Angeles boat is operated by a crew of 130 officers and men. It is capable of diving to a depth of 800+ feet and is fitted with four 21-inch torpedo tubes as well as twelve vertical launch tubes for the Tomahawk cruise missiles it carries. The final 23 Los Angeles-class 688 I boats utilize an advanced combat system. They are quieter than their predecessors and are configured for under-ice operation in that their forward diving planes have been moved from the sail structure to the bow, and the sail has been strengthened for breaking through ice.

In September 2000 I went to sea for a day as a guest of the US Navy aboard the USS *Jefferson City*, SSN 759, a Los Angeles-class fast attack submarine that is homeported in San Diego. It was a family day, or dependents' cruise, in which several relatives of the boat's crew were invited to spend a day at sea to learn something about the routine and the sort of life their husbands, sons, boyfriends, brothers or fathers experience in their submarine careers.

Crossing the gangplank onto the deck with its coating of black anechoic decoupling tiles, I was aware of how low the 360-foot hull lay in the water. It seemed like a black iceberg, with the bulk of its mass hidden from view beneath the surface of the bay. The black tiles have been fitted to all hull surfaces except the hatches, control surfaces and the sonar dome. They seem to flex very slightly when you walk on them. They are intended to defeat hostile active sonars and minimize any noise that emanates from the *Jefferson City*.

We gathered first in the enlisted mess area where coffee and doughnuts were served at 7 a.m. Roughly 48 crew members can sit down for a meal at one time in this room which, as the largest communal space on the boat, also serves as a game room, study area, video theatre and meeting room. Everyone was given an extra styrofoam coffee cup and asked to write his or her name on it in ink, and to write or draw anything else on it if we wanted. The cups were then collected and put into a large plastic bag. By this time we were under way on the surface out of San Diego Bay.

We were allowed to visit various areas in the forward half of the boat—the after parts and stern being off-limits. I doubt that any of us cared much about getting close to the nuclear reactor anyway. Most of us spent some time in the control room where we were all able to look through the two periscopes. As we departed San Diego, they provided a fascinating view of the city, harbour and other ships and small craft which we had to avoid. A colour television system showed the same view. The two periscopes (search and attack) are located on a platform in the centre of the room. This is also the watch station of the officer of the deck who oversees the status of virtually everything in the room, from periscopes to radar to ship control to weapons control—the BSY-1 (Busy One) combat control system. Navigation and plotting, including the Global Positioning System (GPS) are down the port side of the room. There is a vertically-mounted automated plotting board, as well as two manual plotting tables where the majority of the submarine's movements are plotted.

Ship control is on the port side at the front of the room. Two enlisted men—a helmsman and a planesman—drive the boat using airliner-style yokes, while a diving officer and the chief of the watch are in charge of the trim and ballast control. The two "drivers" take orders from the diving officer, who stands behind them. To his left is the

right: The USS *New York City* (SSN 696) under way in 1979.

180

station of the chief of the boat.

Of the two periscopes, the Type 18 Multi-function Search scope is certainly the most interesting. It provides readouts for the Electronic Support Measures (ESM) receiver at the top of the periscope mast; it contains the antenna for the global positioning system; it has a 70mm camera installed for photographing images through the periscope, and it is able to project a television picture onto monitors throughout the sub. The masts of the two periscopes project up through the sail/fairwater structure and are covered with a radar-absorbent coating to minimize their radar signature.

We watched as control room crewmen steered the boat, navigated and monitored radar screens. The room is illuminated with fluorescents by day and in the late afternoon a series of small red lights come on in the 'rigged for red' mode. This allows for a gradual acclimation to a lower light level, essential should the boat be required to surface rapidly and key crew members have to go immediately to the top of the sail. The actual day and night of the surface world has little significance for the crew, which tends to see the passage of time in terms of working 'watches', meals and sleep. Through a door from the control room was the sonar room, another off-limits area to visitors.

A little later in the morning the captain, Commander Ron Steed, of Atlanta, Georgia, spoke to us about the mission of the *Jefferson City*. He then presented performance awards to several of his crew members, some of whom were proudly receiving them in front of their relatives.

Having cruised away from the California coast on the surface, it was soon time to submerge. I fully expected to hear the aaa-ooo-gaaa tone of a klaxon (there is one) warning of the impending action, but what we got instead was someone's calm and delberate tones on the public address system ordering, "Prepare for diving." When it happened, it was a almost a non-event. The

Within the Navy, "interviews" with Admiral Rickover are rather famous or, perhaps, infamous. Almost anything can happen. At one time, for example, the Admiral kept a special chair for interviewees, the front legs of which were shorter than its rear legs. It was always placed in such a position that, with an easy flick of the Venetian blinds, the Admiral could focus the bright rays of the sun in the interviewee's eyes. Many young naval officers sat in the chair blinded by the sun, sliding forward, all the while being pummelled by questions that had no easy answer or perhaps no answer at all.
— from *Nautilus 90 North* by Commander William R. Anderson with Clay Blair, Jr.

right: A night view of the USS *Seawolf* (SSN 21) under construction and ready for her rollout at the Electric Boat Corporation facility, Groton, Connecticut

submarine just slid gently beneath the waves and descended to periscope depth, where the crew stabilized it. We then continued down to 150 feet and spent most of the day at that depth, except around midday when the crew took the boat down to 1000 feet for about half an hour. Again there was virtually no sensation, either during the descent or at that depth. The boat did not incline noticeably, nor was any sort of pressure change felt. And being nuclear-powered, there was no engine, shaft or propeller noise. When cruising submerged the beautifully designed boat gives a glassy-smooth ride, while up on the surface, depending on sea conditions, the ride can be far more stimulating.

Some of us spent our deep submergence time in the surprisingly large torpedo room, which is where the line started to form for lunch. It wound its way out into a corridor, then up a near-vertical flight of stairs to the next deck before snaking around a corner and down another corridor into the mess room. There one was assured of a very good meal thanks to the US Navy's determination to offer its submariners the best food it can. On this day the chef and his staff had prepared *Boeuf Bourguignonne* and it was very good indeed. There was a variety of vegetables and desserts and a well-stocked salad bar. Beverages ranged from coffee, tea, or milk, to the traditional fruit-flavoured "bug juice". Due to the narrow aisles and limited space, beverages were served to the diners by crew members for efficiency's sake. After the meal, I talked with Lieutenant JG Todd Nelms, of Jacksonville, Florida. Lt Nelms is Supply Officer on the *Jefferson City*, a position he has held for the last three of his thirteen years in the Navy.

"We feed meals every six hours. We do a breakfast, a lunch, a dinner and a 'mid-rats' [at midnight], which is a combination of everything we offered throughout the day plus maybe luncheon meat or beanie weenies . . . something to tide the guys over until breakfast. Because we are on an eighteen-hour work day, we always have one group getting off [watch]. They then sleep through two meals so when they get up they're usually pretty hungry.

"Our menus go through review boards once a quarter. We don't ration food at all. The submarine force gives us so much money to feed our people that I can't even spend it all. We do steak, lobster and shrimp every Sunday. Hamburgers, the most popular meal, is on Fridays. The night before we pull into port, we always have pizza. Usually the divisions rotate around and go in the galley and make calzones and their own personal pizzas. That's how you get the crew involved in the crew's mess, by letting them come in and cook a meal now and then.

"I have a Mess Division of eight people—a Chief, a First Class and six cooks. We probably make fifty loaves [of bread] an evening. We serve just about anything you would eat at home. When we are out at sea we make our own doughnuts, coffee cakes, biscuits, banana nut bread . . . we always have morning pastry and with every meal there are always fresh rolls or bread. We get a kind of milk which can last us up to forty days because it doesn't have to refrigerated. I can store that back in the engine room. As long as it's cold it tastes just like pasteurized milk. When we go on a Westpac we get a special kind of egg that has a coating around it to seal it, like a wax sealant. If we can't get to the next port in three to four weeks on real eggs, we use a lot of dehy [dehydrated] eggs. I have bags to put vegetables in that are supposed to keep them crisp and extend their shelf-life up to 21 days, depending on what kind of vegetables they are. I can keep enough beef, fish and poultry on board for six months. Everything is quick-frozen, which keeps it fresh. This last Westpac, I had enough ground beef for the whole time. I learned on my first Westpac that foreign ground beef is nothing like what we eat in the US. There were a lot of complaints on the hamburgers then.

"The recipe cards that we use are taken right out of *Bon Appetit* [magazine]. We adjust the quantities, and have to censor them as we can't carry all the wines and the different herbs that are called for, so we have to substitute some. We have a Thai night, an Italian night, a Mexican night and a Greek night every week. Mexican is by far the most popular. We make our own burritos, tacos, enchiladas, Spanish rice and refrieds."

The early afternoon agenda called for a period of "angles and dangles", in which the submarine was to be put through a series of high-speed climbing and diving turns. Few among the visitors on board knew what to expect, and wisely elected to remain seated in the mess room at the communal tables during the exercise. As the relatively severe manoeuvring began, two women who were talking at one end of an aisle separating the mess tables, suddenly found themselves at the high end of a profoundly tilted room. Physical forces took over and they were unceremoniously deposited on the floor, sliding like bowling balls to the other end of the room. They (and we), thought it hilarious, and they quickly picked themselves up and repeated the performance to loud applause.

After the floorshow, I went to the torpedo room to meet with David Noel, Torpedo Mate First Class. "We call exercising the torpedo system 'shooting waterslugs'. We are just cycling the ejection pump through it's firing stroke and forcing water out of the torpedo tube, hence the term 'waterslug'. We do it to keep moisture from building up inside the various air pipings that are on the tube. That moisture can start rusting on the inside and degradation of the valve components, eventually causing one of the valves to explode. We shoot waterslugs once a week. With guests on board today we will probably shoot about fifteen or twenty of them so everyone will get a chance to pull the trigger on a warship. We'll use just one tube today,

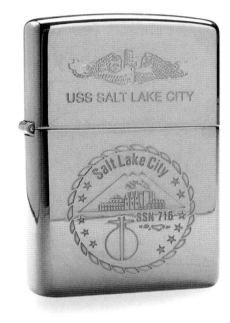

I was astonished to see the food supply for eight weeks disappear between pipes and valves, ribs and machines, closets and ducts. Huge smoked hams were hung in the control room. Staples such as whipped cream, butter, coffee and tea were locked up for distribution by the Captain. The fueling of U-557 was accomplished on May 10. On May 12, we received loads of fresh vegetables, eggs, bread and fresh water. We squeezed the crisp loaves into the last unoccupied crannies and filled three hammocks with the rest, letting them swing free in the bow and aft compartments.
– from *Iron Coffins* by Herbert A. Werner

right: Ernest Borgnine and Glenn Ford in the movie *Torpedo Run*.

but for the actual maintenance we shoot them out of each tube to keep them all exercised and up to speed." The first visitor to fire a waterslug stepped up to the torpedo tube and was coached by David Noel on the procedure. She was about twelve, the daughter of a crew member, and was obviously excited by what she was about to do. On Mr Noel's command, with all in readiness, the young lady hollered a countdown, "three . . . two . . one . . . " and triggered off the slug which is said to make the same exact sound as that of an actual torpedo being fired. It was so loud that everyone in the room had to wear earphones for protection.

"Depending on our mission, we carry up to 28 weapons in the torpedo room, torpedoes and Tomahawk cruise missiles combined. Where our mission is going to take us determines what kind of load-out we will have. If our mission is going to be more 'anti-surface ship', we'll carry more torpedoes. If we are going more 'land attack', we'll take more Tomahawks.

"Serving on submarines is a whole different way of life. I started out in the middle of the Cold War, then did a tour in Desert Storm and now I'm on my way out. I've got a few more months to go 'til I retire and spend the rest of my life with my wife and kids."

All the old submarine movies lead one to believe that keeping clothes and body clean and presentable cannot be the highest priority in the confines and limited facilities of a sub. Actually, they manage pretty well nowadays with only a single washer and dryer to handle the laundry of 130 men. How do they do it? By very careful scheduling.

The medical care of the crew on a US Navy attack submarine is the charge of the senior pharmacist mate whose tiny office is just off the crew mess. Medical supplies are kept and dispensed there. If a crewmember should become seriously ill or injured, the pharmacist will confer with the captain about possibly surfacing the boat in order

to make radio contact with a Navy doctor for consultation. The option of calling for a helicopter to pick up the patient and take him to a properly-equipped surface ship or shore facility for appropriate care rests with the skipper.

At various times of the day I noticed one or more sailors on errands to retrieve stored items such as canned food, toilet paper or supplies of one sort or another. They located these items in storage lockers, drawers and closets throughout the boat. No space is wasted in these vessels. Only the need for replenishment of food and other consumables, and relief for the crew, keeps these nuclear-powered submarines from staying out on virtually endless patrols.

Forward from the enlisted mess area, on the port side passageway, is a large area of berthing spaces for enlisted men. The aisles and companionways in the submarine are extremely narrow, requiring personnel to sidle past one another. Personal space and privacy, are minimal, with three-tier bunks the rule. The bunk itself is relatively comfortable and measures about six feet long and three feet wide with a little over two feet of vertical space between the bunks. Like the dark blue coveralls worn by the enlisted crewmembers, the blankets used on the bunks are of a synthetic material designed to not create lint which would get into and clog the air filters of the boat. Each bunk is equipped with a fresh air blower, a reading light and a privacy curtain. Each man's personal gear is stored in a six-inch-deep tray under the bunks. The Los Angeles-class sub was not designed with enough berthing space for all the enlisted personnel of the crew, so a certain amount of "hot bunking" is required on a shift ratio of about three men for every two bunks.

In operating completely independently of the earth's atmosphere, nuclear submarines must produce their own air and water. The oxygen is generated through the process of electrically hydrolyzing sea water and the air quality is

No man can have society on his own terms. If he seek it, he must serve it too.
— from *Journals* by Ralph Waldo Emerson

Howsoever every man may complain of the hardships of his condition, he is seldom willing to change it for any other on the same level.
— from *The Rambler* by Samuel Johnson

preceding spread: The USS *Alabama* (SSBN 731) in the waters near Bangor, Washington. right: HMS *Valiant* under way in 1969.

continually monitored to assure the right blend of oxygen, nitrogen and carbon dioxide. A system of mechanical "scrubbers" operates at all times to clean the carbon dioxide from the air. The system also expells the gaseous hydrogen by-product into the sea employing a diffuser to prevent large, highly visible bubbles from showing on the surface.

Submariners serving in the vessels of the 1940s had to make do with very little water for their personal use and were normally able to shower only about once a week. In nuclear submarines water is more plentiful, but the manner of taking a shower is similar. One is required to get in, get wet and turn off the water before lathering up with soap and then turn the water on again to rinse the soap off.

The senior enlisted mess and berthing spaces are located on the starboard side of the sub. This area is referred to as the "goat locker". Beyond it is the officer's wardroom where they take meals, meet and study. It is well-appointed and the tone is usually less formal than that of surface ship wardrooms.

Late in the afternoon we were heading back to San Diego and the guests were going to have the privilege of riding part of the way in with the two lookouts at the top of the sail/fairwater. When my turn came I was rigged up in a harness as it is necessary to be hooked to a railing while on the sail for safety. Getting up to the lookout position is easier said than done, especially if you are carrying cameras as I was. It involves a climb of about 25 feet up a vertical ladder through the sail structure, with a couple of sharp turns on the way, before hauling yourself out of the hatch and onto the lookout level. Once up there, however, the view and experience are spectacular.

The space at the top of the sail is tiny, with just enough room for three close friends, without luggage. I took up the rearmost position, behind the two lookouts and just forward of the sensor

far left: The USS *Alabama* heading into San Diego Bay. top left: Seaman Ted Fanning at the coffin locker of his bunk which lies beneath a torpedo aboard the attack submarine USS *Tucson*. left: Fire Technician 3rd Class Shea Keesee at the missile launch console of the USS *Seawolf*. below left: Machinist Mate Fireman Brian Zitt "driving" the USS *Tucson* on deployment in the Persian Gulf in support of Operation Southern Watch.

Baked Tuna and Noodles
Yield: 100 portions
2 1/3 gals tuna, canned
Drain tuna, flake and set aside for use later.
4 lb 3 oz noodles, egg
2 1/4 gals water, boiling
1 1/3 tsp salt
Cook noodles in boiling salted water 8 minutes or until tender. Drain. Set aside for use later.
1 1/4 qts flour, wheat, general purpose, sifted
2 2/3 tsp salt
1 qt shortening, melted, or salad oil
Blend flour, salt, and shortening or salad oil together using a wire whip; stir until smooth.
2 qts milk, nonfat, dry
2 1/2 gals water, warm
Reconstitute milk; heat to just below boiling. DO NOT BOIL. Add milk to roux, stirring constantly. Simmer 10 to 15 minutes or until thickened. Stir as necessary.
1 gal celery, fresh, sliced
continued on page 196

2 cups onions, dry, finely chopped.
Add celery and onions to sauce. Bring to a boil, stirring constantly.
1 2/3 cups pimientos, canned, drained, chopped
Combine tuna, noodles and pimientos with sauce. Mix well. Pour about 6 1/2 qts mixture into each greased pan.
3 cups bread crumbs, dry
3/4 cup butter or margarine, melted
3 tbsp paprika, ground
Combine crumbs, butter or margarine and paprika. Sprinkle about 1 cup over mixture in each pan. Bake about 45 minutes or until lightly browned and bubbly.

above right: Admiral Hyman G.Rickover addressing guests at the keel-laying ceremony for the nuclear-powered fast attack submarine USS *La Jolla* (SSN 701) at the Electric Boat facility in 1976. far right: A deck party of the USS *Michigan* handling ropes on their return from a patrol. following spread: The Trident submarine USS *Georgia* (SSBN 729) at Bangor.

masts with the search and attack periscopes, communications and radar. After the crowded decks below, the sudden isolation was exhilarating. There was only the wind, the sea and the great black submarine cruising awash beneath us, its bow wave rolling unbroken across the rounded, nose-down front of the boat—a formation that is unique to current submarine hull design, and a mesmerizing phenomenon.

In the late-day gloom, the USS *Jefferson City* approached Point Loma, the long, high peninsula that shields San Diego and its superb deep-water harbour from the Pacific. We fortunates who had spent the day on board gathered one last time in the mess room to talk about the unique adventure we'd had. A few of the ship's crew brought in a large plastic bag and began placing the contents on a shelf for all to see. Here were the styrofoam coffee cups that we had signed and adorned with various graphics. Now the cups were about a third of their original size. They had been placed in an unpressurized part of the sail prior to our descent to 1000 feet and the pressure at that depth had compressed them to the size of whisky shot glasses, an impressive example of what can happen to something at such depths without the protection of the boat's pressure hull.

By 5 pm the boat had been secured at a pier in the Submarine Squadron Eleven base and our little band of tired, happy civilians departed with memories of a very special experience.

The Los Angeles-class fast attack submarine was born in the late 1960s. The then-Director, Naval Reactors, Vice Admiral Hyman Rickover, believed strongly that the US Navy needed a high-speed nuclear attack submarine to replace the boats of the Sturgeon class. His view was in conflict with that of Naval Sea Systems Command (NAVSEA), which was in charge of the specification and design for the next generation SSN. NAVSEA favoured

something called the Conform-class sub which, though slower than Rickover's design choice, would be quieter and would afford better habitability for the crew.

The admiral had considerable support both in the Navy and in Congress and that, together with a widespread belief at the time that the Soviet November class attack submarine was actually very much faster than western "experts" had previously thought, coalesced the support Rickover needed to win the day and get the sub he wanted. The Navy was authorized to proceed with the new class of twelve boats. To secure the vital congressional votes for funding the purchase, Rickover offered to break with Navy tradition and, instead of naming the new submarines after fish, he said that he would name them after the home towns of the twelve congressmen who agreed to vote his way. He reputedly commented later: "Fish don't vote."

196

WHY I DO IT

right: Officers having coffee in the wardroom of USS *Batfish* (SS 310) as the submarine returns to base after a war patrol, May 1945.

" 'COMMANDER,' said the Mayor. 'Tell me something I've always wanted to know about submarines.' "

"The Bodger composed himself to answer the usual chestnuts on claustrophobia and escape from sunken submarines.

" 'Why do men, like yourself for instance, go into submarines? What sort of man would do a thing like that?"

" 'You might just as well ask why do people become missionaries or shoplifters. I suppose the extra money has something to do with it but I'm sure that basically it all comes down to the question of which would you rather do, run your own firm, however small, or help to run someone else's, however big. Would you rather be a small cog in a big machine or a big cog in a small machine. Most of our ship's company are big cogs in a small machine. They're nearly all specialists. They have clearly defined jobs and in most cases they're the only man for that job, although all of them can do the basic things in a submarine which everybody should be able to do.' "
– from *Down The Hatch* by John Winton

"We operate with impunity in virtually any body of water we choose to go in. That's what attracted me to submarines as a midshipman, and the opportunity to do real-world things instead of just practising with other members of the US Navy. I wanted to go against the real opponent in the real environment, and that's exactly what I've gotten the opportunity to do in the last four years, and after four years of doing the attack submarine business I'm very confident in our ability to go where we want without anyone finding us.

"My mother was a Navy brat. Her father was a captain and her brothers were all officers in the Navy. All three of them were graduates of the Naval Academy. As a little kid I used to visit my grandparents in Key West, Florida. There was a submarine base there at the time and my grandfather, who had been on submarines in the 1920s, took me on tours of the submarines. He had the book *Submarine Operations in World War II*, by Theodore Roscoe, the authoritative history of sub operations in that war. I would lie there on the floor looking at the pictures in it every time I visited them. That stuck in the back of my mind. When other kids got spacecraft toys, I got submarines that would shoot missiles and torpedoes and you could take them in the pool.

"I always wanted to go to the Naval Academy, and once I got there I pretended that I was going to be open-minded, but in fact, it was a foregone conclusion that I wanted to go into submarines. I never doubted that decision. I look back on my career with absolutely complete satisfaction. I've gotten to go everywhere, operate in every body of water, to do every one of the submarine operations. I've had all the moments of excitement that I hoped I would.

"In the submarine business, you are an independent operator, on your own. You have to solve your own problems. You don't get on the radio, call home and ask them for help with a technical problem, fixing a piece of equipment. 'What do you want me to do now, boss?' You can't have a helicopter fly in a part to you. You can't get the technical representative to fly out to the ship to help you. You can't get any prints or drawings that you don't have. You have to figure it out yourself. The 23-year-old kids on your ship have got to sort out the problem, figure out how to fix it. Very often they have to figure out how to use parts that were meant to do something else; how to put them together to serve the function in the piece of gear that we don't have parts for. That kind of creativity, self-sufficiency and resourcefulness—you're out there on your own and you have to solve the problem yourself. It's been very satisfying. You can't do that without a great bunch of guys. I was told before I came into

top and above: Former Royal Navy submariners Colin Tucker-Watts and Colin Way, respectively. far right: Crew members of the Trafalgar-class nuclear-powered attack submarine HMS *Turbulent* in February 2001.

submarines that I would work with the cream of the crop of sailors. The enlisted guys, and the officers, are super-aggressive, hard-working, smart and dedicated. I found that to be true. It's very easy to do a hard job like this when there is no question that everyone is pulling on the same end of the rope. I don't look forward to going into the private sector one day and having to worry about who is on my side, competing with people in my own company. On a submarine there is no doubt that everybody is on the same side and that everyone wants the right thing to happen. They don't worry about who gets the credit. They just do the right thing. It's a fantastic environment.

"My own experience has all been attack submarines and I'm very proud to have been on them. It's a harder job [than on missile subs]; everyone will tell you that it's a harder job. The schedule is more flexible, constantly changing. The operations are more intense and demanding. The amount of space in the boat is much more compressed. It's harder: harder on the sailors, harder on the officers. There is no question but that some guys flourish in that kind of environment. That's what I like. That's what I came in for, the challenge. You've got to bob and weave with the problem, sort it out on the fly, that kind of thing. That's the stuff I love about this business. I don't think I would enjoy being on a ballistic missile submarine. For other people, being on a missile submarine, where the schedule is predictable, where they can get everything set up and go for a fixed period of time, come back and be back for a fixed period of time, that works out best for them. That's great. I think that probably more than half of the boomer guys will recirculate back to a boomer. Certainly more than half of the attack submarine guys will recirculate back to an attack submarine. Probably one fourth of one's career will be on the other kind of ship than the one that you spend most of your time on. I'm an oddball because I have been on attack

submarines for all four of my tours. That's very unusual. Less than ten per cent of submariners are in that situation, spending all of their tours on one type or the other. I wear some kind of warped 'badge of honor' that I've done the hard job for four consecutive tours."
– Commander William Hoeft, skipper of the USS *Salt Lake City,* SSN 716.

"Why did I join the Submarine Service? I am not quite sure. In our centenary year we now have several fourth-generation submariners who have followed their fathers into submarines, but I am not one of these. I was not entirely a volunteer either, but there was a distinct shortage of submarine officers when I did my training back in 1957 as an entire training class of seamen and technical officers had perished when HMS *Affray* went down in 1951, and this deficiency ran on for several years. I was easily persuaded and have not regretted this decision for one moment. It certainly wasn't for the money (half a crown [12 1/2 pence]a day extra pay in those days).

"Responsibility at an early age, the opportunity to command as a Lieutenant, small ship comradeship with each depending on the other. Tremendous 'regimental' pride and lifelong friendships extending to an international brotherhood of those who do their business beneath the surface. Operational professionalism of the highest order, quite a bit of excitement and, of course, a touch of glamour—but I was very fortunate to have served when I did as the advent of the larger, comfortable nuclear submarine made the service a little more impersonal despite the huge technical challenge. What a lucky fellow I am to have served when I did, starting in conventional/diesel submarines, spending most of my time abroad, and eventually graduating to an SSN."
–Commander Mike Sizeland, Royal Navy (Ret)

"In 1948 it was in vogue to join some part of the

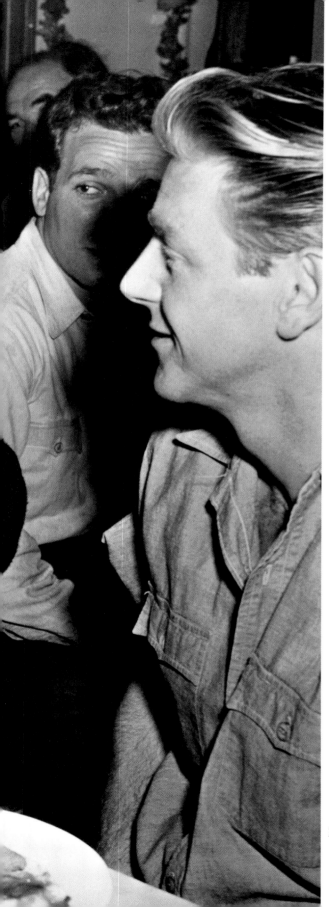

military . . . besides, there was conscription. I went to recruit training and then to Engineman (diesel mechanic) school. After graduating my orders were to report to submarine school in New London, Connecticut. I don't remember ever volunteering, as they say you have to do. After sub school I went to Panama to a World War II boat, the *Conger*, and found that I was serving with some fine people. That never changed. We ate better than most and, of course, back then we received a lot more money than the surface people did. The people in charge looked out for us and we were more than just a number. I served as an enlisted man and then as an officer for more than 20 years, on several different submarines. There isn't a day goes by that I don't miss some part of that period of my life."
— James W. Gibson, former US Navy submariner

"A friend of mine, who was serving on a submarine tender, told me that while he was eating hot dogs on the tender, the guys on the submarines were eating steak. Of course, the fact that I would be getting half again as much base pay for hazardous duty sat pretty well with me too. I believe, though, that I would have remained in submarines even if these things had been eliminated. I found such a sense of 'family' serving on the boats, that I made a 20-year career out of it."
— Norm Wehner, former US Navy submariner

"When I joined the Navy in 1970, the training package was that you spent a year at Dartmouth [Britannia Royal Naval College], then a year at sea as a midshipman. Then you went back again into the Navy for a year's worth of academics before you had to make a decision as to which branch you would go into, even though you wouldn't necessarily go straight into that branch.
  "In 1970 the Fleet Air Arm in the British Navy was declining. The decision had been made in 1969 that fixed-wing flying was no longer going to be part of the Navy, eliminating that as a good route

Youth! youth! how buoyant are the hopes; they turn like marigolds toward the sunny side.
— from *The Four Bridges* by Jean Ingelow

left: John Garfield in a scene from the movie *Destination Tokyo*.

through the Navy. To my mind, submarines, especially the SSN fleet, represented the battleships of the future. It was a growing force. We had a large number of conventional submarines and the nuclear submarine was coming on line in a big way. The attraction of early command was significant in that you could take command of a conventional submarine at age 28 or 29, if you were moving, and a conventional submarine was a fairly potent weapon. It was certainly more impressive than a mine-sweeper, which is the equivalent of what I would have got if I had stuck in the flotilla. So, early command, early responsibility, and an attraction to what appeared to me to be the expanding branch of the Navy, in a business which was expanding, were very much the driving forces [behind my choice of submarines].

"I went to sea from Dartmouth in a conventional submarine just for a day to give me an insight into it, and it all looked good to me. It's a very different life. I read physics at university. Physics was the only subject I was ever any good at and the nuclear aspects of it were the spark that tied very neatly into my career. I was ambitious enough to think that this degree would be useful to my career. I then went back into the Navy and did some courses, and went into the submarine world joining HMS *Swiftsure* in 1976. I served with her much longer than normal, until 1979, and during that time I qualified as a submariner and got these submarine brooches [dolphins], and I remember the enormous pride in getting them. I then went back into the conventional submarine world in HMS *Orpheus*, which was an odd route. Most people had grown up through the conventional submarines. I was the Sonar Officer. During my time in *Swiftsure* I was the Torpedo Officer and then the Communications Officer. After *Orpheus* I went back to another S-boat, *Superb*, for about two years as the Torpedo and Anti-Submarine Officer, and I went straight from there to the

Perisher Course. I then was given HMS *Orpheus* to command just after the Falklands War, and took her down to the Falklands. From there I went to Captain Submarines Sea Training Organization as one of the training staff. I then got promoted to Commander and was given HMS *Splendid*, in command for two years. I went from there to become the teacher of the commanding officers qualifying course [Perisher] for two years. Then, after nine months in the Ministry of Defence, I went to become Captain Submarine Sea Training, in charge of the workup of all of our submarine fleet. [In later years Rear Admiral Stanhope, as Captain Stanhope, commanded the aircraft carrier HMS *Illustrious*.]
– Rear Admiral Mark Stanhope, Royal Navy

"I had read all this stuff about the World War II submarines and the concept of how the machines worked. That's why I came in. The machine is cool. The mechanics of it have always impressed me. When you get something that's designed to take the pressure and the abuse that this thing takes, and it still works time and time again, that's like, wow! They say that the most complicated piece of gear in the world is the space shuttle. The second is the submarine. When you think that you have all of these systems that work together, hydraulic, electrical, pneumatic, air, servos, all the computer stuff, the reactor, all that stuff back aft, it's all got to work together to make this thing go forward, take you down and bring you back up."
– Douglas Cushman, sonarman, USS *Jefferson City*, SSN 759.

"My childhood hobby was woodwork. When I was about ten, my father set up a shop for me, and soon I began to turn out such items as lawn chairs and tables, which I sold. Sometimes I worked on other projects. I built a couple of rowboats, which were launched in the small river that ran close to home. James Beckham, a boyhood friend, and I

converted one of the rowboats into a crude submarine. We found that by covering most of the deck we could turn the boat upside down and submerge it with air pockets inside that permitted us to breathe. Thus we played at being U-boat captains.

"My performance at the [Naval] Academy was about average. I was neither an athlete nor a brain. World War II broke out soon after we entered, and the class was accelerated. When I graduated in 1942, standing in about the middle of our class of six hundred men, I found that certain restrictions had been relaxed, and that Annapolis graduates were allowed to apply straight for submarine school. Our class had made one summer cruise— in 1940—on the battleships *Texas*, *New York*, and *Arkansas*, and I had come away with the impression that I would not like the spit and polish of a large ship. Because they were small and informal, and because responsibility would come sooner, submarines appealed to me. I put in an application and was lucky enough to be among the first forty Annapolis men selected directly for submarines."
– from *Nautilus 90 North* by Commander William R. Anderson, USN, with Clay Blair, Jr. Commander Anderson was skipper of the USS *Nautilus* when it made the first trans-polar voyage, from the Pacific Ocean to the Atlantic, in August 1958.

"I grew up in an Army town, the world's largest basic training camp for Infantry. Enough said.
"I was seventeen years old when I went aboard my first submarine. I was an only child and had had a very easy life. My first assignment was as a Mess Cook. My day started at 5:30 each morning and ended at around 8:30 that night. I washed dishes for all three meals and served 24 people at a time. I set table for each meal and made salads. Before the Navy I had never had my hands in soapy water, let alone washed dishes, platters, bowls and assorted pots and pans. This went on

God and our sailors we adore, When danger threatens, not before. With danger past, both are requited. / God forgotten, the sailor slighted.
– Old saying

far left: Heather and Bill Walders. Bill is a Fire Control Technician on the USS *Salt Lake City* based in San Diego. above: Commander Jeff Tall, RN (Ret), was a submarine skipper and is now Director, The Royal Navy Submarine Museum at Gosport, England.

I have been called a lot of names in my lifetime and the one of which I am proudest is Submariner. That's submar<u>ee</u>ner, not sub<u>ma</u>riner.

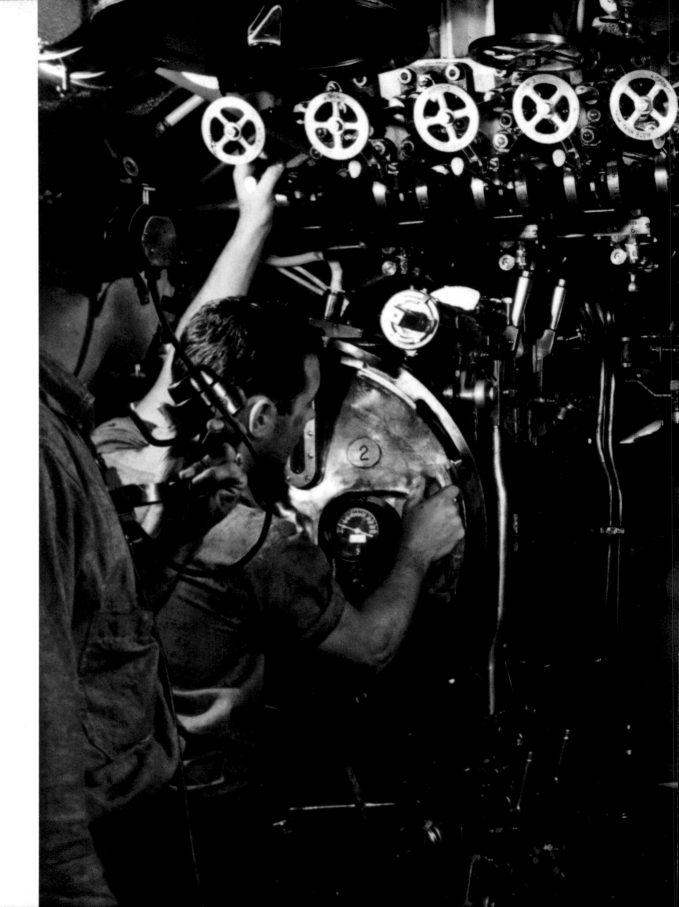

right: Crewmen in the torpedo room of the USS *Cero* (SS 225) on patrol in the western Pacific in August 1943.

for six weeks. I look back on it now as an initiation although at the time it was Hell. My new shipmates made sure I crossed my Ts and dotted my Is. If I spilled sugar or missed the opening while filling a salt shaker, or dropped a dish, I soon heard about it from everyone on board. The pressure was intense for learning to turn the other cheek and keep on working. The last job of my long day was to scrub the floor in the mess area with coffee, since coffee is an acid that cut the grease and oil that had been tracked in from other compartments. I made the grade and went on to become an Electrician Striker, my next assignment.

"I had had experience with automobile electrical components as a high school kid, so it was no stretch to become an 'electrician'. My duties soon became equal in pain and discomfort to those of mess cook. The battery wells were located below the walking deck and everything done in them had to be done on your hands and knees. The batteries required about a quart of water a week per cell. It was dispensed through a garden hose with a special nozzle that fitted down inside the top of the battery. It was easy to get a very potent electric shock if you accidentally touched one of the steel I-beams that ran just 20 inches [maximum] above your head and, for the upper tier, just ten inches. Those batteries, which were charged nightly, got very warm and steamed off small amounts of sulphuric acid which caused grounds that had to be removed by washing the cell tops, 252 in all, with baking soda and then rinsing them with fresh water. You can imagine how sore backs, knees and stomach muscles got, and this had to be done every day for eight months.

"I'll never forget that first six weeks. I learned so many lessons of life that I consider them priceless."
— Harry Farmer, former US Navy submariner

"I was a young sailor on a frigate in Singapore. It was my first ship after my initial training. I was in the clerical branch, a Writer, as they call it in the Royal Navy. I was having the time of my life as this frigate was going round the world. It was 1967.

"One day this black thing came churning into the harbour—one of the old diesel submarines—and tied up alongside us. Emerging from it were these monster people, long hair, unshaven, unwashed, and I thought, 'That's what it's like to serve in submarines.' At the time, submarines didn't carry writers, but then came the nuclear submarine era and the complement then included a Leading Writer, and I was one of the first writers to join the submarine service. They had to have someone on board to handle the increase in paperwork, pay and records, and to write all the patrol reports.

"I joined HMS *Conqueror* in 1978 as the Leading Writer and remained on her until 1984. It was around April 1st in '82 and the phone rang. I'd only been home about three days having just come back from a patrol, and thought this phone call telling me to come back to the boat was an April Fool's joke, but no, we stored quickly and off we went down to the Falklands. We were ordered to attack the *General Belgrano* on Sunday, May 2nd. We carried out the attack. Afterwards, there was a sense of celebration, but also a lot of sadness. We had been ordered to do it and we did it. I was in the control room, on the forward planes, driving her. The lads all did their jobs well.

"When it was all over and we left the area on our way home, the captain had a signal saying there was going to be a mail drop on the way back when we were off Cuba. As we came into the area of the drop we put the periscope up and there was this big Nimrod floating above us and he dropped about 35 containers of mail for us. We surfaced and we all went up and out the hatch for the first time in about eight weeks and there was all this mail around us. In addition to the mail there were newspapers, fresh strawberries and milk. When we saw the newspapers, it all came home to us about what we'd done and everyone

The wealth of nations is men, not silk and cotton and gold.
— from *Peace* by Richard Hovey

To be alive at all involves some risk.
— Harold Macmillan

far left to right above: The Chief of the Boat, Weapons Officer and a Fire Control Technician of the Trident missile submarine USS *Michigan*. far left below: A Fire Control Technician and a cook, also aboard the *Michigan* at Bangor in January 2001.

right: Students learning to repair and assemble torpedoes at the US Navy Submarine School, New London, Conn. in August 1943.

knew that it was *Conqueror*. The submarine service has always been run on secrecy and we never even knew what we'd be allowed to say [about the attack on the *Belgrano*] when we got home, and there it all was in the bloody *Sun* the next day.

"What I liked most about serving in submarines was the comradeship. Like my old captain used to say, it's the greatest private club in the world. I thoroughly enjoyed every minute of it."
— Colin Way, former Royal Navy submariner

Colin Watts-Tucker is a veteran of 30 years service in submarines of the Royal Navy. In his last two attack submarines he was the Tactical Officer of the Watch, the chief petty officer in charge of all the people in his branch. In that capacity he sat in the operations seat, taking in all information from all the sensors, the sonar and electronic warfare equipment and visual information, processing through the computers to provide the captain with a full tactical picture. "I was advised to serve in submarines. I joined the Navy in 1965 and served in two ships; the last one was the *Bulwark* and while there I was very disatisfied with the Navy and I was thinking of leaving. The only way to get out was to have done six years of a nine-year engagement. Then I met a gentleman who was an ex-submariner and had been invalided out of the submarine service on a medical discharge, and he persuaded me to go into submarines. He said it was a good life and that when you went ashore you were all one big family. You were treated completely differently in submarines and you felt as though you were wanted. When you went on watch you were doing a vital job all the time. He said to try it and once I had been there awhile I would know what he meant. I volunteered for submarines in November 1969 and my whole attitude towards the Navy changed completely.

"If I had sons growing up and they showed some

interest in serving in submarines, I would certainly encourage them. Although, the work is very hard and it's very demanding on family life—extremely demanding. That's why my first marriage broke up, because I got no support from my first wife."

"I'm Petty Officer Chris Worton. I'm a Third Class Torpedoman on the USS *Michigan* [SSBN]. I think what attracted me to submarines is that they are elite. Not too many people know what submarines do. There are a lot of jokes going around about submariners, but when you actually know them and spend time, you find they are really close knit. It's like a big family. You may not like all the guys you work with, but the respect factor is there. You know that that guy beside you is gonna save your life one day if need be, in case of war or casualty or something. My brother joined the Navy about a year and a half before I did, and he told me about the submarine force, and that's what guided me to be a submariner. I've been in it about four years. Once you get your fish [the dolphins pin] it's like a whole new world."

"I knew from a pretty early age that I would go in the military. When I was a small boy in kindergarten, one of my best friend's father was a colonel in the Army during the Viet Nam war. For some reason that appealed to me. When I got into college I had to decide which service to get into, and the Navy was most appealing to me then. In the summer of my third year in college, I went on a cruise on the USS *Guardfish*, a submarine which was based in San Diego. It was a great summer and that was a really good time, and a good crew. I decided that was the life that I wanted."
— Commander Ron Steed, skipper of the USS *Jefferson City*, SSN 759.

"What attracted me to submarines was that it seemed like a more involved thing to do than

being on a surface ship. I was told that I would have more responsibility and there would be greater requirements placed on me, so it was the challenge and the thrill to do something different. I was in them for eight years. There was no other place for me to go after I'd seen submarines."
– John Lily, former US Navy submariner

"When I entered the submarine force it was making history on a day-to-day basis. It really appealed to me to be in a position where I could, potentially, be out on a submarine influencing history as opposed to reading about it in a newspaper. I liked the engineering aspect of it: the fact that a submarine is really a science laboratory, the broad spectrum of engineering systems that exist on a submarine, from hydraulics to electrical to the nuclear reactor plant. I liked the fact that a submarine officer, as a general officer, is really involved in everything that is going on on the ship, unlike other warfare communities where you really get focused on, let's say, flying your plane if you're an aviator. If you're a surface warfare officer as a junior officer in operations or in weapons, you really spend most of your time in that area and you're not as aware of what's going on in the rest of the ship. A submarine officer, due to the size of the wardroom—its relatively small number of officers—by necessity each officer has to play a part in everything that goes on at a very, very early age. Once he gets qualified, a junior officer could come in in the morning and start up the reactor plant, get relieved of that, go forward and become the officer of the deck on the bridge, actually drive the submarine out on the surface, reach the dive point, go below and submerge the submarine, get relieved, have dinner and then attend an brief given by the operations officer in which he is describing the upcoming weeks operations. So, that junior officer, at the early age of 24 or 25 years old, is really involved with everything, and that really appealed to me. I didn't see that type of involvement any place else that I looked. I can honestly say that, during my submarine tours, I looked forward to going to work every day.

"The way that the submarine career path is laid out, there is so much variety, so much exposure to leadership and responsibility at an early age. Submariners are known for being very close as a group. There is a lot of *ésprit de corps* and there's less formality on a submarine. You interact very closely with the enlisted troops, you get involved very much with their lives. I've done trips on surface ships, very professional platforms, but there was a very distinct difference in the officer's country and the rest of the ship. There wasn't as much interaction. An enlisted person on a surface ship felt less comfortable talking with an officer, whereas a submariner, even a junior enlisted guy who has just reported would feel very comfortable knocking on the commanding officer's door and coming in upon his invitation and talking about a problem he has."
– Captain Michael King, Chief of Staff, Submarine Group Nine, Bangor, Washington

"All the movies and the recruiting stuff I saw, I wanted to be a submariner. I didn't want to get lost in the shuffle of a carrier where you've got 5000 people. I was offered the job of being a fire control technician, shooting torpedoes and missiles; it seemed really appealing to a nineteen-year old kid. Once I got into submarines I heard all the horror stories and I was really apprehensive. I went through two years of training before I ever set foot on a submarine. Two weeks after I got to my first boat I went on deployment for five months. I qualified for submarines in three months and got a really good head start. You make a lot of good friends. You can't help but like other submariners."
– Bill Walders, US Navy submariner and member of the crew of the USS *Salt Lake City*, SSN 716

Teddy Roosevelt was the first American President to go aboard a submarine and make a dive. The boat was the USS *Plunger* (SS 2), the second US submarine, on 25 March 1905 in Long Island Sound, New York. Prior to this event, the US Navy hierarchy considered submarine duty to be neither unusual or dangerous. In fact, they classified it as "shore duty" and the rate of pay for submariners at the time was 25 per cent lower than that paid to sailors serving at sea in destroyers, cruisers and other warships. In that two-hour trip in *Plunger*, Roosevelt became convinced that the payment policy was unfair and discriminatory, describing submarine duty as "hazardous and difficult". He declared that submariners "have to be trained to the highest possible point and show iron nerve in order to be of any use in their positions." By executive order he directed that submarine officers be equated with those on surface ships, and that enlisted men who were qualified in submarines receive ten dollars per month in addition to the pay of their rating. They were also to be paid an extra dollar for every day in which they were submerged while underway. Enlisted men assigned to submarines, but not yet qualified, were to receive an additional five dollars per month. From that moment, submarine pay was established.

left: The fast attack submarine USS *Columbia* (SSN 771) under way.

GALLERY

left: The USS *Capelin* (SS 289) running at slow speed off the coast of New London, Conn. during World War II. following spread: The ballistic missile submarine USS *Florida* (SSBN 728) at Bangor.

left: Lieutenant Larry Caldwell and the crew of the first American submarine in June 1901. above: Captain Edward L. Beach, CO of the USS *Triton* (SSN 586) during the first submerged circumnavigation of the world. overleaf-left:Lance Reynolds of the USS *Pogy* during a 1996 arctic exercise. overleaf right: Lookouts on the sail of the USS *Salt Lake City*.

above: On deck with the captain of a U-boat in 1942. right: Captured members of a U-boat crew in the care of the US Coast Guard.

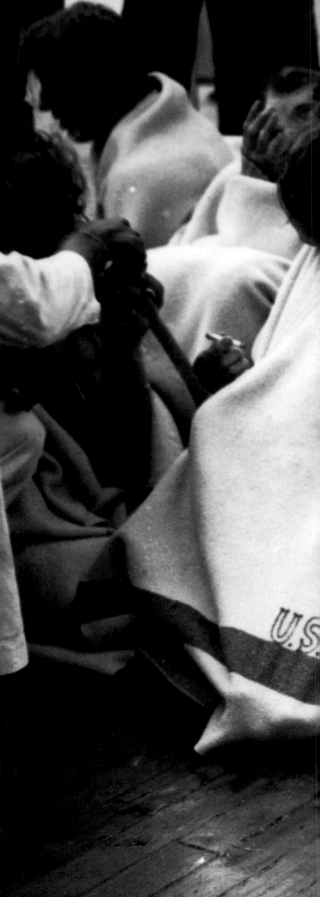

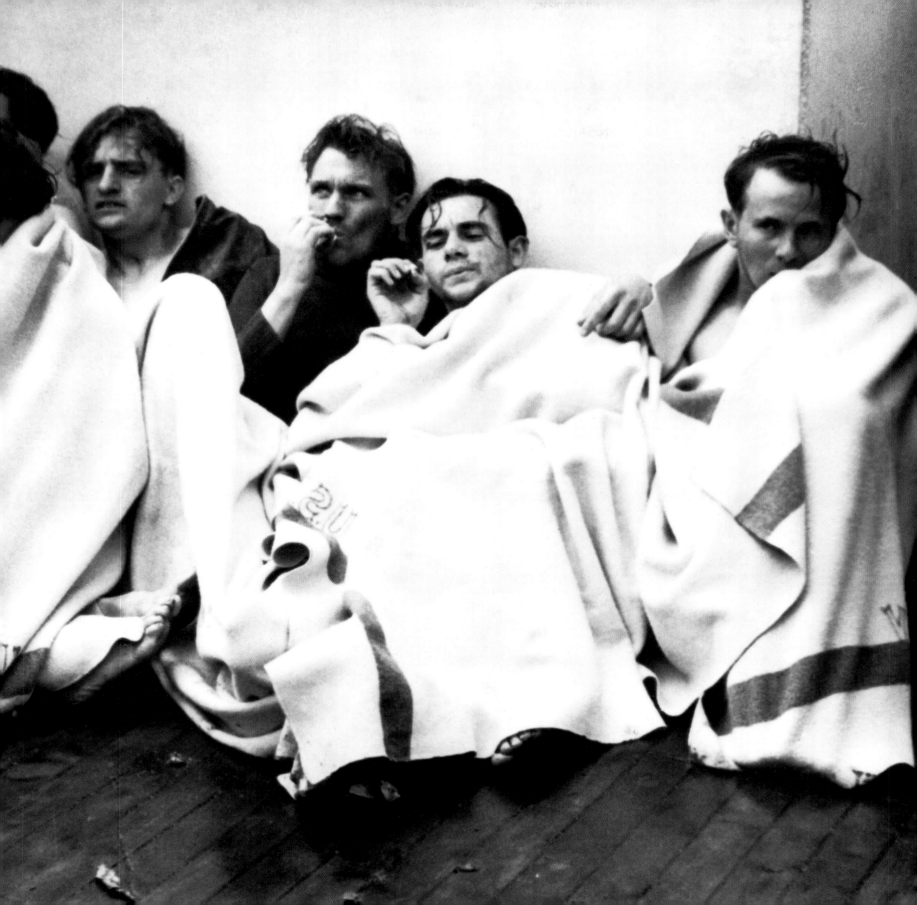

left: The USS *Alabama* at her Bangor, Washington base.
below: A torpedo tube on the World War II USS *Pampanito* (SS 383) in January 2001.

above: Crewmen of the
USS *Pampanito* (SS 383)
in September 1945.
right: Mrs Harold Allen,
sponsor for the USS
Barbel launching on 14
November 1943 at the
Electric Boat Company.

right: The watercolour *Submarine R-10* was painted at St Thomas, Virgin Islands during World War II by Commander Albert K. Murray, United States Naval Reserve. Murray was a well-known portrait painter before being commissioned a Lieutenant with the US Navy Combat Art Section. Attached to the Fourth Fleet in the South Atlantic, and later to the Eighth Fleet in North African waters, he often sketched in the heat of battle and was awarded the Bronze Star for bravery.

above: A U-boat officer at
the periscope in a 1944
drawing. right: A U-boat
is rocked by the
explosion of a bomb
dropped by a US Navy
Liberator in World War II.

preceding spread: The Trident ballistic missile submarine USS *Alabama* moves to the Explosives Handling Wharf at the US Naval Submarine Base, Bangor, Washington, in May 1998.

Picture Credits

Photographs by Philip Kaplan are credited: PK. Photographs from the author's collections are credited: AC. Photographs from the United States Navy are credited: USN. Photographs from the United States National Archives are credited: NARA. Jacket front: USN /Jim Brennan-courtesy Electric Boat Corporation, jacket back: Royal Navy, jacket back flap: Margaret Kaplan. Front endsheet: Royal Navy Submarine Museum, Back endsheet: NARA, P2: Craig Peterson-USN, P5: NARA, PP6-7: Dale Barber-USN, P10: PK, P11: PK, PP12-13 all: USN, P14: Royal Navy, P15: Dale Barber-USN, P18 left: courtesy US Postal Service, P18 right: courtesy Royal Mail, P19: USN/Jim Brennan-courtesy Electric Boat Corporation, P20: AC, P22: AC, P25 both: AC, P26: AC, P29 all: AC, P30: AC, P31: AC, P32 top and centre: AC, P32 bottom: Royal Navy Submarine Museum, PP34-35: Thomas Hart Benton-US Navy Art Collection, PP36-37: AC, P38: NARA, P39: PK, PP40-41: British Film Institute, P42 all: AC, P43: NARA, P44: AC, P45: NARA, P46 left: AC, P46 right: Georges Schrieber-US Navy Art Collection, P47: PK, P49 both: Royal Navy Submarine Museum, P50: Thomas Hart Benton-US Navy Art Collection, P51: NARA, P52 both: NARA, P53: NARA, P54: AC, P55: AC, P56: AC, P56: AC, P57: AC, P60: AC, P61: AC, P62: Royal Navy Submarine Museum, P63 both: AC, P64 all: AC, P65: all: AC, P66 both: PK, P67: PK, P69: AC, P70: AC, P71: AC, PP 72-73: Vernon Howe Bailey-US Navy Art Collection, P74: Jeffrey S. Viano-USN, P75 all: The Darkroom, P78 all: PK, P79 top: John E. Gay-USN, P79 bottom: August Sigur-USN, P81 both: NARA, P83 top: Jeffrey S. Viano-USN, P83 bottom: USN, P85: NARA, P86: USN, P87 top: Royal Navy Submarine Museum, P87 bottom: NARA, P90: The Darkroom, P91: PK, P92: Royal Navy Submarine Museum, P93: Royal Navy Submarine Museum, P94: Jeffrey S. Viano-USN, P95: PK, P98 both: PK, P99 both: PK, PP100-101: NARA, P102: John Charles Roach-US Navy Art Collection, P103: Wendy Hallmark-USN, PP104-105: Royal Navy Submarine Museum, P107 left: AC, P107 right: The Darkroom, PP110-111: David C. Duncan-USN, P114 all: USN, P117: NARA, P118: USN, P119: Dale Barber-USN, P122: courtesy Electric Boat Corporation, P123: The Darkroom, P126: Wendy Hallmark-USN, USN, P135: Alan P. Goldstein-USN, P138 all: USN, P139 all: USN, P140: British Film Institute, P142 all: PK, P143 all: PK, P146 all: Royal Australian Navy, P147 all: Royal Australian Navy, P149 all: USN, PP150- 151 all: USN, P153: NARA, P154: PK, P155: The Darkroom, P156-157: courtesy Bill Walders, P158: The Darkroom, P159 top left: USN, P159 top right and bottom: Wendy Hallmark-USN, P160: NARA, P162: PK, P163: Wendy Hallmark-USN, PP164-165: NARA, P166: Wendy Hallmark- USN,P167: Wendy Hallmark-USN, P168: NARA, P170: Wendy Hallmark- USN, P171 both: Wendy Hallmark-USN, PP172-173: NARA, P174 both: PK, P175 top left: courtesy Heather and Bill Walders, P175 top right and bottom: PK, PP176-177: NARA, P178: Wendy Hallmark-USN, P179: Wendy Hallmark- USN, P181: NARA, P182-183: courtesy Electric Boat Corporation, P184: NARA, P185 all: NARA, P186: USN, P187: The Darkroom, P189: British Film Institute, PP190-191: Wendy Hallmark-USN, PP192-193: courtesy Peter Wright, P194: Mark A. Correa-USN, P195 top left: Chris Desmond-USN, P195 top right: John E. Gay-USN, P195 bottom: Jeffrey S. Viano-USN, P196: NARA, P197: Wendy Hallmark-USN, PP198-199: Dale Barber-USN, P201: NARA, P202 both: PK, P203 all: PK, PP204-205: British Film Institute, P206: courtesy Heather and Bill Walders, P207: PK, PP208-209: NARA, P210 all: PK, P213: NARA, P214: Electric Boat Corporation, PP216-217: NARA, PP218- 219: Wendy Hallmark-USN, P220: Royal Navy Submarine Museum, P221: NARA, P222: USN, P223: H. Wolfgang Porter-USN, P224: AC, P225: US Coast Guard, P226: Wendy Hallmark-USN, P227: PK, P228: AC, P229: NARA, PP230-231: Albert K. Murray-US Navy Art Collection, P232: J. C. Schmitz-Westerholt-US Army Art Collection, P233: NARA, PP234-235: Brian Nokell-USN.

Acknowledgments

The author is particularly grateful to the following people for their kind help in the development of this book: Tim Altevogt, William Anderson, Jon Archer, Brian Barber, Malcolm Bates, Susan Bergquist, Joann Bromley, Piers Burnett, Tami Calhoun, Liz Campbell, Joseph Cereola-Commander, USS *Ohio* (Blue), Brian Coval-Commander, USS *Michigan* (Blue), Andy Duff, Rob Dunn, CB Eagye, Jonathan Falconer, Harry Farmer, John Gale, Flo and David Garetson, James Gibson, Keith Gill, Patrick Hannafin, William Hoeft-Commander, USS *Salt Lake City*, Eric Holloway, David Jones, Hargi Kaplan, Margaret Kaplan, Neal Kaplan, Michael King, Albert Konetzni, John Lily, Christopher Madden, Sarrah Malone, Robert Mehal, Mitchell McCaffrey, Judy and Rick McCutcheon, Elise McCutcheon, Steve Nichols, David Noel, Michael O'Leary, Merle Olmsted, Peter Padfield, Doug Prince-Commander, USS *Helena*, Jim Rodrock, Brian Sewell, Wendy Shaw, Christina Sheaff, Susan Sirota, Mike Sizeland, Jan Stanhope, Mark Stanhope, Ron Steed-Commander, USS *Jefferson City*, Kevin Stephens, Everett Stoops, Lloyd Stovall, Jeff Tall, Mark Thistlethwaite, Heather and Bill Walders, Colin Watts-Tucker, Colin Way, Norm Wehner, David Werner, James White-Commander, USS *Ohio* (Gold), Chris Worton, Peter Wright, and Dennis Wrynn.

Grateful acknowledgment is made to the following for the use of their previously published material:

Evans Brothers: Excerpt from *The Golden Horseshoe*, by Terence Robertson.

Evening Standard (London): For *Burial by bureacracy*, article by Brian Sewell. Reprinted by permission of Brian Sewell.

Henry Regnery: Excerpts from *Twenty Million Tons Under The Sea*, by Rear Admiral Daniel V. Gallery, United States Navy

Hodder and Stoughton: Excerpt from *Nautilus 90 North*, by Commander William R. Anderson with Clay Blair, Jr.

Houghton Mifflin Co., Excerpts from *The Second World War*, by Winston S. Churchill.

Hollywood Pictures: Quote from the motion picture *Crimson Tide*.

Holt, Rinehart and Winston: Excerpt from *Iron Coffins*, by Herbert A. Werner.

John Murray: Excerpt from *War Beneath The Sea*, by Peter Padfield. Reprinted by permission.

Konetzni, Rear Admiral Albert H., United States Navy: Remarks.

Michael Joseph Ltd: Excerpt from *Down The Hatch*, by John Winton.

Penguin Books Ltd: Excerpts from *The Cruel Sea*, by Nicholas Monsarrat.

Tempus Publishing Ltd: Excerpt from *U-Boat Commander*, by Gunther Prien. Reprinted by permission.

United States Department of Defense: Excerpts from *Conduct of the Persian Gulf War (1992).*

Bibliography

Anderson, Commander William R. and Blair, Clay, Jr., *Nautilus 90 North*, Hodder and Stoughton, 1959

Bagnasco, Erminio, *Submarines of World War II*, Cassell, 1973

Beach, Edward L., *Run Silent, Run Deep*, Henry Holt & Co., 1955

Beaver, Paul, *U-Boats in the Atlantic*, Patrick Stephens Ltd., 1979

Bekker, Cajus, *The German Navy 1939-1945*, Dial Press, 1974

Bishop, Chris, *Firepower Sea Warfare*, Grange Books, 1999

Blair, Clay, *Hitler's U-Boat War*, Cassell, 1998

Blake, Bernard, ed. *Jane's Underwater Warfare Systems 1990-91*. Jane's Information Group, 1990

Botting, Douglas, *The U-Boats*, Time-Life Books, 1979

Broome, Jack, *Convoy Is To Scatter*, William Kimber, 1972

Buchheim, Lothar-Günther, *The Boat*, William Collins, 1976

Burn, Alan, *The Fighting Commodores*, Leo Cooper, 1999

Canby, Courtland, *A History of Ships and Seafaring*, Leisure Arts Limited

Cantwell, John C., *Images of War-British Posters 1939-45*, HMSO

Carmer, Carl, *Jesse James of the Java Sea*, Farrar & Rinehart

Churchill, Winston S., *The Second World War*, Houghton Mifflin Co. 1948

Clancy, Tom, *SSN*, Berkley Books, 1996

Clancy, Tom, *Submarine*, Berkley Books, 1993

Compton-Hall, Richard, *Submarine Boats*, Windward, 1983

Cope, Harley F., *Serpent of the Seas*, Funk and Wagnells, 1942

Crane, Jonathan, *Submarine*, BBC, 1984

Cremer, Peter, *U-Boat Commander*, Naval Institute Press, 1985
Crowther, J.G., and Whiddington, R., *Science At War*, HMSO, 1947
Crouch, Holmes F., *Nuclear Ship Propulsion*, Cornell Maritime Press, 1960
Dallies-Labourdette, Jean-Philippe, *U-Boote*, Histoire & Collections
Dickison, Arthur P., *Crash Dive*, Sutton Publishing Ltd., 1999
Dönitz, Karl, *Memoirs*, Greenhill Books, 1990
Dunham, Roger C., *Spy Sub*, Onyx Book, 1997
Edwards, Bernard, *Dönitz and the Wolf Packs*, Cassell, 1996
Enever, Ted, *Britain's Best Kept Secret-Ultra's Base At Bletchley Park*, Alan Sutton, 1994
Farrago, Ladislas, *The Tenth Fleet*, Drum Books, 1962
Franks, Norman, *Dark Sky, Deep Water*, Grub Street, 1997
Friedman, Norman, *Submarine Design and Development*, Naval Institute Press, 1984
Gabler, Ulrich, *Submarine Design*, Bernard & Graefe Verlag, 1986
Gannon, Michael, *Operation Drumbeat*, Harper Perennial, 1990
Genat, Robert and Robin, *Modern US Navy Submarines*, MBI Publishing, 1997
Giese, Otto, *Shooting The War*, Naval Institute Press, 1994
Gray, Edwin, *The Devil's Device*, Seeley, Service and Co., 1975
Gray, Edwin, *The Killing Time*, Scribners, 1972
Guske, Heinz, *The War Diaries of U-764*, Thomas Publications, 1992
Hadley, Michael L., *Count Not The Dead*, Naval Institute Press, 1995
Hampshire, A. Cecil, *The Blockaders*, William Kimber, 1980
Harris, Brayton, *The Navy Times Book of Submarines*, Berkley Books, 1997
Harris, Marshal of the Royal Air Force Sir Arthur, *Bomber Offensive*, Collins, 1947
Hervey, Rear Admiral John, *Submarines*, Brassey's, 1994
Hickam, Homer, *Torpedo Junction*, Naval Institute Press, 1989
Hill, Rear Admiral J. R., *Anti-Submarine Warfare*, Ian Allen, 1984
Hirschfeld, Wolfgang, *Modern Sub Hunters*, Cassell, 1996
HMSO, *The Battle of the Atlantic*, 1946
HMSO, *Coastal Command*, 1942
Holmes, Harry, *The Last Patrol*, Airlife, 1994
Horton, Edward, *The Illustrated History of the Submarine*, Sidgewick and Jackson, 1974
Hoyt, Edwin P., *Bowfin*, Burford Books, 1983
Hoyt, Edwin P., *The U-Boat Wars*, Robert Hale Ltd., 1984
Huchthausen, Peter, *Hostile Waters*, Arrow, 1997
Humble, Richard, *Undersea Warfare*, New English Library, 1981
Ireland, Bernard and Grove, Eric, *Jane's War At Sea 1897-1997*, Harper-Collins 1997
Jackson, G. Gibbard, *The Romance of the Submarine*, J. B. Lippincott
Jackson, Robert, *Submarines of the World*, Grange Books, 2000
Jenkins, Geoffrey, *Hunter Killer*, Fontana Collins, 1966
Jones, Geoffrey, *Defeat of the Wolf Packs*, William Kimber, 1986
Jones, Geoffrey, *Submarines Versus U-Boats*, William Kimber, 1986
Kaplan, Philip and Currie, Jack, *Convoy*, Aurum Press, 1998
Kaplan, Philip and Currie, Jack, *Wolfpack*, Aurum Press, 1997
Kaufman, Steve and Yogi, *Silent Chase*, Airlife, 1989
Kaufman, Yogi and Stillwell, Paul, *Sharks of Steel*, Airlife, 1993
Kemp, Paul, *Convoy Protection*, Arms and Armour, 1993
Kemp, P. K., *H. M. Submarines*, Herbert Jenkins, 1952
Kemp, Paul, *Submarine Action*, Sutton Publishing, 1999
Kimmett, Larry and Regis, Margaret, *US Submarines in World War II*, Navigator Publishing
Lavo. Carl, *Back From The Deep*, Naval Institute Press, 1994
Lawliss, Chuck, *The Submarine Book*, Burford Books, 1991, 2000
Lewin, Ronald, *Ultra Goes To War*, McGraw-Hill, 1978
Lederer, Commander William J, *The Last Cruise*, William Sloane, 1950
Lund, Paul and Ludham, Harry, *Night of the U-Boats*, NEL, 1974
Maas, Peter, *The Terrible Hours*, Harpertorch, 1999
Macintyre, Donald, *The Battle of the Atlantic*, Pan Books, 1961
Margolin, V., *Propaganda: Persuasion in WWII Art*, Chelsea House, 1976
Mars, Alastair, *Unbroken*, Pan Books, 1953
Mason, David, *U-Boat: The Secret Menace*, Ballantine Books, 1968
Meisner, Arnold, *U.S. Nuclear Submarines*, Concord Publications, 1990
Mendenhall, Rear Admiral Corwin, *Submarine Diary*, Naval Institute

Press, 1991
Messenger, Charles, *World War II in the Atlantic*, Warfare Books and Toys Ltd., 1990
Middlebrook, Martin, *Convoy*, Penguin Books, 1978
Miller, David and Jordan, John, *Modern Submarine Warfare*, Salamander Books, 1987
Miller, David, *Submarines of the World*, Salamander, 1991
Monsarrat, Nicholas, *The Cruel Sea*, Penguin, 1951
Morison, Samuel Eliot, *The Two-Ocean War*, Atlantic Little, Brown, 1963
Mulligan, Thomas P., *Lone Wolf-Werner Henke*, Praeger, 1993
Neitzel, Sonke, *Die Deutschen Ubootbunker und Bunkerwerften*, Bernard & Graefe Verlag, 1991
Ogden, Graeme, *My Sea Lady*, Hutchinson & Co., 1963
O'Kane, Rear Admiral Richard H., *Clear The Bridge!*, Presidio, 1977
Padfield, Peter, *War Beneath The Sea*, Pimlico, 1995
Past Times, *Swinging The Lead & Spiking His Guns*, 2000
Preston, Antony, *Submarines*, Bison Books, 1982
Polmar, Norman, and Allen, Thomas, *Rickover*, Simon and Schuster, 1982
Polmar, Norman and Noot, Jurrien, *Submarines of the Russian and Soviet Navies 1718-1990*, Naval Institute Press, 1991
Prien, Gunther, *U-Boat Commander*, Tempus Publishing
Rawls, Walton, *Wake Up, America!*, Abbeville Press, 1988
Robertson, Terence, *The Golden Horseshoe*, Evans Brothers, 1955
Rossler, Eberhard, *The U-Boat*, Naval Institute Press, 1989
Runyan, Timothy and Copes, Jan, *To Die Gallantly*, Westview Press, 1994
Schmeelke, Karl-Heinz and Michael, *German U-Boat Bunkers*, Schiffer, 1999
Schwab, Ernest Louis, *Undersea Warriors—Submarines of the World*, Crescent Books, 1991
Shattuck, Thomas, *A Mother's Gift To A War-Torn Nation*, Minerva Press 1999
Showell, Jak P. Mallmann, *The German Navy in WWII*, Naval Institute Press, 1991
Showell, Jak P. Mallmann, *U-Boats Under the Swastika*, Naval Institute Press, 1987
Sontag, Sherry and Drew, Chris, *Blind Man's Bluff*, Harper, 1998
Squadron/Signal, *US Ballistic Missile Subs in Action*, 1993
Stern, Robert C., *Battle Beneath The Waves*, Arms & Armour, 1999
Stern, Robert C., *Type VII U-Boats*, Arms & Armour, 1998
Syrett, David, *The Defeat of the German U-Boats*, University of South Carolina, 1994
Tall, Commander Jeff, *Submarines*, Ticktock Publishing Ltd., 1998
Tarrant, V.E., *The U-Boat Offensive 1914-1945*, Naval Institute Press, 1989
Terraine, John, *Business in Great Waters*, Leo Cooper, Ltd., 1989
Van Der Vat, Dan, *Stealth At Sea*, Orion, 1994
Vause, Jordan, *Wolf*, Airlife, 1997
Waters, John M., *Bloody Winter*, Naval Institute Press, 1967
Werner, Herbert A., *Iron Coffins*, Holt, Rinehart & Winston, 1969
Westwood, David, *The Type VII U-Boat*, Naval Institute Press, 1984
Wheeler, Keith, *War Under The Pacific WWII*, Time-Life, 1981
Williamson, Gordon, *U-Boat Crews*, Osprey, 1995
Winton, John, *Down The Hatch*, Michael Joseph Ltd., 1961
Winton, John, *Never Go To Sea*, Michael Joseph Ltd., 1963
Winton, John, *The Fighting Téméraire*, Michael Joseph Ltd., 1971
Winton, John, *The Submariners*, Constable, 1999
Winton, John, *Ultra At Sea*, Leo Cooper, 1988
Wolfe, Brian R. and Alexander, John, *From The Sea*, Osprey, 1997
Yokota, Yutaka, *Suicide Submarine*, Ballantine Books, 1962
Young, Edward, *One of our Submarines*, Penguin, 1952

British midget submarines played a dramatic role in World War II in both Asia and Europe. They took part in the vital reconnaissance of the Normandy beaches in June 1944; the September 1944 attack on the German battleship *Tirpitz* in Norway, and in attacks on Japanese cruisers at Singapore in 1945. While the little subs built for the Asian operations were slightly larger than those used in Europe, their specs were generally similar. With a crew of four or five, they displaced between 30 and 40 tons and were powered by one 42 hp diesel engine and one 30 hp electric motor. They had a surface speed of 6.5 knots and a submerged speed of 6 knots. Their armament was two side units, each containing 4480 pounds of explosive which could be released under a target vessel and detonated by a time fuse. The midget subs built for use in the Far East had the addition of an airlock, air-conditioning, and spring-loaded legs which could be deployed to help stabilize the sub on the seabed.

INDEX